Anastasios Theofilou • Georgiana Grigore • Alin Stancu
Editors

Corporate Social Responsibility in the Post-Financial Crisis Era

CSR Conceptualisations and International Practices in Times of Uncertainty

palgrave
macmillan

Editors
Anastasios Theofilou
Bournemouth University
Poole, Dorset, United Kingdom

Georgiana Grigore
Bournemouth University
Poole, Dorset, United Kingdom

Alin Stancu
Bucharest University of Economic Studies
Bucharest, Romania

Palgrave Studies in Governance, Leadership and Responsibility
ISBN 978-3-319-40095-2   ISBN 978-3-319-40096-9   (eBook)
DOI 10.1007/978-3-319-40096-9

Library of Congress Control Number: 2016957154

Cover illustration: © blickwinkel / Alamy Stock Photo

Printed on acid-free paper

This Palgrave Macmillan imprint is published by Springer Nature
The registered company is Springer International Publishing AG
The registered company address is: Gewerbestrasse 11, 6330 Cham, Switzerland

Contents

.

Notes on Contributors

Ana Adi is the Head of the Department of Corporate Communications at Quadriga University of Applied Sciences (Berlin, Germany) (https://www.quadriga.eu/). She defines herself as a digital humanist whose research covers, among others, digital storytelling and corporate digital discourses.

Kyungmin Baek is Assistant Professor of Sociology and Anthropology at Nazarbayev University, Kazakhstan. His research interests include corporate social responsibility, environmental management, work–family programs, diversity management, and statistics. Recent publications include *Asian Business & Management, Law & Social Inquiry*, and *Journal of Business Ethics*.

Maria Castillo is a PhD candidate at KEDGE Business School (Marseille, France). She holds an MBA from Arizona State University. Her research interests include corporate social responsibility, business model innovation, sustainability, and international business in developing countries. She can be reached at maria.castillo@kedgebs.com.

Athanasios Chymis is a research fellow at the Centre of Planning and Economic Research, (KEPE) in Athens, Greece. He holds a PhD from the University of Missouri-Columbia in Agricultural Economics. He is interested in the connection between Ethics and Economics and, currently, his research is focused on how social responsibility could be infused in the public administration sector as well as in all organizations, both of the private and the public sectors.

Camelia Crisan is a senior lecturer at the College of Communication and Public Relations (www.comunicare.ro) Bucharest, Romania. She believes in the power of social networks to craft the common good and researches on how employees' storytelling increases the corporate citizenship behavior.

Paolo D'Anselmi is a practitioner of management consultancy and policy analysis. He teaches Corporate Social Responsibility at the University of Rome Tor Vergata, Italy. He is a graduate in Engineering (Sapienza, Rome) and in Public Policy (Harvard). He is working on extending Corporate Social Responsibility to Public Administration.

Nathalie Gimenes is a PhD student affiliated with the Magellan Research Center at Lyon. She is also Medical Manager in Janssen France, a medical subsidiary of Johnson and Johnson. Nathalie's thesis focuses on the responsible business model deployed by Janssen France to facilitate the access of revolutionary molecules for everyone.

Georgiana Grigore is Senior Lecturer in Corporate and Marketing Communications at Bournemouth University, UK. In 2012, Georgiana co-founded an annual international conference in 'Social Responsibility, Ethics and Sustainable Business', and in 2015, she co-edited two academic monographs on responsibility and ethics.

David McQueen is Lecturer in Politics, Media and PR at Bournemouth University. His research interests include public relations, news and current affairs, political communications and media management. He is researching various lobbying and 'greenwashing' campaigns by the fossil fuel industry and the presentation of fracking in the news.

Mike Molesworth is a Principal Teaching Fellow at the University of Southampton. He has been teaching digital marketing for almost 20 years with an emphasis on ethical and critical aspects of technology. His research interests include emerging online practices and the use and possession of digital consumption objects.

Christina Nizamidou is a PhD Candidate in the Department of Business Administration at the University of Macedonia, Thessaloniki, Greece. She has working experience in private sector in administrative and consulting positions. She is Member of the Academy of Management (USA). Her research interests include crisis management, human resources management, corporate social responsibility, and business ethics.

Fragkoulis Akis Papagiannis is a senior lecturer at Liverpool Business School, Liverpool John Moores University. As a consultant, for over 25 years, he delivered several European Union-funded projects involving strategic planning and redesign. His research interests relate to innovation and entrepreneurship, business strategies, change management, and enterprise architecture.

Marielle A. Payaud is an associate professor at the University of Lyon III (France), within the Lyon Graduate School of Business (IAE Lyon). Her research centers on management and marketing strategies at the bottom of the pyramid (BoP), sustainable development, and corporate social responsibility (CSR). www.bopmap.net.

Wybe T. Popma is principal lecturer at Brighton Business School in the UK. His research interests relate to managerial ethics, decision making, CSR, and competition. He has worked at universities and business schools in the Netherlands, the UK, and Switzerland. He also holds an appointment at the University of Montpellier (France).

Rutherford was previously a director of communications for non-profit groups, and since 1999, has designed and led programs in advertising and corporate communications. His essays on the influence of the visual presentation of information on our perceptions ('mental pictures') of products, policies, and the right priorities have appeared in peer-reviewed academic journals, newspapers, and magazines. Rutherford's website: http://www.theshadowofthephotographer. co.uk/.

Maria Anne Schmidt is a lecturer at the HTW Berlin University of Applied Sciences in the area of communication studies and corporate social responsibility. Her research interests focus around social business, religion, and quantitative projects. She is writing her PhD thesis on the topic of religion and business ethics expectations.

Richard Scullion has a PhD from the London School of Economics on 'The meanings that consumers ascribe to their consumer and political choice practices'. His research interests include the intersection of consumer culture and civic culture, and the issues of voice and marginality linked to the Paralympics. He is Member of the Promotional Cultures & Communication research group: http://promotionalculturescommunication.org.

Alin Stancu is Associate Professor of Corporate Social Responsibility and Public Relations at Bucharest University of Economic Studies, Romania. He is the co-founder of The International Conference on Social Responsibility, Ethics and Sustainable Business (from 2012), and he also organized the 4th Organisational Governance Conference.

Christos Triantopoulos is a research fellow at the Centre of Planning and Economic Research, (KEPE) in Athens, Greece. He holds a PhD from Athens University of Economics and Business. His interests lie in the area of Political Economy and Financial System. He also does research on Financial Supervision, Institutions and Economy and Public Finance, and he regularly does consulting at the Ministry of Finance.

Virginie Vial is an associate professor at Kedge Business School (Marseille, France) and an affiliate researcher at the Lyons Institute of East Asian Studies (ENS de Lyon). Her research deals with the measurement and determinants of economic growth, economic welfare, and human well-being in the context of emerging economies.

Andreea-Angela Vonțea is Assistant Professor of Marketing and Social Marketing for undergraduate courses at the Bucharest University of Economic Studies, Romania. Her research interest concerns aspects referring the nonprofit organizations' strategic and tactical approach of fundraising, as well as the general fields of non-profit marketing and corporate social responsibility.

Fotis Vouzas is an associate professor in the Department of Business Administration at the University of Macedonia, Thessaloniki, Greece. He is a senior researcher at Lancaster University (UK) in part of the European Union Research Project Human Capital and Mobility Programme. He is also a participant in various European Union projects ADAPT, TEMPUS specialized in Total Quality Management-related issues.

Rebecca Watkins is Lecturer in Marketing at Cardiff University. Her research explores the impact of digital media upon consumer culture, in particular the ownership and possession of digital consumption objects. Rebecca's work has previously appeared in the *Journal of Consumer Culture, Journal of Marketing Management*, and the *Journal of the Association for Consumer Research*.

List of Figures

List of Tables

Introduction

As there is a general consensus that global economy is recovering from the *great* recession, the focus of this book is to investigate how corporate social responsibility (CSR) is perceived in this new era of uncertainty. The consequences of the financial crisis (2007–2008) and the global recession (2008–2012) have severely affected the everyday operation of both for-profit and non-profit organizations not to mention societal stability. Cutbacks, layoffs, and strategic changes have been on the top of the organizational agenda leading occasionally to the question of whether or not CSR is a necessity or a commodity and what is really the role of for-profit organizations in society.

In the aftermath of every crisis, one should look for opportunities. This financial crisis has provided organizations with the space to re-conceptualize and re-configure the role of CSR within the everyday business practice. It has created the ground for organizations to actively demonstrate that a business may go beyond making profit.

The book breaks down into three parts: moral discussions, institutionalization, and case studies. Key observation for the chapters included in this book is the diverse perspective and different angle presented, which on its own is a consequence of the financial crisis, that is, the necessity to practice and research CSR differently than before. All chapters of this book are based on data collected during or after the global recession, offering insight on current trends and future directions of CSR.

The first part of this book involves a more philosophical discussion around CSR with authors expressing new views and paradigms. Rutherford and Scullion (Chap. 1) putting education in the very center consider the implications, opportunities and challenges of embedding the principles and practices of CSR in the design and delivery of advertising, marketing communications and public relations programs. Schmidt (Chap. 2) observed that in times of uncertainty, a turn to religion may break out as form of solidarity. Grigore et al. (Chap. 3) argue that responsibility in the use of digital technologies requires more than just legal compliance and address a need to theorize responsibilities derived from the use of technologies that have been previously silent in CSR literature. Crisan and Adi (Chap. 4) explore the debate of whether or not after the financial crisis and in the context of the social movements which are becoming political movements too, there will be a paradigmatic conviction or conversion. In Chap. 5, Papagiannis attempts to design an ontologically innovative framework entailing long-term Critical Success Factors (CSFs) necessary for a sustainable CSR design, secondly, to identify Key Performance Indicators (KPIs) necessary for the implementation of a CSR strategy, and finally, to realize internal and external socioeconomic and political forces of the indicated stakeholders that shape the CSR policies and collaborations.

In the second part, the necessity for institutionalization arises. The financial crisis has directed, as Baek (Chap. 6) observed, toward having a code of business ethics to respond to institutional pressures and to improve their market competeveness. Popma (Chap. 7) brought to the surface the value of an oath as an important and peculiar new element of CSR within the organization when discussing the case of the Banker's Oath. In this second part of the book, as an integral part of institutionalizing CSR, it becomes also apparent that there is a necessity for CSR to expand from private sector to public administration as suggested by Chymis et al. (Chap. 8) and even explore the importance of maintaining operational sustainability, and returning to normality through an integrated crisis management model adopted by private/public organizations in order to enhance CSR (Nizamidou and Vouzas in Chap. 9).

Finally in Part III, some particularly interesting case studies are presented upon reflection of the financial crisis. Castillo and Vial (Chap. 10) found significantly low percentage of multinational enterprises (MNEs) operating in Mexico to be exploiting social media drawing theoretical as well as practical implications. Gimenes and Payaud (Chap. 11) describe CSR projects of pharmaceutical companies' contribution toward society, while McQueen (Chap. 12) investigates the proposed introduction of fracking in the UK. Last but not least, Vontea and Stancu (Chap. 13) analyze the manner in which the corporate organizations interact with non-profit organizations in terms of the fundraising activity during the forthcoming timeframe to the financial crisis.

It is the editors' and authors' aim to bring together through this book normative and instrumental CSR conceptualizations, practice-based examples, and international case studies post-financial crisis. We hope that we played our part in the creation of knowledge in the field.

Poole, UK   Anastasios Theofilou
Poole, UK   Georgiana Grigore
Bucharest, Romania   Alin Stancu

.

Part I

Corporate Responsibility in the "Post-Financial Crisis": A Moral Discussion

1

Embedding Social Responsibility in HE Corporate Communications Degrees. The Place of CSR in Teaching Corporate Communications Programs (Advertising, Branding and Public Relations)

Rutherford and Richard Scullion

1.1 Introduction

Corporate social responsibility (CSR) is a politically, morally, economically and culturally loaded concept, not simply a niche area of contemporary business practice. This chapter will consider the implications of CSR for the design and delivery of advertising, marketing communications and public relations programs, including the opportunities and challenges for fostering ethical corporate behavior. We suggest that there are two main issues: *How we can enhance our students' knowledge and understanding of CSR* and *how we can engender their commitment to the application of its objectives, principles and practices.*

Rutherford (✉) • R. Scullion
Corporate and Marketing Communications,
Bournemouth University, Bournemouth, Dorset, UK

© The Author(s) 2017   **3**
A. Theofilou et al. (eds.), *Corporate Social Responsibility in the Post-Financial Crisis Era*, Palgrave Studies in Governance, Leadership and Responsibility, DOI 10.1007/978-3-319-40096-9_1

As observed by the editors of this volume, consumers as well as the broader civic community increasingly demand that companies demonstrate a commitment to creating what Porter and Kramer (2011) term 'shared value'. In addition to the impact of CSR on competitive advantage, customer loyalty, staff morale and the ability to attract and retain staff (Webb 2016), the Organisation for Economic Co-operation and Development (OECD) reports (Nieuwenkamp 2016) that even access to finance will increasingly depend on companies' demonstrable commitment to ethical policies and practices such as sustainable design, social justice, the ethical treatment of animals and environmental responsibility. As a consequence, CSR metrics have become a standard feature of corporate annual reports (Waller and Lanis 2009).

> [A] cursory glance at the websites of large multinationals such as British Petroleum, Shell, British American Tobacco and BT [reveals that] many industries and sectors create much fanfare around their corporate responsibility initiatives. Indeed [...] Corporate Social Responsibility is now a key marketing and branding reference point for most large and medium sized corporations. (Hanlon and Fleming 2009)

Despite the evidence that CSR is increasingly important in ensuring the goodwill of both consumers and communities, public confidence in the professed commitment of the corporate sector is regularly undermined by reports that, in the pursuit of maximized profits, many major corporations are prepared to ignore or actively flout popular notions of social justice and environmental responsibility with little or no regard for the consequences for their reputations.

> A big part of the problem lies with companies themselves, which remain trapped in an outdated approach to value creation [...] optimizing short-term financial performance in a bubble while missing the most important customer needs and ignoring the broader influences that determine their longer-term success [including] the well-being of their customers, the depletion of natural resources [and] the economic distress of the communities in which they produce and sell [...]. (Porter and Kramer 2011)

In the wake of the economic recession of 2007–08 which led to government spending cuts and a reduction in public services, already rising levels of social inequality (OECD 2016) have been exacerbated by the spread of predatory employment practices such as the use of 'zero-hour' contracts (up 19 % during 2014—Office for National Statistics). During the same period, the public has seen executive pay expand while the pay of workers stagnates, enormous bonuses paid to bankers widely blamed for both the financial crash of 2007–08 and the resulting austerity measures imposed by the same governments that countenance, or even tacitly support, 'aggressive' corporate tax avoidance and the use of tax havens which reduce the revenues needed to fund healthcare, education, social programs and infrastructure. As acknowledged by the Chair of the OECD Working Party on Responsible Business Conduct, however, 'Corporate tax responsibility […] is most often not on the radar screen of a CSR manager' (Nieuwenkamp 2016).

> [A]ccording to a survey of the British public […] four out of five people agreed that tax avoidance by multinationals made them "feel angry" [and] that a third of Britons say that they are boycotting companies which do not pay their "fair share" of tax in the UK. In a 2012 IBE survey carried out by Ipsos MORI, 'tax avoidance' was the second most important ethics issue that the British public think business needs to address. (Institute of Business Ethics 2013)

Media reports of large-scale protests, boycotts, petitions, social media campaigns and various forms of public 'shaming' attest to public anger in response to what are deemed unacceptable corporate behaviors. The increase in both the number and frequency of such actions indicates that the public is both more likely to be informed about—and less willing to tolerate—the indifference of corporations to the consequences of their policies and practices on lives, communities, the natural environment and the climate. The claim that '*We're all in this together*' has transmogrified from just another political platitude to become a rallying cry in the growing demand for meaningful change.

> [T]he tide of public opinion is visibly turning. Even 10 years ago, news of a company minimising its corporation tax would have been more likely to be inside the business pages than on the front page. In September 2009, the Observer ran with the headline: "Avoiding tax robs our public services, declares minister". (Barford and Holt 2013)

In light of growing public anger, cynicism and increasingly well-organized campaigns able to channel this into effective action, empty claims by companies of ethical practice behind which it is 'business as usual' risk being promptly and publicly exposed with potentially devastating consequences for both reputations and share value. (It will be instructive to see how long it will take for Volkswagen's reputation for environmental responsibility to recover from the discovery of having 'cheated' in emissions testing.) The OECD has warned of the consequences should the public come to see CSR 'primarily as a PR tool [and] merely a greenwashing exercise' (Nieuwenkamp 2016), especially where such assurances are used as an argument against government regulation. The authors take the position that, to ensure public goodwill, CSR initiatives must reflect a demonstrable commitment to ethical policies and practices.

As a major influence over the attitudes and behaviors of graduates (Stes et al. 2010; Parsons et al. 2012), we argue that educators have a responsibility to foster students' understanding of—and commitment to—the principles of CSR. Following a brief examination of the role of CSR in corporate communications, we consider how Higher Education (HE) communications programs might achieve this.

1.2   CSR in Corporate Communications

While the relevance of CSR to business and management is gaining acceptance, Kendrick et al. (2013) note that less attention has been paid to its application to, and its implications for, corporate communications. While CSR has an important role in guiding the management of companies (for example, in their procurement and HR policies), corporate communications has an equally important role in creating constructive relationships between customers and brands as a means to enhance social justice and environmental sustainability.

At the heart of corporate communications is the notion of compelling narratives: the 'stories' told about brands, products and services, as well as politicians, policies and the Right Priorities. Through the affective use of emotionally resonant words and images, corporate communications is able to present clients' products as the solution for the audience's desire for popularity, worthiness and success, thereby subtly influencing the way in which audiences define their desires and 'mentally picture' their fulfillment. As a result, despite the contribution of advertising, marketing communications and public relations agencies to constructive social change through *pro bono* work on campaigns to reduce smoking, domestic violence and climate change, the corporate communications industry is often associated in the public consciousness with less positive influences.

> [T]he social impact of advertising is often viewed as detrimental [with] criticism ranged from promoting commercialism, intrusion and irrationality, reinforcing sexual stereotypes, trivializing language, and provoking negative feelings. (Kendrick et al. 2013)

The persuasive influence of the presentation of information on our perceptions is well known.

> The effect of making men think in accordance with dogmas, perhaps in the form of certain graphic propositions, will be very peculiar: I am not thinking of these dogmas as determining men's opinions but rather as completely controlling the *expression* of all opinions. People will live under an absolute, palpable tyranny, though without being able to say they are not free. (Wittgenstein 1937)

However, as companies come to realize the extent to which their ability to differentiate their brands, and so protect their share value, depends on their public *persona*, communications agencies have begun to provide more substantial services than the design and production of materials that influence the perceptions and behaviors of consumers. As 'the first step towards developing a CSR mentality is to redefine the principles of the company' (Camilleri 2016), to assist clients in responding effectively to the market's demand for sustainable design, social justice and environmental responsibility, advertising, marketing communications and public relations agencies are increasingly called upon to lead clients through a fundamental re-conception of who they are and how they 'prove' it.

In undertaking this work, creative agencies have both an opportunity and responsibility to assist clients in recognizing the extent to which their current definition of 'success' and the pursuit of short-term financial goals have got them 'stuck' in policies and practices which, by damaging the environment and the social and economic well-being of the communities in which they operate, threatens to undermine their continued viability.

But of course, in preparing to undertake such an ontological task (*Help us to become something else … something better …*), the corporate communication industry must ask its own 'raison d'être' questions. Thus, just as the rise of social media fundamentally changed both the purpose and practices of advertising, branding, marketing communications and public relations (from creating persuasive messages and visual materials for defined target markets—to engaging diverse audiences in meaningful conversations and relationships), the demand for socially responsible practices and 'corporate citizenship' is once again obliging communications agencies to comprehensively re-evaluate the nature of the relationships between brands and their customers, including what and how they communicate, to whom—and for what purpose.

In his 1964 manifesto *First Things First*, British designer Ken Garland spoke for many corporate communications professionals who had grown increasingly uneasy with supporting—and thereby implicitly endorsing—their influence on the ways in which 'citizen-consumers speak, think, feel, respond and interact', arguing that this had led to 'a reductive and immeasurably harmful code of public discourse' (Garland 1964). Revised by Barnbrook et al. in 1999, 33 visual communicators renewed the call for an urgent change of priorities:

> Unprecedented environmental, social and cultural crises demand our attention. […] We propose a reversal of priorities in favour of more useful, lasting and democratic forms of communication—a mindshift away from product marketing and toward the exploration and production of a new kind of meaning. The scope of debate is shrinking; it must expand. Consumerism […] must be challenged by other perspectives expressed, in part, through the visual languages and resources of design. (Barnbrook et al. 1999)

1.3   Teaching CSR in Higher Education

This impetus for more reflective approaches and more socially conscious practices by communications professionals demands a meaningful response from higher education. In considering our role in shaping the knowledge and perspectives of graduates (what they understand and how they use this understanding), institutions of higher education must also reflect on our societal purpose beyond merely supplying the next generation of skilled workers.

Despite—or perhaps in response to—the failure of many companies to embed CSR practices, HE business and management programs have begun to include ethics, CSR and sustainability into their curricula (Brennan 2012) to equip students/graduates with the knowledge and skills necessary to assist their future employers in responding to the growing pressure to contribute to (or, at least, to be seen to contribute to) the well-being of the community. 'The companies that hire our graduates are demanding it, our students need and usually want it, and our economy and society rely on it' (Ikenberry and Sockell 2012).

Despite this, however, there is evidence that the inclusion of CSR into HE business and management programs has been uneven. Although a majority of the top 50 global MBA programs (as rated by the Financial Times in their 2006 Global MBA rankings) now include CSR in their curricula, a 2003 survey of European business schools found an 'intellectual bias against business ethics' (Matten and Moon 2004), that CSR is often relegated to the status of 'an elective or optional track of studies' (Hasrouni 2012), and that, '[r]egardless of what is happening in the top […] MBA programs, there is a trend toward less ethics education overall' (Nicholson and DeMoss 2009). Furthermore, consistent with the findings of Kendrick et al. (2013) that less attention has been paid to the role of CSR in corporate communications as a means to promote social justice and environmental sustainability, the literature on CSR in HE has likewise given relatively little attention to its integration in (or its implications for) the curricula of corporate communications (advertising, marketing communications and public relations) programs.

If HE programs are to serve the national economic interests (Mandelson 2009), our programs must enable our graduates to understand and respond effectively to the changing socio-economic environment in which companies—their future employers—now operate. This will require more than just new modules inserted into existing curricula (Nicholson and DeMoss 2009; Turker et al. 2016); it demands a fundamental reconsideration of the purpose of professional education, including what and how we teach—and for what purpose. It requires a critical review and re-evaluation of what these 'national economic interests' should (and could) be.

> [E]thics and corporate social sensitivity is not just a core curriculum issue. [The] ethical culture of a business school is pervasive. It is reflected in the context of courses, in expectations of ethical student conduct (and repercussions for unethical behaviors) [...] and in the projects and programs to which the school devotes its energies and resources. (Nicholson and DeMoss 2009)

We argue therefore that those who teach the corporate leaders of tomorrow have a responsibility, not only to our students and their future employers, but to the broader communities whose lives will be affected by their values and behaviors. Embedding the values of social and environmental responsibility within the teaching and learning environment is therefore essential, not only to improve our graduates' career prospects but also to encourage 'business students to critically evaluate, analyse and question the basic premises underlying contemporary business practices' (García-Rosell 2012) and their impact on the lives of those who will be affected by the policies and practices they will help to shape. This, in turn, will both encourage and enable our students to redefine the concept of 'successful business practices' and what it means to engage in these.

> The question is no longer whether CSR should have a place in the business curricula, but how it should be incorporated and what role business schools play within the wider "business in society" debate. Students, the marketplace, the community, government and civil society are increasingly demanding that business schools rethink their traditional role. (Haski-Leventhal 2014)

> The oft-cited argument is that higher education has educated the politicians, managers, teachers, scientists and engineers who have taken us to our current and generally unsustainable position, and it is the education of future groups of these folk that will enable us to step up to new levels of sustainability. On this basis, curriculum change towards sustainability, for all students and not just those who choose to study sustainability-related topics, is the next critical stage. (Shepard 2015)

In a recent review of CSR teaching in European business education, Turker et al. (2016) report that the wide variations in the way in which CSR is taught (and, by inference, the wide variations in the way in which it is defined) have significantly influenced students' perception of the topic. As observed by Boulding (1956), the way in which we IMAGiNE, define or 'mentally picture' what something 'is' shapes our (often subconscious) assumptions about what it is 'for', and this, in turn, informs the decisions we make in our efforts to achieve it (Rutherford 2015).

> [W]e are bound to take a view of […] higher education, whether or not we articulate it and whether or not we are conscious of it. In that case, the models and approaches that we develop […] will take on the form of an ideology [that] contain hidden interests, bound up with our assumptions about the fundamental purposes of higher education. (Barnett 1992, p. 15)

It follows therefore, that way in which we 'mentally picture' the purpose of teaching CSR will shape the way in which we present it to our students (what Entwistle 2003, termed our 'ways of thinking and practising in the subject'), and this, in turn, will influence our students' assumptions about the reasons we are teaching it. If we wish to encourage our students' commitment to the principles of CSR and its role in establishing a new, constructive relationship between the corporate and social spheres, we must consider carefully *our* 'mental picture' of CSR and our beliefs about the purpose for including it in the curriculum. Do we 'see' CSR as just another promotional tactic for short-term economic advantage, and therefore just another professional skill our students will need if they are to improve their 'marketability' to future employers—or do we 'see' CSR as a means to engage our students, as citizens and professionals, in a debate about the contribution of affective communication to social justice, environmental responsibility and community health? (To 'build value in people's lives, rather than plant messages in consumers' heads', Johnson 2013.). In the way in which we 'see' (and so present) the purpose of teaching CSR, we believe that HE programs have an opportunity to re-claim and re-invent our historic role as a critical friend and a source of radical social reform.

As explicitly endorsed by the Mission Statements of many universities, a central objective of higher education is to encourage our students to see themselves as more than just aspiring professionals, consumers and tax payers, but as human beings and citizens with a responsibility to contribute to the well-being of the communities in which they will live and work. In our efforts to foster this attitude among students, we submit that advertising, marketing communications and public relations programs have a clear positional advantage over many other business disciples.

If we are to help our students to understand how to use communications to influence the ways in which audiences IMAGINE or 'mentally picture' brands, products, services, ideas and events, it is necessary to encourage (and assist) them in identifying—and in reflecting critically upon—how the narratives implicit within commercial messages have influenced *their* perceptions. In other words, if we are to teach students *How We* (as advertisers) *Do It to Audiences*, it is necessary to lead them to consider *How They* (advertisers) *Do It to Us* (Rutherford 2012). If our students are unable to recognize how and why *they* have been affected by certain campaigns, we argue that they will be at a significant disadvantage in being able to make informed and appropriate decisions in the conception and execution of materials that will likewise affect others.

In designing our programs to foster, or even require, such on-going reflection and analysis on the part of students, we must encourage (and equip) our students to 'look around the frame' of the current neoliberal dogma in order to recognize—and question the implications of—the values and assumptions reflected by, and implicit within, corporate campaigns and messages. In this way, we not only encourage and validate the integration of professional and civic objectives, but simultaneously assist our students in developing the critical, imaginative and creative problem-solving skills upon which the future of their employers and clients will depend.

In the effort to achieve this, there are two inter-related issues: *How we can enhance our students' knowledge and understanding of CSR* and *how we can engender their commitment to the application of its objectives, principles and practices.*

1.3.1 Enhancing Students' Knowledge and Understanding of CSR

New dynamics, as well as changing consumer values and expectations have radically changed the communications industry (Johnson 2013). If students are to develop the cognitive, strategic and practical skills needed for a career in the communications industry, they must understand how to 'build value in people's lives, rather than plant messages in consumers' heads' (Johnson 2013) and develop the ability to translate that understanding into action (Ikenberry and Sockell 2012).

According to numerous studies (Hidi and Harackiewicz 2000; Crumpton and Gregory 2011; Entwistle et al. 2002; Hockings et al. 2008; Sanacore 2008; Thomas and Jamieson-Ball 2011; Yorke and Longden 2008), the single most important influence on students' willingness to engage with a subject is the extent to which they perceive it to be 'relevant' to their lives and careers. To assist our students in *understanding* the ways in which CSR contributes to 'shared value', we must provide opportunities to witness its impact through practical examples, case studies and live projects.

As identified by Haski-Leventhal (2014), students studying business subjects are keen to see how CSR issues can be incorporated into 'real life' business situations (Fig. 1.1).

1.3.2 Engendering Students' Commitment to the Objectives, Principles and Practices of CSR

We believe however, that it is not enough that students *understand* the ways in which CSR contributes to 'shared value'. To encourage our students' commitment to the aspirations of CSR, we advocate that we must do more than 'teach' it: We must 'practice what we preach' by demonstrably embedding CSR in the design and delivery of our programs (Entwistle's 'ways of thinking and practising in the subject'), including the nature of the projects we set and the criteria by which we assess these by ensuring that a passing grade requires the appropriate and effective application of its principles and practices and, at higher levels, the ability to critique these.

We must also embed its principles and practices in the management of our institutions. While the widening participation agenda is often cited as a prime example of the incorporation of CSR in the management and delivery of UK higher education, as universities now reply for their funding on student tuition, 'widening participation' has become an economic necessity in order to ensure an adequate revenue stream.

	Level of agreement in general
Bring in experts and leaders as guest speakers on these topics	85.1%
Encourage professors to introduce more applicable case studies in classes	80.4%
Educate recruiters on the importance of these themes in the MBA curriculum	72.6%
Integrate social and environmental themes into the core curriculum	70.7%
Provide students with internships related to corporate responsibility / sustainability	68.6%
Create a concentration on sustainability and corporate social responsibility	59.4%
Increase the number of electives that focus on social and environmental themes	55.6%
No changes are required	25.5%

Fig. 1.1 Levels of agreement by 1250 international MBA and Masters of Business students to proposed changes in responsible management education (adapted from Haski-Leventhal 2014)

1.4 The Challenges in Embedding CSR in HE

A number of the changes introduced into the UK HE sector since the 2007–08 economic recession pose significant challenges for the effective integration of CSR into our institutions and for the design and delivery of corporate communications programs.

As a direct consequence of the reduction in state funding, there has been a significant increase in the tuition fees at UK universities (from

£1000 in 2006 to £9000 in 2010). This reflects the government's stated intention to shift the cost for HE from the state to 'the individual who benefits' (Briefing Paper: *HE in England from 2012—Funding and finance*). This has resulted in two significant changes in HE: the need for universities to attract and retain customers, and the shift in the perceptions of students as to the role and purpose of higher education.

1.4.1   The Need To Attract and Retain Customers

Central to universities' recruitment and retention strategies in this increasingly 'marketized' sphere is the need for evidence that students achieve high marks as 'proof' of high quality teaching and learning (Molesworth et al. 2010; Kahu 2013). And so, as assessment of practice-based skills tends to produce higher marks and 'customer satisfaction' statistics (Brown 2001), the shift toward assessment of HE programs weighted toward practical skills identified by Stevens (1999) is likely to only intensify (Rutherford 2015).

As the business and industry leaders brought in as guest speakers regularly remind our students however, the effective application of CSR in corporate communications demands knowledge and understanding of several complex factors as well as the ability to translate this understanding into appropriate solutions for diverse and complex problems. Despite this requirement to foster greater cognitive skills, several recent trends driven by the need to attract and retain customers (including grade inflation and efforts to reduce failure rates, increased student choice of optional units in which students gravitate toward their comfort zones, and the rise in importance of student satisfaction as a driver of HE policies [Molesworth et al. 2010]) are all likely to adversely affect students' capacity for critical thinking, structural analysis and the ability to develop innovative solutions.

As a result, the changes in the design and delivery of HE programs driven by the market forces which now dominate the discussion of the role of HE are likely to undermine both our graduates' career prospects and the ability of industry (their future employers) to respond to consumer demand for meaningful change, thereby reducing the value of our programs and, ultimately, the long-term prospects of our institutions.

1.4.2 Students' Perceptions of the Role and Purpose of HE

Under the neoliberal paradigm, the purpose (or 'mental picture') of higher education has been 're-framed'. Once seen as an opportunity to acquire knowledge and understanding esteemed in their own right (Collini 2012), HE is now increasingly 'seen as' a mercantile service (Newstead and Hoskins 2003) and a financial investment in the acquisition of professional qualifications and skills which can be 'sold' in the market (Fitzmaurice 2008). And, with 'economic advantage' its purpose, it follows that, as its primary beneficiaries, students should be expected to bear the burden of its costs and be treated primarily as consumers (Molesworth et al. 2010).

This new conception of 'HE as a mercantile service' has coincided with an increase in resistance to difficult/complex assignments by both students and university management. Students (for whom the objective is now *the degree* rather than the subject knowledge and understanding to which it used to attest) oppose them because they often lead to less-than-laudatory grades. University management resists them because they are obstacles to the high student marks desired for recruitment and retention strategies. These pressures will have to be addressed if we are to encourage a greater proportion of students to engage with the inherently complex challenges of social justice and environmental protection.

But those of us who teach communications are in the business of changing frames of reference, and we must accept the challenge. We might begin by encouraging our students to 'see' themselves as more than just aspiring professionals—but as human beings and as citizens and to accept the responsibility for considering carefully both the origins and implications of the assumptions they carry around in their heads—because these will not only determine the lives they will lead, but the shape of the world they will leave behind.

1.5 Case Study: CSR Embedded in Higher Education Persuasive Communications Programs

The following case study briefly outlines one department's pedagogic approach to embedding the underlying principles of CSR into its teaching and learning environment for a variety of a BA (Hons) degree programs (Advertising, Public Relations, Marketing Communications and Marketing). We offer this as an example/illustration of how one department has attempted to address (Higher Education Institution) department has attempted to address/embed these issues. Both the philosophical underpinning and its practical manifestations are outlined. We are not claiming extraordinary outcomes as a result of these recent efforts; however, we believe that this case demonstrates a commitment to embed the principles outlined in this chapter and illustrates some of the issues, and recommendations that flow from it.

This case study describes a recent revalidation process and the outcomes for three well-established undergraduate degree programs taught in a post-92 south coast university. The revisions were made in response to a number of sources, including a comprehensive review of the offerings of competitors, constructive input from industry contacts, and an evaluation of student and alumni feedback. In this, we have responded to our stakeholder groups: one of the cornerstones of acting in a socially responsive manner. The changes are also the result of efforts by the academic team to enhance the current suite of programs to ensure they are 'fit for purpose' in the current and anticipated future environment (including the industries with which we align, as well as their current and *potential future* practices). In preparation for this revalidation, the department undertook a reflective and reflexive mirroring process to ensure that we recognized the nature of the relationships HE has and *should have* with the society in which we operate in order to 'practice what we intended to preach': designing our offering with due consideration to both its current—and crucially, its potential and future societal impacts.

Our stated aim was:

to provide an environment in which we can help to produce visionary Advertising, Marketing Communications and Public Relations practitioners and to facilitate and support our graduates in becoming independent, creative, entrepreneurial, ethical and enlightened practitioners, able and committed to define new industry practice and benchmarks for excellence in their fields, and so capable of contributing to the transformation of their industries.

This is bold, ambitious and purposefully challenging: features which we believe characterize CSR-informed programs committed to improving the societal role of business. We are asking our students and ourselves to go beyond knowing 'what is happening' in the commercial world, to recognize why this might be and so to be able to imagine ('mentally picture') alternatives. One of the intended consequences of our revalidation is to help locate CSR (and indeed other corporate and organizational practices) within a socio-historical context. Thus, CSR is not treated as the newest trend for building (possibly undeserved) reputational goodwill, but as a complex and multifaceted way of thinking and practicing communications that offers a new way to learn.

Our pedagogy is based on a learning hierarchy of *knowledge*, then *doing*, then *practice* and finally, *critical creation* through which students are expected to first, learn *about* their discipline (its foundations, structures, roles and processes), then *apply* these knowledges and skills in practical projects, before *demonstrating* their transferability in a year-long professional placement. In their final year, they are expected to have both the ability and the confidence to generate—*and demonstrate*—the capacity for innovative thinking and practice. The distinctions between each phase are reflected and reinforced in the bases for assessment in the following ways:

Year 1   Students are assessed on their ability to describe and explain the foundational theories of CSR and the industry roles, structures, processes and practices in this area of business.

Year 2   Students are assessed on their ability to apply existing methods and processes in designing and implementing CSR projects in a given context.

Year 3   Students take into their placement this appreciation of CSR and are tasked at the end of the year with reflecting on how CSR does/could play a prominent role in the organization they are working for.

Year 4   Students are assessed on their ability to demonstrate potential in contributing to CSR thinking and practice that builds on existing modes, and to actively critique and challenge existing practice through the prism of an appropriate intellectual lens (i.e. using notions of consumer as citizen or 'prosumers').

Central to our commitment to embed a professional practice ethos within the curriculum in a way that both encourages and assists students to place their leaning in a wider active context is the year-long placement required of all students on all three programs. As part of their reflection on this experience as they start their final year of study, students are expected to consider the impact and implications of the CSR practices in which the organization either was engaged, had considered, or in which the students believe it should have been engaged.

This placement is aligned with the newly revised unit *Innovation and Enterprise* required of all students in their final year and tailored to the specifics of each of the three programs: Advertising, Marketing Communications and Public Relations. Here, notions of enterprise culture and 'the enterprising self' are explored in ways that allow and encourage students to consider their own agency as they prepare to become active members of a societal workforce to which they must both adapt and begin to influence. To this end, we have also developed bespoke units/modules for these revalidated programs that speak directly to the impact and implications of CSR for the practice of Advertising, Marketing Communications and Public Relations. These bespoke units/ modules require our students to consider various practices—and their actions within these—through an ethical lens, such as social communications, consumer culture, advertising and society and transcultural communication.

While the final year outlined above may sound overly ambitious for undergraduates, we define the notion of 'creation' as stretching across a continuum, breaking, to various degrees, with existing practice and thinking. For some, this will mean developing the ability to make tangible recommendations on ways in which to improve existing CSR programs for a specific company, organization or even an entire industry—while for others, it will involve developing a radical departure from existing ways of thinking and practice.

Conclusion

At the core of CSR is the expectation that organizations will recognize and respond proactively by being prepared to act on both the ideals and the 'deliverables' of social justice and environmental stewardship.

Higher education has an essential role to play in contributing to this development by encouraging—and engaging our students in—a thorough review of the current orthodoxy which values short-term financial goals at any cost. If we wish to encourage and enable our students/graduates to do their part and to integrate citizenship with corporate objectives, we must begin to consider carefully the impact of the ideological 'frames of reference' which have driven recent changes in the design and delivery our programs, and be prepared to undertake the same radical 're-imagining' of both our purpose and practice that society now demands of the business sector our graduates must be prepared to lead.

A commitment by academics and senior management to the principles of CSR and the meaningful integration of its practices in the design and delivery of our programs will allow us to identify, reflect on—and, most importantly, to challenge—currently short-sighted modes and models of corporate and organizational practices and priorities and, in doing so, enable us to reclaim and re-invent our historic role as a critical friend and a source of radical social reform.

References

Barford, V., & Holt, G. (2013, May 21). Google, Amazon, Starbucks: The rise of 'tax shaming'. *BBC News Magazine*. Retrieved March 8, 2016, from http://www.bbc.co.uk/news/magazine-20560359

Barnbrook, J., et al. (1999, Autumn). First things first manifesto 2000. *Eye Magazine*. Retrieved March 10, 2016, from http://www.eyemagazine.com/feature/article/first-things-first-manifesto-2000

Barnett, R. (1992). *Improving higher education: Total quality care*. Bristol: Open University Press.

Boulding, K. (1956). *The image*. Ann Arbor, MI: University of Michigan.

Brennan, R. (2012, February 10). *Teaching marketing at university level*. Higher Education Academy Report. Retrieved March 1, 2016, from https://core.ac.uk/download/files/125/9256646.pdf

Brown, G. (2001). *Assessment: A guide for lecturers* (Learning and Teaching Support Network (LTSN) Generic Centre Assessment Series Number 3).

Camilleri, M. A. (2016). Reconceiving corporate social responsibility for business and educational outcomes. *Cogent Business & Management, 3.*

Collini, S. (2012, February 24). The threat to our universities. *The Guardian.*

Crumpton, H. E., & Gregory, A. (2011). "I'm not learning": The role of academic relevancy for low-achieving students. *The Journal of Educational Research, 104*(1), 42–53.

Entwistle, N. (2003). *Concepts and conceptual frameworks underpinning the ETL project.* Occasional Report 3, 3–4.

Entwistle, N., McCune, V., & Hounsell, J. (2002). *Approaches to studying and perceptions of university teaching-learning environments: Concepts, measures and preliminary findings of the ETL project.* Occasional Report 1: Enhancing Teaching-Learning Environments in Undergraduate Courses. Retrieved July 21, 2012, from http://www.etl.tla.ed.ac.uk/docs/etlreport1.pdf

Fitzmaurice, M. (2008). Voices from within: Teaching in higher education as a moral practice. *Teaching in Higher Education, 13*(3), 341–352.

García-Rosell, J.-C. (2012). Struggles over corporate social responsibility meanings in teaching practices: The case of hybrid problem-based learning. *Management Learning, 0*(0)1–19.

Garland, K. (1963). *First things first.* Retrieved March 10, 2016, from http://www.designishistory.com/1960/first-things-first/

Hanlon, G., & Fleming, P. (2009). Updating the critical perspective on corporate social responsibility. *Sociology Compass, 3*(6), 937–948.

Haski-Leventhal, D. (2014). MBA student values, attitudes and behaviors: A cross-cultural comparison of PRME signatory schools. *SAM Advanced Management Journal, 79*(4), 29.

Hasrouni, L. (2012). Cultivating values—How business schools can plant the seeds of change. *Responsible Business,* July–September, 54–67.

Hidi, S., & Harackiewicz, J. M. (2000). Motivating the academically unmotivated: A critical issue for the 21st century. *Review of Educational Research, 70*(2), 151–179.

Hockings, C., Cooke, S., Yamashita, H., McGinty, S., & Bowl, M. (2008). Switched off? A study of disengagement among computing students at two universities. *Research Papers in Education, 23*(2). Retrieved July 21, 2012, from http://www2.wlv.ac.uk/celt/Projects/RPiEAcademic_Feb08.pdf

Ikenberry, D. L., & Sockell, D. (2012). Occupy our business schools. *Bloomberg Business.* Retrieved March 25, 2016, from http://www.businessweek.com/business-schools/occupy-our-business-schools-01112012.html

Institute of Business Ethics. (2013). *Tax avoidance as an ethical issue for business.* Issue April 31.

Johnson, S. (2013). *The future of sustainability is design, not communication.* Retrieved February 23, 2016, from http://www.sustainablebrands.com/news_and_views/communications/future-sustainability-vdesign-not-communication

Kahu, E. R. (2013). Framing student engagement in higher education. *Studies in Higher Education, 38*(5), 758–773.

Kendrick, A., Fullerton, J. A., & Kim, Y. J. (2013). Social responsibility in advertising: A marketing communications student perspective. *Journal of Marketing Education, 35*(22), 141–154.

Mandelson, P. (2009, December 22). *Letter to Tim Melville-Ross, Chairman, Higher Education Funding Council for England.* Retrieved October 24, 2010, from http://www.hefce.ac.uk/news/newsarchive/2009/HEFCE,Grant,settlement/

Matten, D., & Moon, J. (2004). Corporate social responsibility education in Europe. *Journal of Business Ethics, 54*(4), 323–337.

Molesworth, M., Scullion, R., & Nixon, E. (2010). *The marketisation of higher education and the student as consumer.* London: Routledge.

Newstead, S. E., & Hoskins, S. (2003). Encouraging student motivation. In H. Fry, S. Ketteridge, & S. Marshall (Eds.), *A handbook for teaching & learning in higher education.* London: RoutledgeFalmer.

Nicholson, C. Y., & DeMoss, M. (2009). Teaching ethics and social responsibility: An evaluation of undergraduate business education at the discipline level. *Journal of Education for Business, 84*(4), 213–218.

Nieuwenkamp, R. (2016, January 22). 2016: CSR is dead! What's next? *OECD.* Retrieved March 9, 2016, from http://oecdinsights.org/2016/01/22/2016-csr-is-dead-whats-next/

Office for National Statistics (ONS). (2015, September 2). *Contracts with no guaranteed hours: 2015.* Retrieved March 23, 2016, from http://www.ons.gov.uk/employmentandlabourmarket/peopleinwork/earningsandworkinghours/articles/contractswithnoguaranteedhours/2015-09-02

Organisation for Economic Co-operation and Development (OECD). 2016. *Inequality.* Retrieved March 24, 2016, from http://www.oecd.org/social/inequality.htm

Parsons, D., Hill, I., Holland, J., & Willis, D. (2012). *Impact of teaching development programmes in higher education.* HEA Research Series. York: The Higher Education Academy.

Porter, M. E., & Kramer, M. R. (2011). The big idea: Creating shared value. *Harvard Business Review, 89*(1), 2.

Rutherford. (2012). Why advertising students should be required to write. *Networks* Higher Education Academy (17).

Rutherford. (2015). Improving student engagement in commercial art and design programmes. *International Journal of Art & Design Education, 34*(1), 89–101.

Sanacore, J. (2008). Turning reluctant learners into inspired learners. *The Clearing House: A Journal of Educational Strategies, Issues and Ideas, 82*(1), 40–44.

Shepard, K. (2015). *Higher education for sustainable development.* Basingstoke: Palgrave Macmillan.

Stes, A., Min-Leliveld, M., Gijbels, D., & Van Petegem, P. (2010). The impact of instructional development in higher education: The state-of-the-art of the research. *Educational Research Review, 5*(1), 25–49.

Stevens, M. (1999). Human capital theory and UK vocational training policy. *Oxford Review of Economic Policy*, Oxford University Press, *15(1)*, 16–32.

Thomas, L., & Jamieson-Ball, C. (Eds.) (2011). *Engaging students to improve student retention and success in higher education in Wales.* York: Higher Education Academy.

Turker, D., Vural, C. A., & Idowu, S. O. (Eds.). (2016). *CSR, sustainability, ethics & governance.* Springer. Retrieved from http://link.springer.com/book/10.1007/978-3-319-26716-6

Waller, D. S., & Lanis, R. (2009). Corporate social responsibility (CSR) disclosure of advertising agencies: An exploratory analysis of six holding companies' annual reports. *Journal of Advertising, 38*(1), 109–122.

Webb, J. (2016, February 11). The "shared value" of corporate social responsibility. *The Financial Times.* Retrieved March 11, 2016, from http://blogs.ft.com/mba-blog/2016/02/11/the-shared-value-of-corporate-social-responsibility/

Wittgenstein, L. (1937/1998). *Culture and value* (G. R. von Wright Ed.). London: Wiley-Blackwell.

Yorke, M., & Longden, B. (2008). *The first-year experience of higher education in the UK.* York: Higher Education Academy.

2

Does Religiousness Influence the Corporate Social Responsibility Orientation in Germany?

Maria Anne Schmidt

2.1 Introduction

Various company scandals in recent years involving also German firms (e.g., emission scandal of Volkswagen or KiK's weak labor conditions in Bangladesh) as well as the financial crisis lead to a loss in credibility in national and international companies. To regain credibility, the business scene intends to direct itself toward more sustainable, philanthropic activities. Consumers search for an alternative to the modern reliance on the economic system. Some find their religious belief to offer this alternative by giving solidarity and breaking out of the fast-moving nature. Whether religiosity plays a role in modern consumers' decisions provides a valuable source of information for directing business toward

M.A. Schmidt (✉)
Faculty of Social and Behavioral Sciences, Friedrich Schiller University Jena, Fuerstengraben 1, Jena 07743, Germany

© The Author(s) 2017   **25**
A. Theofilou et al. (eds.), *Corporate Social Responsibility in the Post-Financial Crisis Era*, Palgrave Studies in Governance, Leadership and Responsibility, DOI 10.1007/978-3-319-40096-9_2

the ongoing challenges. Also researchers address this development by broadening the cultural and geographical context of studies and inter-disciplinary co-operations including economics, ethics, theology, psychology, and sociology. Schlegelmilch and Öberseder (2010) especially mention religion and marketing ethics as one of the most promising research streams. Dyck (2014) goes the extra mile and speaks about a recent "theological turn" in the management and organizational literature. Nevertheless, the literature leaves an inconsistent picture about the connection between religion and corporate social responsibility (CSR) due to different measurement methods, benchmarks, or even findings. Some studies revealed that individuals not involved with religion tend to hold what Agle and Van Buren (1999) refer to as a narrow view of CSR (Quazi 2003; Singhapakdi et al. 2000). In contrast, religious people are more likely to understand CSR in a broader way, as suggested by Carroll (1999). Still, many articles conclude with nuanced results and authors call for more research in the area of religion and CSR (Jamali and Sidani 2013; Weaver and Agle 2002). Moreover, not much is known so far about the understanding of CSR from consumers' perspective (Maignan 2001). Especially in Western economies, religion and religiousness might be presumed to lack a profound influence in the evaluation of consumers regarding the CSR activities of firms. This chapter addresses the research gap between religion and business ethics understanding and expectations from a consumer point of view. With the goal to analyze religiousness as a factor influencing the corporate social responsibility orientation (CSRO) of respondents, the author tries to understand individual differences in CSR expectations in Germany.

After introducing the current literature on CSR and religiousness as well as the model that is applied here, the main results of the study are presented. Religiousness of business students is not found to be a critical factor to influence the CSR orientation. Moreover, a second perspective on religiousness is offered. The author compares affiliated with unaffili-ated students to recheck the results. Also here, findings remain similar. Comparing the study with former writings, it contributes to a more refined understanding of the link between religion and business ethics.

2.2 Theoretical Background

Current literature focuses more and more on the connection between religion, culture, and individual factors that influence entrepreneurs, consumers, or even companies within or across borders, in business to business or business to consumers situations. Especially, religion as a factor influencing the business ethics culture is a research stream that attracts the recent management literature (Parboteeah et al. 2014). While a growing body of empirical research has linked religion with ethical behavior in a business context (Angelidis and Ibrahim 2004; Ibrahim et al. 2008) and in management decision-making (Agle and Van Buren 1999; Longenecker et al. 2004), only a few authors so far analyzed the effect of religiousness on social behavior and management decisions (Angelidis and Ibrahim 2004; Dusuki et al. 2008; Ibrahim et al. 2008; Ramasamy et al. 2010; Wiebe and Fleck 1980). Moreover, wide differences in research methods and in findings lead to mixed results and an unclear knowledge on the connection between religion and ethical behavior. In addition, researchers see a considerable diversity in the attitudes of religious individuals of different faiths. Due to the research focus of this chapter, findings related to Christianity are outlined. Still, results remain diverse and inconclusive.

On the one hand, Quazi (2003) highlights that Australian managers with some level of religious belief are more likely to understand CSR in a wider perspective (going beyond regulatory requirements). Singhapakdi et al. (2000) find out that religiousness significantly influences the personal moral philosophies of marketers in the USA. Wiebe and Fleck (1980) examined the religious orientation of Canadian university freshmen and found that religious people tend to have a greater concern for higher moral standards than nonreligious students. Schneider et al. (2011) find religiosity to have a significant positive influence on ethical consumer behavior. On the other hand, there are numerous studies that see only a small influence of religiousness on business ethics or none at all (Agle and Van Buren 1999; Brammer et al. 2007).

These diverse results might come from definitional vagueness of the terms religion, religiosity, or even spirituality.[1] Religiosity is defined as a "belief in the existence of God and a commitment to attending to and complying with rules that members of that religion believe have been defined by God" (Schneider et al. 2011, p. 32). Others perceive religiosity "as exercising control over beliefs and behaviors" (Vitell et al. 2005, p. 175). In this chapter, the author follows Voland (2009) in his definition of religiousness. For him, it can be defined as the "individually varying psychic and behavioral manifestation of religiosity" (Voland 2009, p. 9). It is about the personal practice of religion (Allport and Ross 1967).

But not only definitional differences remain, also a wide range of research methods impacts the diverse results. Acknowledging that religiosity does play a role not only in economics but also in sociology, theology, or ethics, there is the need to limit the investigation. The business ethics literature is assumed to be the relevant field of study. Thus, the author concentrates on results from this research area and the application of methods.

Angelidis and Ibrahim (2004) were the first to test the relationship between the degree of religiousness and the CSRO of individuals. With their study, they follow an approach developed by Aupperle (1982; Aupperle et al. 1985) for a quantitative study. In Aupperle's framework, participants are requested to rate the importance of economic, legal, ethical, and philanthropic responsibilities of a firm with a forced-choice instrument, thereby constituting a scale of relative importance. These responsibility dimensions date back to Carroll (1979, 1991), who developed his theory in 1979 and considered previous conceptualizations of CSR. For him, a company "should strive to make a profit, obey the law, be ethical, and be a good corporate citizen" (Carroll 1999, p. 43). Carroll originally proposed this theory of a pyramid-like relation with economic obligations as the foundation of a firm's activities and subsequently legal, ethical, and philanthropic obligations as additional factors of decreasing importance.[2] Angelidis and Ibrahim (2004) use the forced-choice instru-

---

[1] The term is currently emerging in business ethics research. Various researchers criticize the Eurocentric perspective suspected behind the terms religiosity and religiousness. Thus, concepts like spirituality or Zen-meditation are used in recent research with the goal to create a universally applicable term.

[2] According to his theory, the assumed relative weighting followed 4:3:2:1 out of ten points.

ment of Aupperle (1982; Aupperle et al. 1985) to check whether the religiousness of students in the USA influences the relative weighting of the four firm's responsibilities economic, legal, ethical, and philanthropic. They found a difference in this importance rating with respect to the economic and the ethical dimension between highly religious and low religious students. Highly religious Christian students in the USA tend to rank ethical obligations more important and economic performance less important than low religious students. In a follow-up study, Ibrahim et al. (2008) reviewed their test with business students and managers and reported mixed results. While religiousness was found to influence the CSRO of students, this was not true for managers.

To summarize, various studies reveal a weak relationship between religiousness and ethical behavior. However, there is still potential to further investigate a clear indication on how CSR perception and ethical awareness are related to religion (Vitell et al. 2005; Weaver and Agle 2002). Jamali and Sidani (2013) see a special need to analyze the correlation between religiosity and CSR since current results remain inconclusive. Schneider et al. (2011) specify this call for future research. They expect interesting results for Germany. This is due to some particularities that show the importance of religiosity research. Although Germany has a Christian majority,[3] more than 70 percent in East Germany and almost 40 percent in West Germany describe themselves as being not religious (Pickel 2013). Allport and Ross (1967), the forefathers of religiosity research in business ethics, pointed to the fact that including nonreligious and antireligious individuals is of *central significance* for religious research. Moreover, 80 percent of Germans think that you can be religious without being a church member (Pickel and Sammet 2014). These data show the importance to include personal religious practice in the research analysis to understand factors around religion influencing the business ethics perception. Thus, this chapter not only provides additional input for the discussion on religiousness and CSRO by reporting empirical results from Germany. The nominal religious surrounding in East Germany, where the study was conducted, offers a unique setting that has never been considered before in CSRO research.

---

[3] Data estimated for 2011 by Pew Research Centre: 68.7 percent are Christians in Germany.

2.3   Method and Sample Description

The data were collected using a survey within a larger cross-cultural study of business ethics (Schmidt and Cracau 2015). To reach the participating business students, classes were personally addressed and the purpose of the study was explained, including anonymity and confidentiality issues.[4]

In the first part of the questionnaire, CSRO was measured with an instrument developed by Aupperle (1982; Aupperle et al. 1985). This is based on the four-dimensional CSR definition proposed by Carroll (1979, 1991) and uses a forced-choice approach. Aupperle et al. (1985) perceived this method as suitable since the forced-choice system minimizes the effect of social desirability on the results. Originally, Aupperle and colleagues used this instrument to determine how chief executive officers (CEOs) view the social responsibility of their firm and sought to provide empirical evidence for the weightings of the four dimensions as proposed by Carroll (4:3:2:1). They had to place relative importance on economic, legal, ethical, and philanthropic activities in their company. Aupperle referred to this emphasis as corporate social orientation (CSO) or CSRO (Aupperle et al. 1985; Smith et al. 2004). It should be noted that CSRO is a construct that "captures one's perception [...] to a firms behaviors with respect to corporate social performance (CSP)" (Smith et al. 2001, p. 267). However, it does not measure an actual performance of a company.

In this context, participants were asked to distribute a maximum of ten points among a set of four statements, where each statement represents exactly one of the four CSRO dimensions (e.g., "It is important for an organization to be committed to being as profitable as possible" for the economic dimension vs. "It is important for an organization to be committed to always following laws and regulations" for the legal one). Following Smith et al. (2004), a total of ten sets of such statements were used.

The second part of the questionnaire consisted of demographic variables including religiousness and religious faith. In particular, the participants' degree of religiousness was measured with items developed by

---

[4]In June and July 2014, 152 students at the HTW Berlin University of Applied Sciences voluntarily completed the questionnaire. The final sample size was 142 since 10 partially completed questionnaires had to be eliminated (response rate greater than 90 percent).

Table 2.1 Correlations and reliabilities—religiousness

Variables	Economic	Legal	Ethical	Philanthropic
Economic	0.92[a]			
Legal	−0.15	0.79		
Ethical	−0.74*	−0.06	0.80	
Philanthropic	−0.57*	−0.43*	0.46*	0.81

$n = 132$
[a]Values on the diagonal are Cronbach's alpha
*$p < 0.01$

McDaniel and Burnett (1990) and utilized by Barnett et al. (1996) as well as Ibrahim et al. (2008). The students had to indicate the extent of their agreement with the following three statements: S1: "I am very religious," S2: "My religion is very important to me," and S3: "I believe in God," on a five-point Likert scale (ranging from five = "strongly agree" to one = "strongly disagree").[5]

For the forthcoming analysis, a sample of 132 German students is used. All of them were undergraduate students in economics and business communication management at the HTW Berlin University of Applied Sciences. The sample consists of 36 (27.3 percent) males and 96 (72.7 percent) females with a mean age of 24 years.

2.4   Results

To validate the sample data, first, reliabilities were calculated, which were tested using Cronbach's alpha. The results are reported in Table 2.1. Cronbach's alpha coefficients fall short of those reported in Aupperle et al. (1985), but are still very satisfactory.[6]

Table 2.1 further depicts the correlations among the four CSRO components. In line with the literature, the economic responsibility reveals a negative correlation with the three other corporate dimensions (Aupperle et al. 1985; Smith et al. 2004; van den Heuvel et al. 2014).

---

[5]A detailed discussion on the problem of measuring religion, religiousness, and religiosity due to a wide understanding of the terms can be found in McDaniel and Burnett (1990).

[6]A coefficient of 0.70 for Cronbach's alpha is average for belief and value constructs, as Peterson (1994) concludes from his meta-analysis.

Thus, respondents strongly separate economic achievements and social activities (reflected by legal, ethical, and philanthropic obligations). The observation that the strongest negative correlation can be found between the economic and the ethical responsibility ($r = -0.74$, $p < 0.001$) also contributes to results from previous studies. Finally, a positive correlation between the ethical and the philanthropic component found in this study is in line with the original research from Aupperle et al. (1985) as well as related works (McDonald and Scott 1997; Burton et al. 2000).

Because the analysis focuses on religiousness, four one-way ANOVAs were used to determine whether differences in each of the four dimensions of CSRO exist between different degrees of religiousness. The independent variable was the degree of religiousness (i.e., the intensity of religious belief, measured on a Likert scale), and the four dependent variables were the points attributed to the economic, legal, ethical, and philanthropic dimensions. It is found that the three statements on religiousness are highly correlated pairwise (rank order correlation S1–S2: $r = 0.91$, S2–S3: $r = 0.77$, S1–S3: $r = 0.75$; all $p < 0.001$). Thus, they yield a reliable approximation for the total religiousness of the students. Before conducting the ANOVA test, the "degree of religiousness" was transformed into a categorical variable. To do so, the author calculated for each individual the sum of points from the three Likert-scale evaluations. Afterwards, the mean score of $M = 5.58$ was used as a threshold value in order to split the sample. As a result, 89 students (67.4 percent) were identified as "low religious" and 43 (32.6 percent) were assigned "highly religious".[7]

It appears that the degree of religiousness influences the ranking of the four CSR dimensions (see Table 2.2). While low religious Germans perceive the economic dimension as the most important of a firm's responsibilities, highly religious Germans rank ethical aspects first. Low religious Germans place significantly higher importance on the economic actions of companies compared to the three social dimensions, namely legal, ethical, and philanthropic obligations (paired t-test: $t = 2.875$, $p = 0.005$; $t = 2.255$, $p = 0.027$; $t = 6.766$, $p = 0.000$). Except for the differences in

---

[7] Using the median ($m = 3$) as a cut-off point, the ranking of the dimensions as well as the differences between the groups remains similar in their structure (group size: 68 low religious vs. 64 highly religious).

Table 2.2 ANOVA results for differences between highly and low religious individuals

| Dependent variables | Group means[a] | | | |
	Low religiousness ($n = 89$)	High religiousness ($n = 43$)	F	p
1. Economic	2.94 (1.25)	2.56 (1.12)	2.89	0.092
2. Legal	2.47 (0.69)	2.37 (0.63)	0.59	0.444
3. Ethical	2.48 (0.77)	2.61 (0.81)	0.83	0.364
4. Philanthropic	1.63 (0.78)	1.87 (0.62)	3.26	0.073

$n = 132$
[a]Figures in parentheses are standard deviations

the ranking observed, ANOVA does not produce significant differences between the two groups regarding the four dimensions of Carroll's pyramid. Thus, the tendencies observed in the study only partially support the findings of Angelidis and Ibrahim (2004), Ibrahim et al. (2008), and Dusuki et al. (2008). All of these studies show that the degree of religiousness appears to somehow have an effect on the ratings of the four CSR dimensions.

In order to add a further perspective, the differences in importance attribution toward corporate actions were analyzed with respect to a difference in religious affiliation. In the German sample, 68 students assigned themselves as unaffiliated (52 percent) and 49 as having a religious affiliation (31 percent Christianity, 4 percent Islam, 2 percent Other Religion). Fifteen students did not answer this question (11 percent). For a comparison, the author thus excluded all participants who did not clearly answer the corresponding question.

As depicted in Table 2.3, reliabilities and correlations in the new subsample remain similar to those reported for the total sample in Table 2.1. Most importantly, the values for Cronbach's alpha are satisfactory, and the significant correlations follow the expected pattern. When splitting the total sample by religious affiliation instead of the level of religiousness, the ranking results show a similar pattern. The unaffiliated students place significantly more importance on economic responsibilities than on the three social dimensions legal ($t = 2.417$, $p = 0.018$), ethical ($t = 1.935$, $p = 0.057$), and philanthropic ($t = 5.367$, $p = 0.000$). These results cannot

Table 2.3 Correlations and reliabilities—subsample religious affiliation

Variables	Economic	Legal	Ethical	Philanthropic
Economic	0.93[a]			
Legal	−0.18	0.77		
Ethical	−0.74*	−0.09	0.80	
Philanthropic	−0.59*	−0.35*	0.59*	0.82

$n = 117$
[a]Values on the diagonal are Cronbach's alpha
*$p < 0.01$

Table 2.4 ANOVA results for differences between unaffiliated and affiliated individuals

Dependent variables	Group means[a]		F	p
	Unaffiliated ($n = 68$)	Affiliated ($n = 49$)		
1. Economic	2.97 (1.40)	2.61 (0.96)	2.35	0.128
2. Legal	2.47 (0.65)	2.53 (0.67)	0.27	0.604
3. Ethical	2.46 (0.87)	2.64 (0.66)	1.55	0.216
4. Philanthropic	1.68 (0.76)	1.70 (0.74)	0.02	0.888

$n = 117$
[a]Figures in parentheses are standard deviations

be confirmed for the affiliated sample ($t = 0.465$, $p = 0.644$; $t = −0.142$, $p = 0.888$; $t = 4.328$, $p = 0.000$). Likewise, ANOVA does not produce statistically significant results for the dataset (see Table 2.4). Still, a difference in attribution cannot be entirely neglected.

2.5   Discussion and Conclusion

The results show that religiousness influences the importance of ranking of the four firm's obligations in the sample in Germany. However, the ANOVA results show no significant differences between the two groups. In Germany, religiousness and affiliation seem not to be a strong driver for the ranking of a firm's responsibilities. This might be due to the nominal religious surrounding in East Germany, where the survey was conducted. In other countries with a higher overall religiousness (e.g., Malaysia), businessmen seem to be more influenced by beliefs when conducting business (Dusuki et al. 2008).

This finding is supported by Parboteeah et al. (2014) who argue that a religious environment influences even those individuals living in the respective country who claim to have no religion. Therefore, the degree of religiousness should be considered by businesses that want to enter a market or even a region within a country. Since highly religious individuals seem to place more importance on the social obligations, this may shape the focus of CSR actions in a country where religion, tradition, and culture are very prominent and influence the daily life. Especially in times where the perception of the dependence of modern society on volatile financial markets still exacerbates a significant impression on consumers, considering their traditional beliefs offers an alternative starting point for focused CSR strategies.

Moreover, the question was raised whether in times of financial uncertainty and company scandals, consumers search for alternatives of the reliability on the economic system. Therefore, in this chapter, expectations of Germans toward economic, legal, ethical, and philanthropic firms' obligations were analyzed. We see that economic stability, profit-making, and long-term financial stability (reflected in the aspect of economic responsibilities) remain the most important aspect for consumers. It might be by experience that consumers not only search for alternatives of the reliance on the economic system but also hang on to financial stability as the most important factor. However, we also see that the social dimensions are highly valued. Thus, Germans expect companies to be profitable but not at the expense of charitable activities and the law. Harmonizing long-term profitability and social responsibilities might be the current challenge of companies in times of financial uncertainty.

A few limitations need to be named that influence the generalizability of the discussed aspects. Extrapolating the results can be delusive since the sample size was modest and comprised of students from a single university in Germany. Still, students as a proxy for consumers are believed to not diminishing the investigation. Most of the students in the survey had work experience and they showed a notable age spectrum (16–34 years). Although anonymity was emphasized and the Aupperle instrument chosen, a social desirability bias cannot be completely ruled out. Moreover, Weaver and Agle (2002) argue that religion is a sensitive topic in surveys and results need to be treated carefully. Since the demographic questions were placed at the end of the survey, at least the latter aspect is not expected to distort the answers. The measurement instrument of McDaniel and Burnett that was chosen for this study is only one possibility to quantitatively identify religiosity. Other instruments seem promising to measure such a subjective, hardly tangible concept. Here, further research is necessary to identify an instrument applicably for the special setting in Germany, where Eastern and Western Germans significantly differ concerning religiosity.

In the chapter, an important research gap was addressed and a new perspective added by analyzing religious affiliation in general. The results of the survey provide a small step in broadening the understanding of the influence of religiousness on CSR. Still, there is no uniform answer to this relationship. In general, a wider understanding of factors influencing a person's CSRO is necessary. Studies with a more profound database seem promising. Since other studies have revealed the effects of gender, age, working experience, or culture, more research on the interaction of these variables and their relative importance when compared to religion and religiousness is needed to create a more comprehensive picture and deeper understanding of an individual's expectations toward CSR efforts. In view of a more globalized but still culturally diverse world, a better understanding of traditions and beliefs of different countries is required.

Acknowledgments I would like to thank Daniel Cracau and two anonymous reviewers for valuable comments that helped to improve the chapter. Furthermore, I thank the audience at the 4th ICSR Conference. Moreover, funding provided by the Berliner Chancengleichheitsprogramm is gratefully acknowledged.

References

Agle, B. R., & Van Buren, H. J. (1999). God and mammon: The modern relationship. *Business Ethics Quarterly, 9*(4), 563–582.

Allport, G. W., & Ross, J. M. (1967). Personal religious orientation and prejudice. *Journal of Personality and Social Psychology, 5*(4), 432–443.

Angelidis, J. P., & Ibrahim, N. A. (2004). An exploratory study of the impact of degree of religiousness upon an individual's corporate social responsiveness orientation. *Journal of Business Ethics, 51*(2), 119–128.

Aupperle, K. E. (1982). *An empirical enquiry into the social responsibilities as defined by corporations: An examination of various models and relationships.* Ph.D. dissertation, University of Georgia.

Aupperle, K. E., Carroll, A. B., & Hatfield, J. D. (1985). An empirical examination of the relationship between corporate social responsibility and profitability. *Academy of Management Journal, 28*(2), 446–463.

Barnett, T., Bass, K., & Brown, G. (1996). Religiosity, ethical ideology, and intentions to report a peer's wrongdoing. *Journal of Business Ethics, 15*(11), 1161–1174.

Brammer, S., Williams, G., & Zinkin, J. (2007). Religion and attitudes to corporate social responsibility in a large cross-country sample. *Journal of Business Ethics, 71*(3), 229–243.

Burton, B. K., Farh, J.-L., & Harvey Hegarty, W. (2000). A cross-cultural comparison of corporate social responsibility orientation: Hong Kong vs. United States students. *Teaching Business Ethics, 4*(2), 151–167.

Carroll, A. B. (1979). A three-dimensional conceptual model of corporate performance. *Academy of Management Review, 4*(4), 497–505.

Carroll, A. B. (1991). The pyramid of corporate social responsibility: Toward the moral management of organizational stakeholders. *Business Horizons, 34*, 39–48.

Carroll, A. B. (1999). Corporate social responsibility: Evolution of a definitional construct. *Business & Society, 38*(3), 268–295.

Dusuki, A. W., Maimunah, T. F., & Yusof, T. M. (2008). The pyramid of corporate social responsibility model: Empirical evidence from Malaysian stakeholder perspectives. *Malaysian Accounting Review, 7*(2), 29–54.

Dyck, Bruno. (2014). God on management: The world's largest religions, the "theological turn", and organization and management theory and practice. In P. Tracey, N. Phillips, & M. Lounsbury (Eds.), *Religion and organization theory (Research in the sociology of organizations*, Vol. 41, pp. 23–62). Emerald Group Publishing Limited.

Ibrahim, N. A., Howard, D. P., & Angelidis, J. P. (2008). The relationship between religiousness and corporate social responsibility orientation: Are there differences between business managers and students? *Journal of Business Ethics, 78*(1–2), 165–174.

Jamali, D., & Sidani, Y. (2013). Does religiosity determine affinities to CSR? *Journal of Management, Spirituality & Religion, 10*(4), 309–323.

Longenecker, J. G., McKinney, J. A., & Moore, C. W. (2004). Religious intensity, evangelical Christianity, and business ethics: An empirical study. *Journal of Business Ethics, 55*(4), 371–384.

Maignan, I. (2001). Consumers' perceptions of corporate social responsibilities: A cross-cultural comparison. *Journal of Business Ethics, 30*(1), 57–72.

McDaniel, S. W., & Burnett, J. J. (1990). Consumer religiosity and retail store evaluative criteria. *Journal of the Academy of Marketing Science, 18*(2), 101–112.

McDonald, R. A., & Scott, V. A. (1997). Attitudes of business and non-business students toward corporate actions. *Teaching Business Ethics, 1*(2), 213–225.

Parboteeah, K. P., Walter, S. G., & Block, J. H. (2014). When does Christian religion matter for entrepreneurial activity? The contingent effect of a country's investments into knowledge. *Journal of Business Ethics, 130*(2), 447–465.

Peterson, R. A. (1994). A meta-analysis of Cronbach's coefficient alpha. *Journal of Consumer Research, 21*(2), 381–391.

Pickel, G. (2013). *Religionsmonitor—Verstehen was verbindet: Religiosität im internationalen Vergleich.* Gutersloh: Bertelsmann Stiftung.

Pickel, G., & Sammet, K. (2014). *Einführung in die Methoden der sozialwissenschaftlichen Religionsforschung.* Wiesbaden: Springer-Verlag.

Quazi, A. M. (2003). Identifying the determinants of corporate managers' perceived social obligations. *Management Decision, 41*(9), 822–831.

Ramasamy, B., Yeung, M., & Alan, A. (2010). Consumer support for corporate social responsibility (CSR): The role of religion and values. *Journal of Business Ethics, 91*(1), 61–72.

Schlegelmilch, B. B., & Öberseder, M. (2010). Half a century of marketing ethics: Shifting perspectives and emerging trends. *Journal of Business Ethics, 93*(1), 1–19.

Schmidt, M. A., & D. Cracau. (2015). *Cross-country comparison of the corporate social responsibility orientation in Germany and Qatar: An empirical study among business students.* No. 150006. Otto-von-Guericke University Magdeburg, Faculty of Economics and Management.

Schneider, H., Krieger, J., & Bayraktar, A. (2011). The impact of intrinsic religiosity on consumers' ethical beliefs: Does it depend on the type of religion? A comparison of Christian and Moslem consumers in Germany and Turkey. *Journal of Business Ethics, 102*(2), 319–332.

Singhapakdi, A., Marta, J. K., Rallapalli, K. C., & Rao, C. P. (2000). Toward an understanding of religiousness and marketing ethics: An empirical study. *Journal of Business Ethics, 27*(4), 305–319.

Smith, W. J., Wokutch, R. E., Vernard Harrington, K., & Dennis, B. S. (2001). An examination of the influence of diversity and stakeholder role on corporate social orientation. *Business & Society, 40*(3), 266–294.

Smith, W. J., Wokutch, R. E., Vernard Harrington, K., & Dennis, B. S. (2004). Organizational attractiveness and corporate social orientation: Do our values influence our preference for affirmative action and managing diversity? *Business & Society, 43*(1), 69–96.

van den Heuvel, G., Soeters, J., & Gössling, T. (2014). Global business, global responsibilities: Corporate social responsibility orientations within a multinational bank. *Business & Society, 53*(3), 378–413.

Vitell, S. J., Paolillo, J. G., & Singh, J. J. (2005). Religiosity and consumer ethics. *Journal of Business Ethics, 57*(2), 175–181.

Voland, E. (2009). Evaluating the evolutionary status of religiosity and religiousness. In *The biological evolution of religious mind and behavior* (pp. 9–24). Berlin, Heidelberg: Springer.

Weaver, G. R., & Agle, B. R. (2002). Religiosity and ethical behavior in organizations: A symbolic interactionist perspective. *Academy of Management Review, 27*(1), 77–97.

Wiebe, K. F., & Fleck, J. R. (1980). Personality correlates of intrinsic, extrinsic, and nonreligious orientations. *The Journal of Psychology, 105*(2), 181–187.

3

New Corporate Responsibilities in the Digital Economy

Georgiana Grigore, Mike Molesworth,
and Rebecca Watkins

3.1 Introduction

Following the financial crisis, governments have looked with enthusiasm toward the digital economy to restore growth, provide competitive advantage, and even achieve sustainability. A highly educated, technology-enabled labor force is lauded as the way to achieve economic success. Yet there has been little attention given to the responsibilities of new businesses and business processes in the digital economy. Some of these responsibilities may be directly related to established agendas in corporate

G. Grigore (✉)
Corporate and Marketing Communications, Bournemouth University,
Bournemouth, Dorset, UK

M. Molesworth
University of Southampton, Southampton, UK

R. Watkins
Cardiff University, Cardiff, UK

© The Author(s) 2017   **41**
A. Theofilou et al. (eds.), *Corporate Social Responsibility in the
Post-Financial Crisis Era*, Palgrave Studies in Governance, Leadership
and Responsibility, DOI 10.1007/978-3-319-40096-9_3

social responsibility (CSR), for example, issues of employment, taxation, and sustainability. Other issues may be identified as ethical concerns, for example, privacy and use of data, transparency in communication practice, and avoidance of regulatory and self-regulatory communication frameworks, but not explicitly framed as new responsibilities. A few areas for corporate responsibility, however, may be entirely new. For example, consumers' rights to digital possessions created through online platforms and employees' right to autonomy—free from digital surveillance and productivity processes. Together, these point to a larger concern: the responsibility of corporations in the digital economy toward human relationships themselves which technology seems to undermine or strip away. In this chapter, we turn our attention to these issues and to ask what it means to be a responsible corporation in the digital economy.

Digital technologies have increased dramatically in their global reach and socio-economic impact in the last 30 years to become key drivers of economic growth that are vital to knowledge economies (EU 2014). Fifty percent of all productivity growth is now linked to investment in such technologies such that the digital economy has grown at seven times the rate of the rest of the economy, and so by 2020, there will be over 16 million information and communication technology-intensive jobs in the European Union alone (EU 2014).

Alongside and quite independent of the rise of the digital economy, CSR is also attracting substantial attention with dominant discourses emphasizing business and society relationships, the moral obligation of corporations "to give something back" or "to do good," and especially the idea that organizations have responsibilities beyond profit making. The proliferation of digital media platforms and content also transforms the practice, and therefore also the theory of CSR, yet until now the rise of digital communications and the interest in CSR have only come together as online CSR communication, disclosure practices, and engagement via new media. Online CSR communication is seen as another tool used to demonstrate social engagement and "care" for stakeholders and society (Idowu and Towler 2004; Junior et al. 2014; Manetti and Toccafondi 2012), with social media enabling "virtual" dialogue with and amongst stakeholders (Korschun and Du 2013; Eberle et al. 2013). This, we argue, represents only a limited and largely instrumental engagement with technology in the context of CSR. For example, when online communication directly to stakeholders is used to rebuild reputation after corporate scandals (Eberle et al. 2013; O'Riordan and Fairbrass 2013), the potential motives may be instrumental, with online CSR deployed only to improve the ability of a corporation to more effectively present its reputation in the way it sees fit, bypassing potentially more critical and/or objective journalistic reporting of events.

When the Internet and CSR are explored in the literature, we also note definitional ambiguity including confusion over both form and purpose. The concept and scope of the use of digital technologies within CSR have varied considerably, including "interactive corporate social responsibility communication" (Eberle et al. 2013) (as if previous CSR did not involve interacting with stakeholders), "virtual corporate social responsibility dialogs" (Korschun and Du 2013) (as if somehow online CSR is not "real," but only virtual, or "imagined"), and "corporate social responsibility in the network society" (Castello et al. 2013) (as if those excluded from online participation are no longer meaningful stakeholders). Such apparent definitional work raises more questions than are answered and to some degree even obscures the actual responsibilities that may be present. For example, is the form of the technology itself what is important, or should we only pay attention to the practices that constitute meaningful interactions with stakeholders regardless of platform? Our view is that academics and practitioners should not rarefy the digital, but rather look for specific consequences of new practices that raise substantive issues for CSR.

To put it another way, there is no "digital CSR," "virtual CSR," or "Online CSR," and so on, but only new ways of communicating existing issues *and* new responsibilities associated with the corporate use of digital technologies. In existing discourse, if there is a transformation in responsible business practice, it is only in the way it is communicated through wondrous new technologies, but this reduces technological developments to a "mere" communication channels for responsible business practice. This prevents broader discussion of the responsibilities corporations have toward society when using digital technology, responsibilities that we propose are worthy of their own analysis.

It is perhaps also significant that, even in its role as a communication tool, Stohl et al. (2015) have suggested that digital media platforms can restrict CSR-related values, obstruct free speech or stakeholder engagement, and lead to enactment of communication practices that conflict with the acknowledged international CSR guidelines (UN Global Compact, ISO 26000, etc.). The authors further question the use of social media communication as an appropriate way to portray CSR undertakings, recognizing the potential for manipulation of information, including through policy designed to control employees use of social media. Thus, even as a communication tool, social media is not a neutral platform for communication, but raises new areas of responsibilities.

In this chapter, we draw attention to new areas of *corporate responsibility in the digital economy*. We contribute to theory by recognizing those responsibilities placed on corporations through the use of online technologies. Drawing from established ethical and policy concerns in other fields, we review the range of potential areas where such new areas for responsibility might be examined. We then identify ways in which these concerns relate to established CSR frameworks.

3.2   CSR Foundations and Digital Technology

Academics have highlighted three dominant discourses showing to whom organizations are responsible (Marrewijk 2001), and we summarize them here to allow us to compare developments in business use of technology with the assumptions each carries about responsibility.

Firstly, Marrewijk (2001) describes the *classical* approach to CSR captured in Friedman's definition that states: "the social responsibility of the business is to increase its profits" (Friedman 1962). From such a perspective, digital technology can be considered as merely an opportunity to increase efficiency, or in terms of opportunities for new sources of profit, presenting no particular responsibilities beyond this. A corporation therefore views digital technology in terms of profit "within the law," paying no attention to any further consequences of changes in business practices for its stakeholders.

Secondly and later, Carroll (1979) notes that there is a natural link between corporations and their stakeholders—*the stakeholder approach* (Marrewijk 2001)—where it is desirable to identify legitimate stakeholders and take into account their rights and interests, and also to delineate how far such obligation extends (Freeman 1984; O'Riordan and Fairbrass 2013). Stakeholder engagement is seen either as an ideal "moral partnership of equals" (Phillips 1997, p. 54) based on the idea of social contract (Rawls 1971) that will create value for stakeholders when considered rightly (Noland and Phillips 2010) or, in contrast, a "morally neutral" practice that is ultimately defined by the motive and virtue of the actor involved in such activity (Greenwood 2007). Stakeholder engagement is also seen as "a necessary prerequisite to socially-responsible action" and so should be integrated in the CSR reporting models and within the corporate mission and values that are communicated to stakeholders (Reynolds and Yutas 2008, p. 58). Here, digital technology may also be seen as an opportunity for stakeholder engagement and indeed this is reflected in emerging studies of CSR. In addition to potential sources of profit or efficiency (which may be limited by conflict with stakeholder interests), the Internet provides new communicative opportunities to listen to and engage with key stakeholders.

Thirdly, the *societal* perspective maintains that companies have a responsibility toward society (Marrewijk 2001). At its most ambitious, this would ask that the use of digital technology should be to make the world a better place. This latest challenge to business ethics requires not simply the assurance that no harm is done to stakeholders, or that their views are considered, but that corporations actively produce a better society (and not just economic growth). Here then we see the strongest normative claims for CSR theory. The legitimacy of corporations is explicitly seen in societal terms. For example, digital technology should be deployed to improve the lives of people, strengthen communities, address inequalities and injustice, and to do so for future generations. Digital technology should improve working conditions, autonomy (e.g. freedom of expression), access to information, services and wealth, and the sustainability of business practices.

We could illustrate these positions in respect to one of the latest areas of excitement in digital technology: big data. Under the classical approach, we can ask about the opportunities to profit from big data.

Under stakeholder theory, we consider potential harm, for example relating to privacy, or manipulation. And, under the societal perspective, we ask if—and how—big data can make the world a better place. With new developments in technology, the limits of these streams of conceptualizations become apparent. As more opportunities and related responsibilities emerge from the use of Internet, it is necessary to explore a *responsibility in the digital economy*, where a new agenda is established that raises questions about underexplored aspects of the classical, stakeholder, and societal approaches to CSR.

Digital technology is much more than a communicative issue, but something that may run through all aspects of an organization and its interactions with society, with previously unheard of opportunities for the most outrageous breaches of trust of a range of stakeholders.

3.3   The Internet and CSR

Alongside the escalating normative ambitions of CSR theory to create a better world, interest in the responsibility of organizations has intensified as a result of scandals in various industries, such as energy, banking, pharmaceutics, and automotive (O'Riordan and Fairbrass 2013). Recently, for example, we witnessed Volkswagen's attempts to balance performance and fuel economy with low pollution that resulted in the illegal use of software created to deceive regulators and "cheat" on emission tests (Plumer 2015) resulting in reputational damage. Elsewhere, there have been protests and boycotts of corporations for their avoidance of tax and/or other financial irresponsibilities and numerous protests about the practices of pharmaceutical companies ranging from their promotion of certain drugs with undesirable side effects to their restriction in the distribution of other drugs to protect profits.

Online CSR has been dominated by communication through reports or corporate websites. In a study that descriptively analyzes Fortune Global 500's CSR reports and their assurance, it is revealed that all organizations provided social or environmental disclosure on their corporate websites as a way to ensure communication between firms and stakeholders (Junior et al. 2014). The Global Reporting Initiative (GRI) is currently the most widely used standard to guide responsible corporate practice and its reporting (Junior et al. 2014; Manetti and Toccafondi 2012), and the Corporate Register is the awarding body for best CSR reports (Crisan and Zbuchea 2015). Indeed, KPMG (2013) highlights that 93 % of the largest corporations communicate about their CSR activities either on the corporate website or through CSR reports, and separately from the annual financial reports. This research illustrates that academics are now preoccupied by the development of assurance services within CSR reporting, sometimes seen as instruments for creating "added value" (Korschun and Du 2013; Manetti and Toccafondi 2012). Research also suggests dynamism and constantly changing assurance tools as a way to meet "industry norms" or in response to the advice of experts (Manetti and Toccafondi 2012). The discourse is therefore related to reporting of CSR practice rather than issues of responsibility themselves, with online media seen as a useful tool for the dissemination of CSR activity to stakeholders.

More recently, academics *have* started to investigate how social media influences firms and their engagement with stakeholders (Adi and Grigore 2015; Whelan et al. 2013), whether this is an effective platform to create awareness of CSR initiatives and to boost reputation (Coombs and Holloday 2015) and to legitimize the role of corporations in society (Castello et al. 2013). Stakeholders can now apparently sanction irresponsible corporate behavior and show their indignation on social media, which may lead to a change for a better society (Crisan and Zbuchea 2015). Whilst only a quarter of global citizens read CSR reports, Cone's (2015, p. 4) data reveal that consumers view social media as a way to "learn, voice opinions and speak directly to companies around CSR issues." The same study encourages companies to "embrace emerging technologies and social channels as effective methods for educating consumers around CSR efforts, creating a dialogue and inspiring them to take action" (Cone 2015, p. 4). Studies seem to suggest an opportunity for dialogue and interaction in the "network" society, but there is limited research that looks at communication disruption, plurality, conflict, and contradictory perceptions between stakeholders, or between companies and stakeholders in such networks. Again, the issue is how online media enables "traditional" CSR processes rather than on any new responsibilities that emerge from engagement with digital technologies.

We argue that the Internet and CSR should not be reduced to issues of communication, but rather that it might encompass new areas of responsibilities that emerge from the rise of digital technology. For example, we could argue that the reduction of digital CSR to a communicative function represents an *othering* of the agency of digital technology (see Law 2004), the ability of digital technology to change the nature of social reality in specific ways. Digital technologies might change networks of communication, but also assemble new products, new forms of labor and labor relations, and new organizational and extra-organizational structures. In the corporate involvement of these new arrangements, there are ethics and responsibilities. An apparent irony here that digital technology as conceptualized in CSR discourse is recognized as important in its ability to transform society and the economy, yet presented as almost benign and trivial, as "merely" a channel of communication. By reducing digital media to a communication role, almost all of these new relationships, and therefore responsibilities, are ignored, or made absent. "Responsible" practice in the digital economy may therefore be counter-productive. Rather than examining business with a view to transforming it into more socially responsible forms, it actually provides an outlet for corporations to hide much of what they do behind reporting and communications functions and opportunities.

3.4   Established Discourses on Responsibility in the Digital Economy

There are established issues of corporate responsibility that we can see as directly relevant to developments in the digital economy. These are transparency in communications, taxation, privacy and data collection and storage, and use or avoidance of regulatory and self-regulatory communication.

In respect to these, existing literature has noted potential ethical concerns surrounding the *transparency of digital communications strategies,* particularly in relation to children (Owen et al. 2012; An et al. 2014; Nairn and Hang 2012; Dahl et al. 2009). For instance, research has found that children as old as 15 struggle to identify advergames as advertising and has called for a new regulatory framework for advergames and new media (Nairn and Hang 2012). UK self-regulatory frameworks require all advertising to be clearly identified as such; however, in addition to advergames, a number of YouTube videos have previously been banned by the Advertising Standards Authority (ASA) for not doing so (Bold 2014), despite recent increased guidance offered to vloggers and bloggers by the ASA (2014, 2015). Other concerns surrounding transparency have emerged in relation to fake "user" reviews, inappropriate targeting (e.g. ads for fast food on Zoella's videos, when she admits that most of her "audience" is under 18). Rather than rejoicing at this new opportunity to talk to key audiences, and/or simply waiting for ASA regulation, responsible firms might regulate this internally in order to actively avoid any potentially misleading/confusing digital communications campaigns. It seems ironic that at the same time as celebrating online CSR reporting, corporations use online communication channels to promote goods and services surreptitiously without declaring their communications as persuasive.

As part of the established discourses on responsibility in the digital economy, we also note issues related to *privacy and data collection, storage, use, and transfer of data*. More specifically, here we can include manipulation of consent and opt-out rights; data sharing/selling; consumer access to their own data, especially in the era of "quantified self"; security of data, especially when re-sold; and the use in behavioral targeting with intrusive algorithms. This is the current focus of rigorous Data Protection legislation and control in European Union, because of the potential harm from irresponsible act. The urgent need for legislation illustrates a lack of responsibility in general in the corporate use of consumer data, yet as technologies of surveillance evolve, there is need to focus on responsibilities beyond legislation that will always lag behind.

When it comes to *taxation*, digital technologies allow various forms of international trade making the avoidance of tax easier. Is this also an evasion of responsibility? Recent campaigns to boycott companies such as Amazon due to tax avoidance (Ethical Consumer 2015) suggest that many consumers percieve this to be the case. Amazon is able to sell across the EU from any of its various EU websites and redirect profits through low tax countries. The movement of goods attracts no additional taxation, and digital technologies make the separate movement of profit more efficient too. However, in addition to denying governments of the revenue required to pay for public goods, both practices disadvantage local business that is subject to a range of local tax regimes, including (e.g. in the UK) business rates and corporation tax as well as VAT. We can see the latter as one of the most contentious aspects of CSR: responsibilities to competitors. The situation is perhaps made worse when the online retailer is aware of, and even exploits or invites "showrooming," where a consumer may use a local retailer for demonstration and viewing of a product, then buy from an online retailer with no such facility and associated overheads (e.g. see Rapp et al. 2015).

Together then we see that the agenda for responsibility in the digital economy may be revised to include the use of technology, and specific areas may be extended (taxation, legal compliance, consumer rights, and even responsibility to competitors).

3.5   New Areas of Responsibility in the Digital Economy

There are also new responsibilities that are currently silent in CSR and business ethics literature. These new responsibilities, we argue, are reflected in issues to do with commodities, contractual agreements, and ownership; exploitation of immaterial labor and fair distribution of rewards; access and equality; and the use of low cost labor and/or artificial intelligence.

3.5.1 Digital Commodities, Contractual Agreements, and Issues of Ownership

Digital media not only presents new opportunities for promoting and distributing material products and offline services; new markets have emerged whereby the "commodity" exists only in digital form. Molesworth et al. (2016, p. 246) argue that recent years have seen the emergence of digital consumption objects, which "possess no enduring material substance but rather exist within digital space (computer-mediated electronic environments), accessed and consumed via devices such as desktop computers, laptops, tablets, mobile phones and videogame consoles." In acquiring, using, and accessing many digital goods, consumers must agree to terms set out in end-user license agreements (EULAs) and terms of use/service contracts, which typically include a range of restrictions on their ownership of these items (Molesworth et al. 2016; Watkins et al. 2016). Such contractual agreements are common in access-based consumption of material items, for instance when renting a car (Bardhi and Eckhardt 2012). However, this is now not the case only for services such as Spotify and Netflix where consumption is clearly positioned as access-based, but in a much wider range of contexts including social media accounts, email accounts, online games, mobile applications, and even downloaded, paid-for content such as digital films, music, and books.

In terms of ownership, business ethics literature has long been preoccupied with digital piracy, the unauthorized procurement, and use of digital media files that infringes copyright and results in loss of revenue to firms (e.g. De Corte and Kenhove 2015). Whilst consumers' ownership rights have received less attention, here we see that consumers' limited ownership of digital items may present significant and yet to be fully realized consequences. Watkins et al. (2016) note that this is particularly problematic given evidence that EULAs and Terms of Service agreements are rarely read by consumers. Even where contractual agreements are read, we might question the extent to which consumers understand them, or may challenge them. Watkins et al. (2016) speculate that a lack of knowledge/understanding of their ownership rights may result in the formation of assumptions based on existing understandings of the relationship between possession and ownership. They may assume, for instance, that they hold the same rights to an ebook that they have become accustomed to in the context of their material counterparts.

This issue stems from a disparity whereby a corporation regards its offering as access to a service, but the consumer comes to perceive the same digital item as a possession. How might companies act responsibly in this area? Under classical CSR, a company would restrict use of digital consumption objects in ways that maximize profit and minimize costs, with no commitment to continuance of access as a way to maximize ongoing profitability with digital goods themselves reducing production and distribution costs.

Under stakeholder theory, however, responsible corporations may need to consider potential harm. For instance, such firms might translate

EULAs into "plain English" to ensure that they are understood. They may also allow consumers to download local copies of digital goods to keep where there is no guarantee of continued access, and encourage them to do so. They might also allow and even help consumers to pass on digital content to friends/family as gifts or heirlooms. These decisions are especially important where there is little or no regulation regarding the types of terms that can be included, or the number of times the terms of such contractual agreements can be updated.

Finally, under the societal perspective, we might further ask if and how digital content can make the world a better place. Given the absence of distribution or manufacturing costs, such consumption objects might no longer be a source of profit at all with large amounts of content made freely available as they have been through various Torrent sites (especially where artists themselves are long dead). In this respect, we might pay more attention to movements that promote open access, and open source as more responsible than the corporate expansion of intellectual property.

3.5.2   Exploitation of Immaterial Labor and Fair Distribution of Rewards

Prosumer-reliant business models have emerged in the digital economy whereby the consumer or "prosumer" largely produces the digital objects that they subsequently consume (Molesworth et al. 2016). For instance, although social media platform Facebook provides the infrastructure within which consumers may create their profiles, owns the servers on which they are hosted, and pays the website developers who create and maintain the platform, the value of the platform is ultimately derived from the user who uploads and tags multiple photographs, fills out personal information, and continuously provides up-to-date socially (and commercially) valuable information. Here, consumers' creation and cultivation of their social media profile increases the platform's attractiveness to other consumers and consequently contributes to maximizing advertising revenue. Whilst some scholars see this as companies presenting a resource for "prosumers" to work with in order to create mutually beneficial value (Prahalad and Ramaswamy 2004; Tapscott and Williams

2006), others argue that companies are in fact establishing new ways to extract value from consumers' free labor (Terranova 2000; Bonsu and Darmody 2008; Ritzer and Jurgenson 2010).

Above we discussed the ways in which business models involve processes of limiting consumer ownership in order to transform digital consumption objects into profitable assets. Consequently, many digital consumption objects created in part by the consumer may not be fully owned by them (Watkins et al. 2016; Molesworth et al. 2016). For instance, whilst Facebook's terms of service declare that "You own all of the content and information you post on Facebook," the consumer simultaneously grants Facebook a "non-exclusive, transferable, sub-licensable, royalty-free, world-wide license to use any IP content that you post on or in connection with Facebook" (Facebook 2015). Within virtual world Second Life, users are also granted intellectual property rights over the items they create, including the ability to sell these items for profit. However, Bonsu and Darmody (2008) describe this as a veneer of consumer empowerment that encourages consumer creativity only to enable the platform to thrive, generating profit for its corporate owners. In this analysis, offering consumers intellectual property rights is simply a means of effectively mobilizing free consumer labor, whilst real control remains with the corporate owners of the platform who regulate behavior and may terminate the platform at any time.

Molesworth et al. (2016) propose that the possession practices that consumers engage in order to enact possession of digital consumption objects are themselves a form of immaterial labor. Singularizing practices that elsewhere de-commoditize (Appadurai 1986; Kopytoff 1986) or sacralize (Belk et al. 1989) mundane objects, severing from the market, here tie in the co-creators of digital consumption objects, producing a phenomenon of consumer ensnarement as consumers become increasingly attached to objects that cannot be separated from company influence (see also Watkins et al. 2016). In some instances, consumers are subject to financial exploitation, as they must continue to pay for access to digital possessions they have in part produced (as in the case of subscription-based online games such as World of Warcraft).

Again, from a classical CSR perspective, this is no more than an imaginative way to minimize labor costs and maximize the value of corporate assets. However, from a stakeholder perspective, there are questions about the transparency, fairness, and accountability of such arrangements with consumers. From the societal perspective, we might consider again how such exploitation and ensnarement might lead to a better society. For example, against celebrations of the empowerment of user-generated content, we might question whether it is responsible and fair to build a business that requires individuals to spend considerable time laboring for free on social media platforms. Put more directly, we might ask if society is improved when corporations design online platforms that encourage extensive uploading of personal information and networking building (with resultant trolling, flaming, and other psychologically destructive activity) for the purposes of selling ads.

3.5.3   Access and Equality

Organizations have recently started adopting web content accessibility guidelines (e.g. ISO/IEC 40500, 2012) to address a social issue (equal access to vulnerable groups) and to ensure compliance with the law (e.g. the Disability Discrimination Act of 1995; the Disability Act 2001). We might see this as comparable with responsible companies that ensure equal access to buildings, jobs, and services. But the use of technology by corporations may still disadvantage certain groups of individuals (the old, and the poor especially) in terms of access to offers, interaction, or customer services. This extends the issues of the "digital divide" that have already been established (e.g. the focus on political engagement, see Ragnedda and Muschert 2013).

For example, does CSR communication via Facebook carry "hidden" assumptions about audiences and their importance? Social media is not accessible to all and is certainly not used by all groups equally. We might therefore consider the implications of using it as a primary communication medium, especially where it is promoted as a way for consumers to feed back to organizations and to hold them to account. Indeed, many organizations might prefer to promote the potential for interaction on their social media in full knowledge that certain groups are unlikely to engage in this way and of the likelihood of "slacktivism," where protest amounts to no more than clicking a "like" button.

More significantly, the range of disadvantages to certain groups where an organization decides to make full use of technologies is overlooked. For example, it is already recognized that where a bank closes branches, but provides online services instead, it may cause problems for the elderly and the poor in a community who are denied access to banking services (Leyshon et al. 2008). In addition, where retailers or services (such as tourist attractions, museums, or public transport) offer online discounts and advance bookings, does this also disadvantage their poorest customers (who must pay more, or be denied opportunities)? Online promotions may be cheap and effective ways for businesses to manage promotional activity and collect data, and they may also allow cost savings in services that can be partially passed on to customers, but is there a responsibility to ensure that an unintended consequence is not an effective penalty for those unable or unwilling to also invest in the latest technology?

Again, a classical CSR approach favors embracing technology for its efficiency. The stakeholder model however may raise questions about equality of access, and the society model might ask larger question about the desirability of a divided society in which many may have cheap and easy access to a range of technologically enabled goods and series, whereas others are increasingly excluded.

3.5.4 Labor, Use of Low Cost, and/or Artificial Intelligence

If our illustrations so far have hinted at how the adoption of technology by organizations may be dehumanizing, this is most obviously seen in aspects of labor. We might first consider the use of technology to extend the working day and workspace of employees. Various reports show how the use of smartphone, tablet, and laptop technologies results in employees adopting 24/7 work practices, answering work emails in the evening, weekends, and whilst on holiday because technology makes them always available. The technology allows flexibility to contact employees, but is it responsible for organizations to do so outside normal working hours? Technology may also be used to monitor employees in various ways including electronic surveillance of daily activity and productivity

(Ball 2010). With new wearable technology, the possibilities to govern all aspects of employees' lives for the "good" of the company are increasingly making the need to consider which approaches are responsible or otherwise even more pressing.

Alternatively, the Internet has allowed various forms of casualization of labor (Uber, Air B&B, Yodel), celebrated under various ideas such as access-based consumption, the "sharing economy," or crowdsourcing (Belk 2014), with new services often described as in opposition to the established businesses which are now accused of merely protecting their own businesses models in order to maintain unreasonable profits. Yet these new businesses deny their employees many of the usual employment rights (as well as evading much legislation, e.g. on access, see above). At the worst, we might consider the responsibilities relating to the use of services like Amazon's Mechanical Turk where labor may be purchased globally in units of a few cents with no commitment to "employees" whatsoever beyond this, driving down labor costs to the global minimum and allowing corporations to avoid almost all the costs associated with employment (an office, holiday pay, sick leave, and pensions, e.g. see Scholz 2012).

Finally, technology can replace the human labor force altogether and indeed has been doing so for some time (Weidel 2015). Now though it is not just manufacturing that is automated (leaving us with growth only in service jobs), but even customer services and sales are subject to cost-saving replacements of humans with machines and software. For example, self-service tills at supermarkets and other shops, touch screen information and ordering points, and automated online and telephone enquiry systems relying on ever-more sophisticated artificial intelligence. In many cases, the result is not just the removal of jobs, but also a denial of what is now apparently intolerably inefficient human contact. Indeed, even with computer-assisted consumer services the employee is encouraged to minimize time spent "idly" chatting to a customer. The market place is becoming too efficiency driven to be a place where employees and customers should "waste time" talking to each other.

Once more then, the classical CSR model might simply note how the move to technologically governed, or even artificial labor is no more that the move to exploit new forms of profit maximization. The stakeholder model on the other hand asks that the rights of employees and customers are balanced against such efficiency. And the society model demands that we consider what sort of society trades human contact, jobs, and working conditions for cost-saving technologies. For example, do we want a society where marketplace interactions are void of human contact altogether and more of our time is spent interacting only with technology?

Conclusion

Although it is difficult to settle on coherent themes within these new responsibilities in the digital economy (hence that broad classification), there are aspects that *can* be identified as underlying features of the digital economy that lead to new areas of responsibility. Specifically, digital technology allows for a blurring of boundaries: for example, between employees and consumers in the case of co-constructed value, through user-generated content or crowdsourcing; between commodities and services in the case of digital consumption objects; and between content and advertising in the case of promotion via social media and celebrity bloggers. Such de-differentiation often renders established legal structures less meaningful. Indeed at times it is as if this is the very purpose of technological developments. In such circumstances, there is a pressing need to define what constitutes responsible business practice.

Under a classical model of CSR, the result is the celebration of new forms of profit, and to a large degree, this is exactly what we see in the business literature and popular press. In this sense, the corporate appropriation of new technology is ethically naïve, lagging behind thinking in terms of social responsibility. Transformation in practice must also raise questions of what is reasonable, ethical, or responsible when it comes to all stakeholders. Disruptive technology is often seen only in how it may enhance business practice and/or lead to new sources of profit, but under the stakeholder model of CSR, we might argue for the need to also consider the appropriate accompanying responsibilities at the very least. Yet even more than this, the ambitious normative move to a societal model of CSR asks us to consider how changes in technology can contribute to a better society. For example, if the distribution of media is now almost free, why would technological efforts go into Digital Rights Management, licensing, and ownership models that are actually more tenuous and less generous than with older technologies? Technology allows almost everyone to access almost all content for almost free, but this is not good for the content business.

Far from seeing corporations accept, explore, and establish new areas for responsibility, what we actually see are attempts to distribute responsibility to other actors: the sellers on eBay, the uploaders on YouTube and the various prosumers of the sharing economy (Uber, Air B&B). Elsewhere, the distribution of agency is toward the code and algorithms themselves, now acting as law (see Lessig "code as law") but without coded moral compasses. For example, did the cheat code in Volkswagen's engine management systems know it was cheating? Does an online account termination know that it has prevented access to important digital possessions? Where a non-human monitors and manages processes ethics may all too easily be evaded as outside the process.

We might question why are these things not already CSR issues, given that they are reported in popular and specialist media and that there is academic work, often outside "business ethics" that already reports the ethical concerns? Finally, we therefore call for further research that recognizes which issues have the greatest range of impacts, for example, where an issue impacts multiple stakeholders, with potentially conflicting interests, dealing with the issue may require more complex management. Doing this may identify the potential for new CSR initiatives as well as potential problems. The opportunities as well as the negative consequences are missed if the connection between CSR and technology is reduced to communicating CSR reports and activity as it currently is. Again, our conclusion is that there needs to be much more dialogue between those critical of the negative consequences of new technologies and those researching CSR.

References

Adi, A., & Grigore, G. (2015). Communicating CSR on social media: The case of pfizer's social media communications in Europe. In A. Adi, G. Grigore, & D. Crowther (Eds.), *Corporate social responsibility in the digital age* (pp. 143–164). Bingley: Emerald Publishing Group.

Advertising Standards Authority. (2014). *Making ads clear: The challenge for advertisers and vloggers*. Retrieved April 15, 2016, from https://www.asa.org.uk/News-resources/Media-Centre/2014/Making-ads-Clear-The-challenge--for-advertisers-andvloggers.aspx

Advertising Standards Authority. (2015). *Video blogs: Scenarios*. Retrieved April 15, 2016, from https://www.cap.org.uk/Advice-Training-on-the-rules/Advice-Online-Database/Video-blogs-Scenarios.aspx

An, S., Jin, H. S., & Park, E. H. (2014). Children's advertising literacy for advergames: Perception of the game as advertising. *Journal of Advertising, 43*, 63–72.

Appadurai, A. (1986). *The social life of things: Commodities in cultural perspective*. Cambridge: Cambridge University Press.

Ball, K. (2010). Workplace surveillance: An overview. *Labor History, 51*, 87–106.

Bardhi, F., & Eckhardt, G. M. (2012). Access-based consumption: The case of car sharing. *Journal of Consumer Research, 39*, 881–898.

Belk, R. (2014). You are what you can access: Sharing and collaborative consumption. *Journal of Business Research, 67*, 1595–1600.

Belk, R. W., Wallendorf, M., & Sherry Jr., J. (1989). The sacred and the profane in consumer behavior: Theodicy on the odyssey. *Journal of Consumer Research, 16*, 1–38.

Bold, B. 2014. *Oreo youtubers ads banned for failing to clearly indicate marketing partnership*. Retrieved April 15, 2016, from http://www.campaignlive.co.uk/article/1323808/oreoyoutubers-ads-banned-failing-clearly-indicate-marketing-partnership

Bonsu, S. K., & Darmody, A. (2008). Co-creating second life: Market-consumer co-operation in contemporary economy. *Journal of Macromarketing, 28*, 355–368.

Carroll, A. B. (1979). A three-dimensional conceptual model of corporate performance. *Academy of Management Review, 4*, 497–505.

Castello, I., Morsing, M., & Schultz, F. (2013). Communicative dynamics and the polyphony of corporate social responsibility in the network society. *Journal of Business Ethics, 118*, 683–694.

Cone. 2015. *Cone communications/ebiquity global CSR study*. Retrieved April 15, 2016, from http://www.conecomm.com/stuff/contentmgr/files/0/2482ff6f22fe4753488d3fe37e948e3d/files/global_pdf_2015.pdf

Coombs, T. W., & Holladay, S. (2015). Two-minute drill: Video games and social media to advance CSR. In A. Adi, G. Grigore, & D. Crowther (Eds.), *Corporate social responsibility in the digital age* (pp. 127–142). Bingley: Emerald Publishing Group.

Crisan, C., & Zbuchea, A. (2015). CSR and social media: Could online repositories become regulatory tools for CSR related activities reporting? In A. Adi, G. Grigore, & D. Crowther (Eds.), *Corporate social responsibility in the digital age* (pp. 197–220). Bingley: Emerald Publishing Group.

Dahl, S., Eagle, L., & Báez, C. (2009). Analysing advergames: Active diversions or actually deception. An exploratory study of online advergames content. *Young Consumers, 10*, 46–59.

De Corte, C. E., & Van Kenhove, P. (2015). One sail fits all? A psychographic segmentation of digital pirates. *Journal of Business Ethics*, 1–25.

Disability Act. (2001). *Special educational needs and disability act 2001.* Retrieved April 15, 2016, from http://www.legislation.gov.uk/ukpga/2001/10/contents

Disability Discrimination Act. (1995). *Discrimination in other areas.* Retrieved April 15, 2016, from http://www.legislation.gov.uk/ukpga/1995/50/part/III

Eberle, D., Berens, G., & Li, T. (2013). The impact of interactive corporate social responsibility communication on corporate reputation. *Journal of Business Ethics, 118*, 731–746.

Ethical Consumer. 2015. *Amazon and tax.* Retrieved April 18, 2016, from http://www.ethicalconsumer.org/boycotts/boycottamazon.aspx

EU. 2014. *Working paper: Digital economy—Facts & figures.* Retrieved April 15, 2016,fromhttp://ec.europa.eu/taxation_customs/resources/documents/taxation/gen_info/good_governance_matters/digital/2014-03-13_fact_figures.pdf

Facebook. *Terms of service.* Retrieved February 1, 2015, from https://www.facebook.com/legal/terms

Freeman, E. R. (1984). *Strategic management: A stakeholder approach.* Marshfield: Pitman Publishing Inc.

Friedman, M. (1962). *Capitalism and freedom.* Chicago: University of Chicago Press.

Greenwood, M. (2007). Stakeholder engagement: Beyond the myth of corporate responsibility. *Journal of Business Ethics, 74*, 315–327.

Idowu, S. O., & Towler, B. A. (2004). A comparative study of the contents of corporate social responsibility reports of UK companies. *Management of Environmental Quality: An International Journal, 15*, 420–437.

ISO/IEC 40500: http://www.iso.org/iso/iso_catalogue/catalogue_tc/catalogue_detail.htm?csnumber=58625

ISO 26000. *ISO 26000—Social responsibility.* Retrieved April 15, 2016, from http://www.iso.org/iso/home/standards/iso26000.htm

Junior, R. M., Best, P. J., & Cotter, J. (2014). Sustainability reporting and assurance: A historical analysis on a world-wide phenomenon. *Journal of Business Ethics, 120*, 1–11.

Kopytoff, I. (1986). The cultural biography of things: Commoditization as a process. In A. Appadurai (Ed.), *The social life of things: Commodities in a cultural perspective* (pp. 64–94). Cambridge: Cambridge University Press.

Korschun, D., & Du, S. (2013). How virtual corporate social responsibility dialogs generate value: A framework and propositions. *Journal of Business Research, 66*, 1494–1504.

KPMG. (2013). *The KPMG survey of corporate social responsibility reporting 2013*. Retrieved April 10, 2016, from https://www.kpmg.com/Global/en/IssuesAndInsights/ArticlesPublications/corporate-responsibility/Documents/kpmg-survey-of-corporate-responsibility-reporting-2013.pdf

Law, J. (2004). *After method: Mess in social science research*. New York: Routledge.

Leyshon, A., French, S., & Signoretta, P. (2008). Financial exclusion and the geography of bank and building society branch closure in Britain. *Transactions of the Institute of British Geographers, 33*, 447–465.

Manetti, G., & Toccafondi, S. (2012). The role of stakeholders in sustainability assurance. *Journal of Business Ethics, 107*, 363–377.

Marrewijk, M. (2001). Concepts and definitions of CSR and corporate sustainability. *Journal of Business Ethics, 44*, 95–105.

Molesworth, M., Watkins, R., & Denegri-Knott, J. (2016). Possession work on digital consumption objects and consumer ensnarement. *Journal of the Association for Consumer Research, 1*(2), 246–261.

Nairn, A., & Hang, H. (2012). *Advergames: It's not child's play. A review of research*. London: Family and Parenting Institute.

Noland, J., & Phillips, R. (2010). Stakeholder enagement, discourse, ethics and strategic management. *International Journal of Management Reviews, 12*, 39–49.

O'Riordan, L., & Fairbrass, J. (2013). Managing CSR stakeholder engagement: A new conceptual framework. *Journal of Business Ethics, 125*, 121–145.

Owen, L., Lewis, C., Auty, S., & Buijzen, M. (2012). Is children's understanding of nontraditional advertising comparable with their understanding of television advertising? *Journal of Public Policy & Marketing, 32*, 195–206.

Phillips, R. A. (1997). Stakeholder theory and a model of fairness. *Business Ethics Quarterly, 7*, 51–66.

Plumer, Brad. 2015. *Volkswagen's appalling clean diesel scandal, explained*. Retrieved April 15, 2016, from http://www.vox.com/2015/9/21/9365667/volkswagen-clean-diesel-recall-passenger-cars

Prahalad, C. K., & Ramaswamy, V. (2004). *The future of competition: Co-creating unique value with customers*. Boston, MA: Harvard Business School Press.

Ragnedda, M., & Muschert, G. W. (2013). *The digital divide: The Internet and social inequality in international perspective*. New York: Routledge.

Rapp, A., Baker, T. L., Bachrach, D. G., Ogilvie, J., & Beitelspacher, L. S. (2015). Perceived customer showrooming behavior and the effect on retail salesperson self-efficacy and performance. *Journal of Retailing, 91*, 358–369.

Rawls, J. (1971). *A theory of justice*. Cambridge: Harvard University Press.

Reynolds, M. A., & Yuthas, K. (2008). Moral discourse and corporate social responsibility reporting. *Journal of Business Ethics, 78*, 47–64.

Ritzer, G., & Jurgenson, N. (2010). Production, consumption, prosumption: The nature of capitalism in the age of the digital "prosumer". *Journal of Consumer Culture, 10* 13–36.

Scholz, T. (Ed.). (2012). *Digital labor: The Internet as playground and factory*. New York: Routledge.

Stohl, C., Etter, M., Banghart, S., & Woo, D. J. (2015). Social media policies: Implications for contemporary notions of corporate social responsibility. *Journal of Business Ethics,* 1–24. Retrieved April 10, 2016, from http://link.springer.com/article/10.1007%2Fs10551-015-2743-9

Tapscott, D., & Williams, A. D. (2006). *Wikinomics: How mass collaboration changes everything*. New York: Portfolio.

Terranova, T. (2000). Free labor: Producing culture for the digital economy. *Social Text, 18*, 33–58.

UN Global Compact. *What is UN global compact*. Retrieved April 15, 2016, from https://www.unglobalcompact.org/what-is-gc

Watkins, R., Denegri-Knott, J., & Molesworth, M. (2016). The relationship between ownership and possession: Observations from the context of digital virtual goods. *Journal of Marketing Management, 32*, 44–70.

Weidel, T. (2015). The "ugliness" of economic efficiency: Technology, species-being, and global poverty. *Ethics & Global Politics, 8*. Retrieved April 16, 2016, from http://www.ethicsandglobalpolitics.net/index.php/egp/article/view/29226

Whelan, G., Moon, J., & Grant, B. (2013). Corporations and citizenship arenas in the age of social media. *Journal of Business Ethics, 118*, 777–790.

4

A New Paradigm: How Social Movements Shape Corporate Social Responsibility After the Financial Crisis

Camelia Crisan and Ana Adi

4.1   Introduction

The impact of the 2007–2008 financial crisis goes beyond currency and economic effects into bringing wider international, societal changes. Among these is a call to redefine the role and responsibility of businesses, organizations and institutions, this being generally expressed through the rise in street protests, civic collective actions and social movements (Occupy from the USA, Indignados from Spain and Uniti Salvam! from Romania). This also brings a new focus on corporate social responsibility (CSR) and questions of whether the new post-financial crisis climate

C. Crisan (✉)
Communication and Public Relations, SNSPA, Bucuresti, Romania

A. Adi
Corporate Communications, Quadriga University of Applied Sciences, Berlin, Germany

© The Author(s) 2017
A. Theofilou et al. (eds.), *Corporate Social Responsibility in the Post-Financial Crisis Era*, Palgrave Studies in Governance, Leadership and Responsibility, DOI 10.1007/978-3-319-40096-9_4

should see the field redefined; not an easy task considering that even before the crisis, both academic literature and practice did not provide a single definition.

Although most scholars outline the relationship between business and society through CSR, CSR is explained in various terms, depending on the area of science authors are coming from: corporate social performance—CSP, reflecting a managerial perspective, focuses on economic and public responsibilities and social responsiveness (Carroll 1999; Sethi 1979; Wartick and Cochran 1985, Gond and Crane 2010). Also from a managerial perspective is Berthoin-Antal and Sobczak's (2014) proposal of renaming CSR as Global Responsibility (GR) and their associated multilevel model which "enables an analysis of the way culture influences how responsibilities are defined and distributed in a culture at a given point in time, and how organizations learn to address new responsibilities in new ways when the context changes. The model starts at the organizational level and zooms in on the individual level as well as outward to the local, national, and international levels".

Other perspectives include Corporate Sustainability (CSu) (Hopkins 2007), reflecting an environmental perspective; corporate citizenship (CC) (Crane et al. 2008), which addresses CSR from a political science perspective; and, more recently, 3C-SR ("ethical and social commitments; connections with partners in the value network; and consistency of behavior over time to build trust" (Meehan et al. 2006, p. 392)) proposed by Meehan, Meehan and Richards from a consumer/marketing perspective.

CSR has also been defined as an evolutionary concept by Frederick (2006) CSR_1, CSR_2, CSR_3 and CSR_4 and Visser (2008) CSR 1.0 and CSR 2.0 as well as a multi-stages learning organization until reaching the civic corporation status by Zadek (2007). The criterion for the concept evolution has been linked both with society's economic and technological development as well as organizational learning as a response to societal problems.

Metaphors and visual representations have also been used to picture CSR. For instance, Caroll (1979 cited in Carroll and Buchholtz 2006) depicts it as a pyramid; Elkington (1994/2007) and Porritt (2007) see it at the crossroads of the triple bottom line economic–social–environmental, McDonough and Braungart (2002) portray it as a relationship between man and environment exploitation from cradle to cradle, while Hawken et al. (1999) describe it as a human activity but not at the expense of the social structure of the natural world.

Definitions of CSR prior to the financial crisis were thus focusing on the extent to which CSR regulated or described the relationship between business and society (the normative versus descriptive approach), but also the extent of the specific difference in defining the terms *social* and the *responsibility*. This chapter aims to explain why understanding both of these is important nowadays, in the post-crisis climate.

In order to understand a complex concept such as CSR, one should consider the *genus proxim* and the specific difference. We believe that the core of the CSR definition is the relationship of responsibility between the business and the society. The specific difference, the one related to the extent to which we view both these terms—social and responsibility—has shaped and continues to shape the way in which CSR has been both defined and theorized about. If we consider these notions on a continuum, we will set one view at the beginning point of an axis (the minimum amount of responsibility toward the minimum amount of people), and at the other end of the axis, we will have the maximum responsibility (toward the largest amount of people). In order to do so, the two most contrasting points of view related to the social responsibility of corporations need to be considered: Milton Friedman's ([1970]2007) (continued by David Henderson (2001)) and Noam Chomsky's (2010, 2011, 2012). These two views will be each, at the beginning, respectively at the end of an axis, with several shades between them; and their description will be elaborated upon in the following section.

4.2   Responsibility at the Minimum Social Level

In his famous article published in The New York Times, Friedman ([1970]2007) questions, if existing, what are the responsibilities of a company: "The social responsibility of a business is to increase its profits." In his view only people can have responsibilities. If a corporation can be considered to be an artificial person (a nexus of contracts), then, as a consequence, it would have only artificial responsibilities. One cannot say about the business environment, taken as a whole, that it has a responsibility, not even in the vaguest of senses. In Friedman's view, in order to clarify the doctrine of business's social responsibility, one must first query what this responsibility entails and who should bare it; in other words, who are the individuals who should be responsible in a business relationship: the owners, the shareholders or the managers? Based on free market philosophy, at whose core lies private property, a manager is the employee of the business' owners. The manager thus has clear and strict legal responsibilities toward those who hired them. These responsibilities are connected to running the business according to the owners' wishes; such wishes are, in general, to make as much money as possible while they are complying with the basic rules of society, as codified by law and ethical principles. In Friedman's view, thus, the managerial responsibility is toward the owners or shareholders—whatever the area of the corporate activity is. Managers may be inclined toward charity or volunteering, and as long as these are being done in their spare time and with their own money, Friedman argues that they are exercising a social responsibility. However, it is an individual one, not a corporate one. Should the manager assume a social responsibility from her/his position as an employee, it means that s/he could end up acting in a manner that may not be in the interest of their employer. For instance, due to social responsibility, a manager may decide not to raise the price in order to contribute to a social objective of preventing inflation, even if raising the price would be in the interest of the corporation. Alternatively, they may spend money on reducing pollution beyond the legal requirements in place or beyond what is needed to protect the company's interests, or they may hire long-term unemployed people instead of other, better qualified candidates, aiming thus to contribute to unemployment reduction. In all the above cases, the manager would spend the money of someone else, concludes Friedman ([1970]2007), for a general social interest. Should the manager's actions of social responsibility reduce profits for shareholders, the manager is spending their money. If the manager's actions of social responsibility increase the prices clients would normally pay for their items, then they are spending their clients' money; if the manager's actions contribute to decreasing the salaries of employees, they are spending their employees' money. In Friedman's ([1970]2007) view, each of these categories—shareholders, employees and consumers—can decide for themselves what to do with the money and on which social cause they would want it spent. However, should the manager decide to spend money on certain social responsibility actions they would be acting as a tax office (taxing the profits of shareholders). Imposing taxes is an activity incumbent to the national states, not to managers. The managers would play the roles of parliament, government and legal system—they may decide whom to tax, how much to tax and for what activity to spend money. When this happens, the manager is not an agent of his employer but a government servant spending private money for social purposes, while claiming to serve private interests. The idea of a social responsibility for the business, Friedman argues, is against the very nature of the free economy ([1962]2002).

Henderson (2001, p. 6) shares Friedman's view, arguing that CSR is nothing but a subversive doctrine "promoting the global salvationism". This, he argues, has been triggered by the development of the stakeholders' theories, globalization and its effects—sometimes real, sometimes just assumed—the increase of the power for the non-profit organizations and the way in which the misbehavior of some companies has been presented in the media. All these pressures and factors have pushed corporations to react: some in a defensive and business-focused manner, and others in a positive manner, focused on their effects on the larger business environment. However, the purpose of these actions has only been a *captatio benevolentiae* in order to protect the business.

New procedures and new forms of corporate governance are being put in place by legislation and thus *the statute of the shareholders is diminished in importance*. CSR regulates behaviors: compensation and benefits for employees, philanthropy, cause-related marketing and public relations. "Taking CSR seriously may lead to substantial changes for the interested parties, while the consequences raise many concerns for the business environment (Henderson 2001, p. 28)." In practical terms, CSR cannot be put into action because, as Friedman argues, managers do not have the mandate to decide *if and how much* can a company's individual actions in the free market contribute to the common good, including the particular actions of commercial companies guided by making profit. The same argument is presented by Sternberg (1999, p. 35) who believes the term social responsibility is wrongly used especially when speaking of non-specific responsibilities that companies should assume in relation with society. In her view, social responsibility is part of larger responsibilities that companies assume for the effects and consequences of their business impact; however, this cannot be demanded as a social responsibility per se, as the companies' sole duty is to reach the objectives for which they have been created and nothing more (Sternberg 1999, p. 36). We too believe that corporations are not persons and hence do not display any intrinsic moral values. The person who is temporarily leading the company operations, whether an agent or a manager, although uses as a steward her/his better judgment, cannot make choices that are not within the mandate the shareholders entrusted them (Crisan 2013).

In *Capitalism and freedom*, Friedman ([1962]2002, pp. 216–217) also suggests that when it comes to issues concerning society such as pollution for instance, the companies are a mere intermediary, a means of coordinating people's behavior in their capacity as consumers and producers. For example, if people want electricity, they must be prepared to pay for it and for the smoke produced as part of burning the fuel to produce it. The consumers are therefore *the guilty party*, due to their demand for such goods and services and hence consumers must be prepared to pay both the direct and the indirect costs, should they want that the electricity production process to pollute the environment as little as possible. Friedman's view, and those of his supporters for that matter, represents the minimum of what one could consider CSR. In this case, the social dimension of CSR comprises both shareholders and consumers, while the responsibility is solely owed solely to the former.

To conclude, Friedman bases his arguments for the minimal corporate responsibility toward society on the concept of property and connected rights or, what Mitchell calls (1986, p. 200), the *shareholder prima facie* theory. In this case, ownership is the only legitimate basis for responsibility, and this responsibility is solely related with the corporations' objectives and purposes as set and stated by its shareholders.

4.3   Responsibility Toward Some Stakeholders

Zenisek (1979) and Fitch (1976) present other views on social responsibility, their approaches being more nuanced then Friedman's and thus further away on our proposed continuum. The latter suggests that to reach a minimum level of social responsibility, corporations would accept utilitarian principles as a basis for judging their current and ideal business circumstances and would thus consider their social responsibility within this framework. A corporation has the responsibility to avoid the costs imposed by their vicinity, be they organizations or individuals. Equally, as a means to stimulate their activities, corporations can exercise their social responsibility in addressing the social problems they create or come across while pursuing their profit making. Fitch (1976) notes however that it is possible that governments would impose laws on corporations when they do not voluntarily accept some responsibilities. In other words, it is better for organizations to voluntarily assume a series of responsibilities to avoid any government-imposed regulations, even if these responsibilities are a result of social pressures.

Stakeholder theories are the next step on our proposed continuum. They pinpoint an increased differentiation and clarification of both *social* and *responsibility* terms. Unlike the previous views, stakeholder theories propose a new focus of the corporations' raison d'être: that to create welfare rather than make profit for their shareholders. Companies would not exist unless they satisfy human needs for which people would pay. Thus, individuals and groups who contribute, intentionally or not, to the process of welfare creation are stakeholders; their contribution may include real inputs (like work or innovation) supporting additional costs, assuming risks and being in the position of incurring losses resulting from company operations. This means that they have something at stake and that they also take risks; it also means that their benefits may be smaller or the consequences of the anticipated dangers higher than assumed (Preston 2001). Freeman et al. (2007, p. 6) define these stakeholders as any group or individual which may affect or can be affected by the corporation in reaching its purpose. Philips (2003) believes that the stakeholders are the groups from which the organization has accepted voluntarily benefits and, as a result, has moral obligations toward them. Building on the arguments of Preston (2001), Philips relates to the common risk taking and, in return, the common sharing of benefits produced by the corporation. The shareholders exercise ownership only on the *residual cash flow* which the corporation produces. They do not own per se the building or the chairs or the cars of a corporation. The ownership of shares does not imply ownership of any of the physical corporation more than it involves the ownership of any other financial tool connected to the corporation (a loan). The corporation is an independent entity whose owner is nobody. In fact, as Post et al. (2002) indicate, the rights of the shareholders nowadays only consist in receiving fractionate distributions from the income that corporations are producing (if the company directors wish it so) and to sell the symbol (token) of ownership to someone else. Thus, if a corporation or another organization is capable of having legal obligations, then it should also be capable of having moral obligations. Fairness is such a moral responsibility: accepting the benefits of a mutual advantageous cooperation relationship, the corporation has also obligations toward those who contribute to its activity. Some obligations are legally binding, while others are not. From this perspective, Philips (2003) argues, shareholders are significant contributors, so the corporations' obligations toward them are also significant; when organizations are well managed, this is usually seen in the corporations' payment of profit shares. The obligations toward other stakeholders are also fairness based, which provides managers with a legitimate argument in favor of appointing organizational representatives to insure the stakeholders' welfare (Philips 2003, p. 156).

Clarke ([1998]2004) and Blair [1995]2004) use similar arguments, when discussing workers' rights and their participation in the decision-making processes of the company. Considering corporate governance processes, they argue that diminishing the shareholders' role in managing the business would lead to a higher recognition of the professional managers' role as well as to a higher contribution of other stakeholder groups to managing the business. Their main argument in favor of increasing the social responsibility of corporations is connected with the diminishing of risks, and as a result, with a reduction of the effects resulting from property rights. They support the idea that, although the stakeholders may not own shares, they are entitled to formulate expectations of higher social responsibilities from corporations in the sense that their interests are listened to and accounted for. From this perspective, shareholders have a statute of *Primus inter pares*, but a *pare*—an equal to the others nonetheless (Crisan 2013). The responsibility of the corporation should therefore be directed only to those who have a stake in it and not to society as a whole. This, in our view, marks the middle position on our CSR definitions continuum.

4.4   Responsibility Toward All Stakeholders

Two developments of the stakeholder theories are also on our proposed continuum: the refined stakeholder model of Yves Fassin (2009) and the social license to operate model of Boutilier and Thomson (2011). They both expand Freeman's (1984) initial model and show how by using them, organizations can legitimize their operations, social capital as well as avoid financial losses. The two models are both instrumental, and they promote a larger extent of the *social* toward whom the business is responsible when doing its operations.

In order to identify stakeholders and practice a more efficient management, Fassin (2009) proposes undertaking a strategic analysis focused on legitimacy of the claims advanced, influence/dominance and responsibility. This would lead to identifying *real stakeholders* which, like in the classical approach, have real stakes in the company, pressure groups which protect and oversee the interests of the real stakeholders (*stake-watchers*) and regulators, who do not have direct stakes, but can impose laws and external controls (*stake-keepers*). All groups influence one another, depend on each other and are each other's stakeholders: for each real stakeholder group, there is a pressure group and a corresponding stake-watcher (associated stakeholder), and for each stake-watcher, there is a specific stake-keeper. For instance, employees (real stakeholders) have the unions as stake-watcher and the government as stake-keeper. Fassin's model (2009) marks the transition of the definitions of *social* toward the end of our proposed axis (society as a whole), because he introduces civil society and the communities in a separate group of associated stakeholders (predominantly in the stake-watcher category). Mass media, along with government, is classified as a distinctive stake-keeper and not as a stake-watcher (Fassin 2009, p. 123) because of its power to require corporations to engage in socially responsible behaviors. However, sometimes media has not been the stakeholder pressing corporations to be responsible for the larger societal issues, on the contrary—it has served the needs of neoliberal institutions. As Herman and Chomsky ([1988]2002, p. 8) put it:

The greater profitability of the media in a deregulated environment ... has forced the managements of the media giants to incur greater debt and to focus even more aggressively and unequivocally on profitability, in order to placate owners and reduce the attractiveness of their properties to outsiders. They have lost some of their limited autonomy to bankers, institutional investors, and large individual investors whom they have had to solicit as potential 'white knights'.

In terms of the social license, the model for engaging stakeholders has been developed as a bottom-up effort, taking into account the mining industry and the challenges it faces when working with local communities. However, as Romania's Rosia Montana Gold Corporation case has shown (Bortun and Crisan 2012), the bigger the organization and its impact, the more stakeholders are needed to give the organization its social license to operate, based both inside the area affected and outside of it, including outside the country. On our proposed continuum, this approach is further up the axis related to expanding the specific difference of CSR, where *social* refers here to the whole territory of a state and sometimes spans to include interested groups from outside its territory and where the *responsibility* demanded from the corporations is oriented toward all the people who feel they have a stake, even a minor one, in the activities of a certain corporation.

4.5   Responsibility Toward Society as a Whole

At the end of our continuum is the maximum social group toward which the corporations must have a responsibility: society as a whole, including the not yet born generations. Using the concept of externalities as a basis, Noam Chomsky (2010) argues that any corporation should be held accountable even by people who do not have any stakes in it, be they direct or indirect. Chomsky argues that the free market is full of imperfections and is inefficient:

> Transactions do not take into account the effect on others who are not party of them. These so-called externalities can be huge. That is particularly so in the case of financial institutions. Their tasks is to take risks, and if well managed, to ensure that the potential losses to themselves will be covered.

To themselves. Under capitalist rules, it is not their business to consider their cost to others. Risk is underpriced, because systemic risk is not priced in the decisions … The pressure is to ignore the impact on others on undertaking transactions, if one wants to stay in the game. In this case, the externalities happen to be the fate of the species, but the logic is the same. (Chomsky 2010, pp. 107–112)

As externalities of business transactions are simply passed on to society—be it the collapse of international financial systems, the laying off of thousands of workers, decreasing the quality of life for children whose parents have an imbalanced work–life relations—everyone belonging to human race will end up paying for these externalities sooner or later. Among these, the most dramatic externalities are the planet's resource depletion and climate change. For this reason, the *social* area of CSR extends beyond the living populations and on to the yet unborn generations (Jonas 1985). Chomsky's argument too is that the responsibility of corporations should be toward society as whole, including its yet unborn generations.

This responsibility is denying even the shareholders' right of prima facie when they aim at having short-term gains to the expense of impoverishing others. Chomsky is thus arguing for a complete restructuring of capitalism, and the renunciation of the neoliberal market fundamentalism. The fact that such externalities are not a subject for public debate is owed to the fact that both the economic and political powers of corporations have increased, while the ideology of the supremacy of the free markets is triumphant in the public debate. As Chomsky (2012) puts it, this ideologic win has meant new taxes and fiscal policies, liberalization and rules of corporate governance which correlate huge bonuses for managers aiming at short-term profits. The wealth accumulated by the rich has led to a greater political power and a vicious circle where 1 percent of the population gets more money, while for the rest of the population, the income has stagnated. In a public speech from 2011, Chomsky is urging people to Occupy the Future! Looking at the financial crisis and quoting from a brochure published by Citigroup in 2005, he is unveiling a situation where the society is divided by big corporations into plutonomy and the rest.

"The U.S., U.K. and Canada are the key plutonomies—economies powered by the wealthy. As for the non-rich, they're sometimes called the precariat—people who live a precarious existence at the periphery of society. The "periphery," however, has become a substantial proportion of the population in the U.S. and elsewhere. So we have the plutonomy and the precariat: the 1 percent and the 99 percent, as Occupy sees it—not literal numbers, but the right picture. The historic reversal in people's confidence about the future is a reflection of tendencies that could become irreversible. The Occupy protests are the first major popular reaction that could change the dynamic" (Chomsky 2011, https://chomsky.info/20111101/).

In the light of the above, what we are proposing is a new paradigm, where business becomes responsible to the whole society and not as a voluntary act, but as an obligation.

Our own definition of CSR is taking into account Chomsky's (2010, 2011, 2012) views, Fassin's (2009) tools derived from the refined stakeholder management and Boutilier and Thomson's (2011) social license.

> Overall, CSR is referring to the relationship between business and society as a whole from the perspective of sustainable development and care for future generations. In particular, CSR refers to the way an organization is managed, where the decision-makers (shareholders, managers, board members) obligatory take it upon themselves to consider, in an equitable manner, in their profit making endeavors the interests of all parties and stakeholder that their activity is affecting. (Crisan 2013, p. 55)

4.6   CSR Paradigms: Friedman and Chomsky

There are fundamental differences between the CSRs proposed by Friedman and those proposed by Chomsky. As their proposed arguments may not find support among their opponents, we argue that the two represent two opposing paradigms. While Friedman's paradigm puts at its center the sacrality of the shareholders' ownership right and exclusivity over the connected rights resulting from business operations, Chomsky's paradigm sits on the premise that shareholders are not entitled to profits and connected rights from business exploitation if they harm the environment and society. In Friedman's paradigm case, the responsibility of the manager is directed inwards (to the shareholders), while in the Chomsky's paradigm, it is directed outwards (to society as a whole). Last but not least, Friedman's paradigm considers that indirect costs associated with corporate responsibilities should be incurred by society while the corporate profits should remain untouched, while Chomsky's paradigm supports the view that companies should decrease profits and incur both the costs and risks of their undertakings, by covering the potential externalities they put on society (Crisan 2013).

Friedman's paradigm is rooted in the economic theory of the firm, while Chomsky's paradigm is rooted in equity on wealth distribution, power of social movements, sociology and anthropology. These two paradigms are in total opposition to one another, so it is no surprise that the arguments in favor of one are the ones used to dismiss the other (Kuhn 1962/2008). These paradigms imply incompatible presuppositions related to the basic concepts of the area they study (CSR), they engage different criteria of delineation for "real" problems and "legitimate" solutions; equally, the observations made by researchers about the same reality yet through either of these paradigmatic lenses are non-comparable. Whether these two paradigms will converge in the future is difficult to predict. Unless the fundamentals of the capitalist system will change and new corporate governance systems for multinational companies will emerge, the two paradigms will remain incompatible (Crisan 2013).

4.7   Social Movements Paving the Way to a Paradigm Change

Interestingly, both Friedman's and Chomsky's paradigms were formulated around the same time: Chomsky's paradigm started, in our view, with the movement initiated by Rachel Carson's essay, The Silent Spring (1962) and the Friedman's with his New York Times essay ([1970]2007). We argue that both paradigms have been shaped by the social movements of their times, which exercised pressure on corporations and governments; the 1970s have equally played an important role in the shaping and further development of both paradigms.

Friedman and Friedman (1980) for instance argued that there is no inconsistency between the free market and helping the vulnerable ones:

> There is all the difference in the world, however, between two kinds of assistance through government that seem superficially similar: first, 90 percent of us agreeing to impose taxes on ourselves in order to help the bottom 10 percent, and second, 80 percent voting to impose taxes on the top 10 percent to help the bottom 10 percent. ... The first may be wise or unwise, an effective or an ineffective way to help the disadvantaged—but it is consistent with belief in both equality of opportunity and liberty. The second seeks equality of outcome and is entirely antithetical to liberty. (Friedman and Friedman 1980, p. 140)

It is around the same time that the *cultural creative* sub-culture emerged, agglutinating views from consciousness, anti-racial, emancipation and feminist movements in the USA (Ray and Anderson 2000, p. 128). Based on anti-system attitudes and the motivational crisis, the cultural creatives moved away from class antagonism to defining themselves as equally capitalists and workers. They manifested interest in corporations targeting profits alone by exploiting poor countries, engaging in extensive layoffs and polluting (Ray and Anderson 2000, pp. 175–192). It is therefore no wonder that some of the new top politicians in Northern Europe and the USA, like Jeremy Corbyn, the new leader of the Labour Party,[1] would espouse a new theory about the relationship between corporations, state and society as his values were crafted in the laboratories of the cultural movements of the 1980s.

The massive deregulation of the 1970s, started during the Reagan administration (Bonner and Wiggin 2009; Reich 2007, Chomsky 2012), based on the economic theories of the Chicago School of Economics (George Stigler, a Nobel Prize winner in Economics and a leader of the Chicago School of Economics alongside Milton Friedman being the major advocate for de-regularization (Stigler and Friedland 1962)), had major effects, leading among others to the concentration of assets in the hands of a few super-rich and the growing number of impoverished

---

[1] "The big question is how to get some of the wealthiest individuals and biggest corporations to pay anything like their fair share" (Corbyn 2015).

populations. This continues to have effects up until today, in the USA for instance "16,000 Americans hold as much wealth as 80 percent of the nation's population—some 256,000,000 people—and as much as 75 percent of the *entire world's* population. The combined wealth of these 16,000 people is more than $9 trillion" (as democratic nominee candidate Bernie Sanders cited Saez and Zucman 2014).

What we have witnessed in the last three decades was a slow but strong transformation of the citizen into a consumer, as Edwards (2008), Reich (2007) and Bonner and Wiggin (2009) indicate. People are faced with rewards such as lower prices if they consume more. However, as civil society members some of them lose jobs as big chains of supermarkets move in, others see the depletion of local resources, while others see how their jobs are being moved to countries with less regulations. This, in turn, leads to higher activism whether organized through non-governmental organizations or the emergence of social movements. The latter can turn into political movements. Schrempf-Stirling and Palazzo (2016) have documented how since the new millennium, due to social pressure, the CSR of companies has changed its scope, depth and management practices. Thus, previous discussions about worker rights have shifted toward human rights, the NGOs from different area of business work with each other to expand the supplier base verification toward what the authors call a full producer upstream CSR.

In the same book, *Freedom to Choose*, Friedman and Friedman (1980, p. 145) argue that

When the law interferes with people's pursuit of their own values, they will try to find a way around. They will evade the law, they will break the law, or they will leave the country. Few of us believe in a moral code that justifies forcing people to give up much of what they produce to finance payments to persons they do not know for purposes they may not approve of. When the law contradicts what most people regard as moral and proper, they will break the law—whether the law is enacted in the name of a noble ideal such as equality or in the naked interest of one group at the expense of another. Only fear of punishment, not a sense of justice and morality, will lead people to obey the law.

Considering the "moral dispense" that the economic theories give businesses as part of Friedman's paradigm, it facilitates the understanding of some corporate misbehaviors recorded in the last decade—from Enron (Sison, [2003]2007) to the financial crises from 2007 with "predatory lending, … opportunistic behavior … acting based on the view that they (bankers) must maximize their own return … they see the real economy as their money supplier" (Spitzek et al. 2012, kindle edition, pp. 463–505) and the newly discovered Panama Papers, which show how big multinational companies have eluded tax regulations, set up ghost companies in fiscal paradises and refused thus to contribute a fair share to the well-being of their societies:

> In 2005, for instance, the European Union implemented a new law called the European Savings Directive, which required banks to withhold taxes on accounts of customers living in European countries. But the savings directive covered only individuals, not corporations. The files show this loophole was seized upon by the banks, which began marketing products that transferred assets from individuals to offshore corporations for tax-reporting purposes. (Chittum et al. 2016)

All these facts are a clear illustration of the classical economic paradigm; this could make Milton Friedman one the ideological gurus and promoters of the current law breaches, should one not be inclined to pay taxes and contribute to society for purposes they do not approve.

In terms of Chomsky's paradigm, a study undertaken by de Graaf and Stoelhorst (2009) shows how the Triodos Bank from the Netherlands has not been affected by the financial crisis because it has responsibly not invested "in structured products, or complex financial constructions based on derivatives" (de Graaf and Stoelhorst 2009, p. 306), but was leading its business based on sound moral principles, using a CSR in action and a governance structure and procedures which were including all the values embedded in the bank's initial mission. It is hard to predict if this *free rider* strategy of the Triodos Bank will be followed by a large number of financial institution; however, if this should happen, it will certainly lead to a major and considerable change in the banking system.

4.8   Friedman versus Chomsky—Convergence or Conversion

We are inclined to conclude that the shift from Friedman's paradigm to Chomsky's is harder to be done than expected. It may be overcome only by the fear of punishment. A new paradigm of CSR will need not only tougher regulations, but also a new relationship between the political establishment, society and corporate environment. As long as the legal requirements and legislation for financing election campaigns favor big capital instead of simple citizens, the only option remains to change the political class and transform the current social movements into strong political ones; Syriza in Greece, Podemos in Spain and Occupy in the USA and elsewhere are showing some success in getting people mobilized. If they are strong enough, our conviction is that they will be capable to change the agenda and bring the priorities from the grassroots level to the mainstream political agenda. For that purpose, the national Occupy—type movements will need to win sufficient power in a large number of states so they transform the whole system of globalized relations. That will set the path to a new relationship between business and society and the premise for applying it within Chomsky's paradigm.

References

Berthoin-Antal, A., & Sobczak's, A. (2014). Culturally embedded organizational learning for global responsibility. *Business & Society, 53*(5), 652–683.

Blair, M. M. ([1995]2004). Ownership and control: Rethinking corporate governance for the twenty-first century. In T. Clarke (Ed.), *Theories of corporate governance: The theoretical foundations* (pp. 174–189). London: Routledge.

Bonner, B., & Wiggin, A. (2009). *The new empire of debt. The rise of an epic financial crisis*. Hoboken, NJ: John Wiley and Sons.

Bortun, D., & Crisan, C. (2012). Levels of corporate community engagement. Who should provide the social license to operate. *The Romanian Economic Journal, 15*(46bis), 41–53.

Boutilier, R. G., & Thomson, I. (2011). *Modelling and measuring the social license to operate: Fruits of a dialogue between theory and practice*. Retrieved September 1, 2012, from http://socialicense.com/publications/Modelling%20and%20Measuring%20the%20SLO.pdf

Carroll, A. (1999). Corporate social performance as a bottom line for consumers. *Business and Society, 38*, 268–295.

Carroll, A. B., & Buchholtz, A. K. (2006). *Business and society: Ethics and stakeholder management* (6th ed.). Mason: Thompson/South Western.

Carson, R. (1962). *Silent spring.* Retrieved April 22, 2016, from http://library. uniteddiversity.coop/More_Books_and_Reports/Silent_Spring-Rachel_Carson-1962.pdf

Chittum, R., Schilis-Gallego, C., & Carvajal, R. (2016). *Global banks team with law firms to help the wealthy hide assets. Leaked records show that hundreds of banks and their subsidiaries and branches registered nearly 15,600 shell companies.* Retrieved April 16, 2016, from https://panamapapers.icij. org/20160404-banks-lawyers-hide-assets.html

Chomsky, N. (2010). *Hopes and prospects.* London: Penguin Books.

Chomsky, N. (2011). *Occupy the future.* Retrieved April 23, 2016, from https:// chomsky.info/20111101/

Chomsky, N. (2012). *Noi cream viitorul. Ocupatii, interventii, imperialism, rezistenta.* Bucharest: Corint.

Clarke, T. ([1998]2004). The stakeholder corporation: A business philosophy for the information age In T. Clarke (Ed.), *Theories of corporate governance: The theoretical foundations* (pp. 189–203). London: Routledge.

Corbyn, J. (2015). *The economy in 2020.* Retrieved April 18, 2016, from https:// d3n8a8pro7vhmx.cloudfront.net/jeremyforlabour/pages/70/attachments/ original/1437556345/TheEconomyIn2020_JeremyCorbyn-220715. pdf?1437556345

Crane, A., Matten, D., & Moon, J. (2008). *Corporations and citizenship.* Cambridge: University Press.

Crisan, C. (2013). *Corporatiile si societatea. Responsabilitatea sociala corporativa intre act voluntar si obligatie.* Bucharest: Tritonic.

de Graaf, F. J., & Stoelhorst, J. W. (2009). The role of governance in corporate social responsibility: Lessons From dutch finance. *Business & Society, 52*(2), 282–317.

Edwards, M. (2008). *Just another emperor. The myths and realities of philanthrocapitalism.* Demos: A Network for Ideas & Action, The Young Foundation.

Elkington, J. (2007). Enter the triple bottom line. In A. Henriques & J. Richardson (Eds.), *The triple bottom line, does it all add up?* (pp. 1–17). London: Earthscan.

Fassin, Y. (2009). The stakeholder model refined. *Journal of Business Ethics, 84*, 113–135.

Fitch, G. H. (1976). Achieving corporate social responsibility. *The Academy of Management Review, 1*(1), 38–46.

Frederick, W. (2006). *Corporation, be good! the story of corporate social responsibility*. Indianapolis: Dog Ear Publishing.

Freeman, E. (1984). *Strategic management: A stakeholder approach*. Boston: Pitman.

Freeman, E. R., Harrison, J. S., & Wicks, A. C. (2007). *Managing for stakeholders: Survival, relation and success*. Delmar, NY: Caravan Books Project.

Friedman, M. ([1962]2002). *Capitalism and freedom*. Chicago: The University of Chicago Press.

Friedman, M. ([1970]2007). The social responsibility of business is to increase its profits. In W. Zimmerli, K. Richter, & M. Holzinger (Eds.), *Corporate ethics and corporate governance* (pp. 173–179). Berlin: Springer.

Friedman, M., & Friedman, R. (1980). *Free to choose. A personal statement*. New York: Harcourt, Brace, Jovanivich.

Gond, J. P., & Crane, A. (2010). Corporate social performance disoriented: Saving the lost paradigm? *Business & Society, 49*(4), 677–703.

Hawken, P., Lovins, A., & Lovins, H. (1999). *Natural capitalism. Creating the next industrial revolution*. New York: Little, Brown and Company.

Henderson, D. (2001). *Misguided virtue: False notions of corporate social responsibility*. Wellington: New Zealand Business Roundtable.

Herman, E., & Chomsky, N. ([1988]2002). *Manufacturing consent. The political economy of mass media*. New-York: Pantheon Books.

Hopkins, M. (2007). *Corporate Social Responsibility and International Development: Is Business the Solution*? New York: Earthscan Publications Ltd.

Jonas, H. (1985). *The imperative of responsibility. In search of an ethics for the technological age*. Chicago: The University of Chicago Press.

Kuhn, T. ([1962]2008). *Structura revoluțiilor stiințifice*. Bucharest: Humanitas.

McDonough, W., & Braungart, M. (2002). *Cradle to cradle. Remaking the way we make things*. New York: North Point Press.

Meehan, J., K. Meehan and A. Richards. (2006) Corporate social responsibility: the 3C-SR model International Journal of Social Economics, 33 (5/6), 386-398.

Mitchell, N. (1986). Corporate power, legitimacy, and social policy. *The Western Political Quarterly, 39*(2), 197–212.

Philips, R. (2003). *Stakeholder theory and organizational ethics*. San Francisco: Berrett-Koehler Publishers.

Porritt, J. (2007). *Capitalism as if the world matters*. London: Earthscan.

Post, J. E., Preston, L. E., & Sachs, S. (2002). *Redefining the corporation. Stakeholder management and organizational wealth*. Stanford: Stanford University Press.

Preston, L. E. (2001). *Consensus statement on stakeholder model of the corporation.* Retrieved December 14, 2008, from http://www.rotman.utoronto.ca/~stake/Consensus.htm

Ray, P., & Anderson, S. R. (2000). *The cultural creatives.* New York: Harmony Books.

Reich, R. (2007). *Supercapitalism. The transformation of business, democracy, and everyday life.* New York: Alfred. A. Knopf, Random House.

Saez, E., & Zucman, G. (2014). *Wealth inequality in the United States since 1913: Evidence from capitalized income tax data.* Retrieved April 22, 2016, from http://gabriel-zucman.eu/files/SaezZucman2014.pdf

Schrempf-Stirling, J., & Palazzo, G. (2016). Upstream corporate social responsibility: The evolution from contract responsibility to full producer responsibility. *Business and Society, 55*(4), 491–527.

Sethi, S. P. (1979). A conceptual framework for environmental analysis of social issues and evaluation of business response patterns. *The Academy of Management Review, 4*(1), 63–74.

Sison, A. ([2003]2007). Enron—Pride comes before the fall. In W. Zimmerli, K. Richter, & M. Holzinger (Eds.), *Corporate ethics and corporate governance* (pp. 129–137). Berlin: Springer.

Spitzek, H., Pirson, M., & Dierksmeier, C. (2012). Introduction. In H. Spitzek, M. Pirson, & C. Dierksmeier (Eds.), *Banking with integrity. The winners of the financial crisis* (Kindle ed.). Houndmills: Palgrave Macmillan.

Sternberg, E. (1999). *The stakeholder concept: A mistaken doctrine.* UK: Foundation for Business Responsibilities.

Stigler, G. J., & Friedland, C. (1962). What can regulators regulate-the case of electricity. *JL & Econ, 5*, 1–16.

Visser, W. (2008, October 7). Comments *CSR 2.0*. In CSR International > Blogspot > 2008 > CSR 2.0. Retrieved December 10, 2008, from http://csrinternational.blogspot.com/2008/10/csr-20.html

Wartick, S. L., & Cochran, P. L. (1985). The evolution of the corporate social performance model. *The Academy of Management Review, 10*(4), 758–769.

Zadek, S. (2007). *The civil corporation.* London: Earthscan.

Zenisek, T. J. (1979). Corporate social responsibility: A conceptualization based on organizational literature. *The Academy of Management Review, 4*(3), 359–368.

5

An Ontologically Innovative Design of CSR Strategies: Enabling Value Added Institutional Collaborations

Fragkoulis Akis Papagiannis

5.1   Introduction

The impact of CSR has become a prominent issue for many corporations in this post-financial crisis era. There is a growing trend for the corporate world to recognise the role of social responsibility and business ethics in their business strategies in order to provide a leading and innovative scope to their competitive advantage (Spence et al. 2003; Kusyk and Lozano 2007). According to Crane et al. (2013), CSR forms a critical strategic parameter, including specific characteristics which are common to most of its definitions and studies. These characteristics assume that CSR (1) is focused on both micro and macro corporate organisational levels for product or service innovation and development; (2) is strategically ori-

F.A. Papagiannis (✉)
Liverpool Business School, Liverpool John Moores University, Liverpool, UK

© The Author(s) 2017   **83**
A. Theofilou et al. (eds.), *Corporate Social Responsibility in the Post-Financial Crisis Era*, Palgrave Studies in Governance, Leadership and Responsibility, DOI 10.1007/978-3-319-40096-9_5

ented to multiple domestic and international stakeholders focusing on collaborating activities; (3) needs to ethically align diverse social (environmental) economic (abbreviated as socio-economic) responsibilities in sustainable managerial decision making; (4) must be embedded to add value to corporate strategy and (5) is beyond philanthropy, focusing on corporate strategic aim and objectives. CSR has gained momentum primarily among multinational corporations (MNCs).

MNCs use the CSR values as a competitive advantage for their strategies (Porter and Kramer 2011; Kusyk and Lozano 2007; Porter and Kramer 2006; Spence et al. 2004). Contemporary research is focused on MNCs due to their formal processes and activities, financial budgeting and compliance with corporate governance practices among the interrelating stakeholders (Grayson 2004). Thus, the conceptualisation of an ethically sustainable and value added CSR is presented to stimulate its major stakeholders towards the formation of a novel and holistic MNC strategic design. This novel strategic design reveals its potential, firstly by creating social and economic value for the MNCs at environmental level, and secondly by improving the managerial and employee morale, green economic sustainability and customer and local community relations. So, the question is: Could CSR become a critical parameter to a MNC strategic business framework, enabling dynamic institutional collaborations? Could MNCs capture a successful CSR value added strategy without a robust conceptual design to address fierce market competition?

This chapter introduces an ontological institutional design providing fertile ground for innovative and successful CSR-related collaborations. Empowered by enterprise ontology (Dietz et al. 2013), it eliminates trivial CSR practices, arising from the lack of strategies or strategic generalities. It catalytically unfolds the strategic competitive advantage and the added value of the CSR. It aims to reveal a CSR model that dynamically integrates with the primary business CSFs adding value to all collaborating stakeholders. The use of ontology enables Institutional Arbitrage (IA) by crossing national and socio-cultural boundaries, allowing MNCs to use knowledge from network partners in foreign countries (Marcus and Anderson 2006). Thus, it could lead MNCs to deliver innovative products and services to the market. It unfolds the CSR qualities, unifying them cohesively at all organisational levels leading to a holistic perspective of diverse corporate strategies. Finally, in an era of post financial crisis, such dynamic social and economic designs address further the needs of the local communities, government stakeholders and business partners (Palazzo and Richter 2005).

5.2   The Background of the Problem

A systematic empirical review over the last three decades of social responsible activities and performance provides evidence of critical links between CSR and specific value added strategies. On the one hand, there is no conclusive evidence indicating how CSR is forming a critical parameter for corporate strategic performance, in a financially measurable way. As a result, it remains in doubt whether MNCs are succeeding in their strategic endeavours because they are socially responsible or whether MNCs which are socially responsible are achieving in their strategic endeavours.

On the other hand, empirical research on CSR reveals significant relationship between corporate social performance (CSP) and corporate financial performance (CFP) in corporate strategies (Margolis et al. 2007). Thus, the argument towards the translation of any socially reliable project concept, including CSR, into a reliable and financially profitable project remains a strong requirement for its economic viability (Girth 2014). Moreover, the existing literature base currently lacks evidence on how CSR could be conceptualised at both corporate micro and macro levels. This chapter aims to eliminate this conceptual gap and thereby create value for MNCs.

At macro level, CSR is reinforcing the complementary concepts of sustainable development (SD) and stakeholder relationship management (SRM) into social- and environmental-sensitive managerial processes and policies. MNCs strive to conceptualise how SD-SRM perspective affects CFP and in what way it relates to the value added strategy of the corporation. Evidence shows a positive correlation between CSP and CFP indicating that CSR practices influence the strength of CSP and CFP (Marc et al. 2003). It also reveals that CSP has a positive impact on CFP and that there is a strong link between CSP and corporate financing both in the UK and USA (Steurer et al. 2005). Current evidence excludes philanthropic activities and environmental programmes from this link between CSP and CFP as they show limited, if any, effect on the CFP indicating a rather subjective CSR concept which primarily influences market indicators and image promotion. Since CSR, including SD-SRM, is still a broad and theoretical concept, MNCs at macro level aim to bridge the gap between CSR and CSP-CFP link. As a result, this novel theoretical network aims to calibrate and align the CSP-CFP link by embedding successfully and profitably CSR into their corporate strategies.

At micro level, systematic empirical evidence reveals that MNCs are seeking for a holistic value added strategy in an effort to achieve product or service innovations. Such innovations could be considered new, not only to the firm but also to the market, based on institutional arrangements between different companies or even countries, referred to as IA (Jackson and Deeg 2008).

According to Clausen (2014), IA assists to the conceptualisation and discovery of new products and services from MNCs among their subsidiaries in different countries or with other MNCs. Contemporary research reveals that a successful outcome from IA is the innovation cooperation in which firms combine new and old knowledge, resources, capabilities and learning experiences from external stakeholders (Powell and Grodal 2005). That way, they could minimise the risk of their new business strategies. A transparent strategic framework for a CSR leads to content-specific IA and clustering, aiding thus to the enhancement of the MNC's competitive advantage (Story et al. 2011). IA links the CSR macro level with the CSR micro level seeking for collaborative strategies strengthening the competitive advantage, based on a framework of institutional rules among the collaborating stakeholders. At this level, empirical evidence unfolds value added activities which are considered critical to a successful CSR strategy, identified as CSFs. These factors primarily include the following:

- Reputation Management (RM): RM is the practice of attempting to shape public perception of an institution by influencing information about the legal entity (Giovinco 2007). Reputation management research, although it does not provide measurable evidence for CFP, is a vital parameter in a corporate valuation;

- Customer Relationship Management (CRM): CRM refers to the management of corporate interactions with existing or potential customers. It is considered as another value added activity of CSR which increases customer satisfaction, especially when it is related to product or service innovation (Du et al. 2007). A product innovation is a new significantly improved product or service introduced to the market (Clausen 2014);

- Innovation Management (IM): Research shows strong links among IM, CSP and CFP (Busch et al. 2011). IM includes two forms of collaboration namely domestic and foreign innovation. Innovation collaboration means active participation in value added activities relating to joint Research and Development (R&D) and other innovative projects with collaborating domestic or foreign organisations (Chesbrough and Crowther 2006).

Concluding, empirical findings underline the importance of a conceptual MNC framework relating CSR strategies to other directly related value added strategies and activities, at macro and micro organisational level. The underlying idea of the problem background indicates the need of CSFs necessary for frameworking measurable performance, linking CSR to CSP. These CSFs change the business as usual way of practising CSR to a responsible corporate governance code of conduct based on KPIs. Such indicators prevent trivial managerial activities focusing on forming collaboration frameworks both domestically and globally. Such MNC strategy frameworks enhance IA by minimising financial and socio-cultural restrictions and maximising CSR performance among diverse socio-economic stakeholders. Thus, they enhance the role of SD of a successful CSR strategic design. The inclusion of CSFs and KPIs to a MNC strategy provides a dynamic and adaptable design to globally diverse collaborating stakeholders (Love et al. 2010). The ontological design of this chapter is valuable for both academics and business consultants of the CSR discourse, as it aids CSR growth and development facilitating IA.

5.3   The Role of Enterprise Ontology

The role of enterprise ontology is critical in the production of a successful and sustainable CSR design. It is evident that the lack of CSP deriving from the absence of CSFs and KPIs embedded to MNC strategic design conceptualisation creates conceptual gaps relating into MNC strategic aim and objectives, jeopardising the SD of CSR. Thus, current CSR-related activities fail to address its promising potential relation with IA. Contemporary ontology, although it preserves its original roots where an "on" according to the Greek philosopher Aristotle is something that exists, also has a very practical role. It assists in developing a common understanding of a business design among stakeholders with diverse socio-economic and scientific backgrounds. As a result, a CSR ontological design provides an innovative approach to strategic decision making. It focuses on the socio-economic essence of the collaborating stakeholders by providing fundamental links between CSR-oriented organisations and conceptually subjective information measures. As outlined in the background of the problem, the main objective of this ontological design is to reveal (1) a transparent design for MNCs; (2) a flexible and ethical socio-economic design for IA and (3) an essential, objectively conceptualised strategic design empowering CSR-related clustering.

Enterprise ontology and its related methodology (Dietz and Hoogervorst 2008) engage a holistic strategic business approach for MNCs due to formal and explicit specification of an objective conceptualisation. This novel ontological design conceptualises at micro and macro organisational level a CSR strategy among diverse stakeholders with a transparent and objective framework. The framework's design is interoperable and expandable with a formal structure and activity based on specified sets of rules. Enterprise ontology and its functionalistic nature dichotomise between the CSR imbalances of collaborating MNCs defining them as subjective or objective. From a constructivist's approach, adopted in this study, a novel scheme of a strategic CSR design should focus on the design interpretation among the participating stakeholders (e.g. customers, suppliers, competitors, collaborating institutions, etc.). It should eliminate ambiguous understanding entailed in the concept of

CSR, enabling its SD-SRM concept (Steurer et al. 2005). Ambiguous, overlapping and subjective interpretations are also responsible for the conceptual gap between SD and CSR. Thus, CSR should extend from the "do no harm" to "create and protect" strategic aim/concept, designated by performance indicators relating to CSFs beyond required set of rules and regulations. Such a conceptual extension will eliminate CSR failures, deriving from the lack of measurable value added increase in corporate strategy and its related managerial activities (Matten and Crane 2005). For such schemes to capture business-oriented semantic gaps, they should link the CSR strategy to a holistic MNC organisational design with a formal, explicit and common understanding conceptualisation. Enterprise ontology provides a potentially successful apprehension of a socio-economic CSR consensus among diverse collaborating stakeholders. It also enables value added activities strengthening MNCs competitive advantage.

5.4   The Novel Ontological Design

Bunge's semiotic triangle (Bunge 2012) and ontological parallelogram (Dietz and Hoogervorst 2008) deliver a White Box (WB) ontological conceptualisation (Barjis 2011) of the CSR concept (see Figs. 5.1 and 5.2).

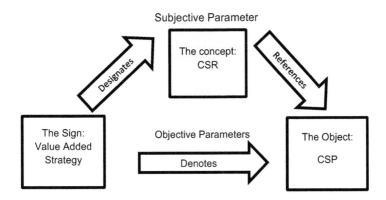

Fig. 5.1 Semiotic triangle: The meaning of a value added strategy

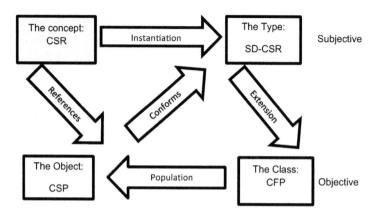

Fig. 5.2 The CSR ontological parallelogram

A sign is an object that is used as a representation of something else. Signs are structures denoting general, mostly subjective, individual things. Thing is a thought or a vision/mission of an object that a subject may have in his or her mind. According to the background of the problem, the broad concept of CSR is conceptualised subjectively unless it is designated objectively by the sign of a specified structure: value added strategy. The sign is also denoted from an object which is an identifiable and measurable individual thing: CSP. The identifiable CSP thing consists of properties (e.g. measurable KPIs). An object is by definition something of an objective structure. Thus, CSP is an object which is populated from an objective structure prohibiting conceptual generalities, as it is referenced by its concept (e.g. selected CSFs for a corporate value added strategy).

Based on the triptych of the semiotic triangle, the subjectively conceived CSR is now designated from the sign of a MNC's value added strategy. A value added strategy consists of value added activities which are denoted from a unique CSP object, differentiating each MNC according to its objectively conceived CSFs. As a result, the semiotic triangle catalytically enhances the competitive advantage of each corporation (e.g. MNCs), under a specified set of rules, defining a selected type of CSR (e.g. SD-CSR).

The ontological parallelogram (see Fig. 5.2) complements the semiotic triangle. It instantiates an individual type of CSR called SD-CSR. A type is a subjective thing that operates as a prescription of a form. The form of an object is defined by the collection of its properties (e.g. objects: KPIs) called a class. Thus, the type of SD-CSR extends to a CFP class of KPIs. These KPIs supporting CFP could populate CSP which is consisted of selected CSFs. Therefore, the object of CSP could conform to the SD-CSR type. It could also simultaneously conform to other embedded types, if selected, which are going to instantiate the concept of CSR.

As a result, the ontological parallelogram explains how a value added strategy sign could be successfully communicated and documented to global organisational stakeholders, regardless of their socio-economic background. Based on enterprise ontology, the ontological parallelogram is fully supported at each organisational level from the organisational theorem.

The organisational theorem (Dietz et al. 2013) provides an innovative design of a CSR strategy which is synthesised from a MNC micro and macro environment (see Fig. 5.3). The micro environment is supported from a datalogical level (e.g. documentation of a set of rules or other related chapter work) which is the organisational foundation supporting the infological level. At infological level, documentation which is received and analysed is based on the documented set of rules to provide evidence for decision making at top organisational level. The datalogical and infological levels form the corporate micro environment level. They both consist of secondary activities supporting the primary value

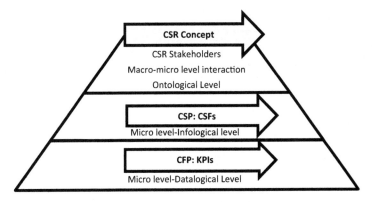

Fig. 5.3 The organisational levels of a MNC relating to CSR

added activities developed at top level. These two levels (datalogical and infological levels) of the micro environment support the corporate level which is called business organisational (B-organisation) or ontological level. This level interrelates micro with macro organisational level. This B-organisation level that this chapter focuses on conceptualises and formulates CSR-related business strategies. The CSR micro level relates to CSP and their CSFs. These CSFs could underline the management of innovation, risk and customer relations analysed at the background of the problem. All organisational levels are managed from different type of stakeholders. At micro level, these stakeholders (e.g. administrative, IT personnel) are not forming any decisions. Managerial decision making is originated from the interaction of micro and macro level stakeholders, at B-organisation level. The CSR concept should be formed at B-organisational level among performa stakeholders (e.g. managers, domestic or foreign entities, collaborating corporations, etc.). Finally, all CSP documentation at the datalogical level should be formed from measurable KPIs (see Fig. 5.3). Objective-oriented information disclosure at infological level, as well as reporting and documentation at the datalogical level, forms a transparent set of rules governing an opaque CSR design for all business stakeholders at the ontological level. Such transparent governance could clearly conceptualise the CSR concept which could be objectively referenced by CSP and supported by the CSFs. CSP object is populated by CFP and its related KPIs. Thus, it justifies how the SD-CSR type of CSR contributes to a value added strategy based on the micro and macro organisational level, as indicated in Fig. 5.3.

Paradigmatically, the ontological approach for a CSR concept could be designated by an informed value added strategy. It should be referenced by selected CSFs (e.g. risk, innovation and customer relations management) of a CSP, which will be objectively populated by measurable CFP and its KPIs (e.g. corporate stock value, return on investment, etc.). So, it could provide a global framework for a SD-CSR type of projects. Figure 5.4 reveals this holistic notion of a value added strategy based on the innovative design of a CSR strategy:

Therefore, this chapter methodologically provides a novel, transparent and globally sustainable conceptual CSR design. It addresses the broad and diverse empirical evidence on CSR strategies, enabling IA among diverse socio-cultural and economic stakeholders.

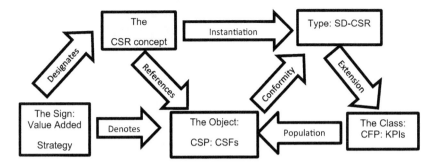

Fig. 5.4   The innovative design of a CSR strategy

5.5   Conclusions and Research Outlook

According to enterprise ontology, the findings of this chapter reveal that CSR could become a critical parameter to a MNC strategic business framework, enabling value added collaborations. It could also address fierce market competition with the proposed innovative conceptual design in order to successfully capture MNCs' CSR strategy. Its essential and concise design empowers ethically information-driven decision making by socio-economic and diverse stakeholders. Thus, it leads to an innovative global view of an international set of rules and guidelines governing successful CSR strategies.

The findings of this study address a plethora of general and non-critical, broad arguments with respect to the design of CSR (MacGregor et al. 2010). It catalytically enables a multiple embedded value added strategic design to overcome problematic financial viability arising from trivial CSR activities (e.g. tactical environmental and philanthropic activities) and lack of IA relating to socio-economic practices and policies (Kusyk and Lozano 2007). Enterprise ontology's organisational theorem, semiotic triangle and the ontological parallelogram objectively support the concept of a CSR strategy, improving heterogeneous managerial CSFs at all organisational levels.

In an era of a post financial crisis, this innovative design of CSR ontologically provides financial efficiency (e.g. CFP) supported from measurable KPIs. From the one hand, the organisational theorem supports primary and secondary activities for diverse stakeholders' roles. It also spans their managerial control that homogenises diverse socio-economic barriers (Kusyk and Lozano 2007; Du et al. 2007). From the other hand, the ontological parallelogram designates successful CSR strategies based on a transparent design that conceptualises value added strategies. These types of strategies align MNC's competitive advantage. They conform to a SD-CSR type of CSR strategy which is objectively denoted from CSFs and populated from KPIs.

As a result, the findings of this study reveal a consistent design providing fertile ground for future research on CSR models in terms of methodology and successful conceptualisation and design. The design's globally oriented collaboration strategy, empowered by its ontological composition, eliminates trivial results, arising from literature generalities (Grayson 2004). The ontological concept design catalytically manages the risk and innovation distribution by justifying financial performance through measurable KPIs (e.g. CFP) that occur among stakeholders at individual level (Busch et al. 2011). It also epistemologically unfolds the added value of IA (Clausen 2014). A successfully designed CSR could attract domestic and international stakeholders as it conceives innovative and technological activities due to its semantic objectivity. It critically improves the socio-economic infrastructure and delivers a mutually inclusive and holistic collaboration. In addition, it contributes to the engineering of successful CSR theory by demonstrating how its holistic conceptualisation is hierarchically disseminating among collaborating stakeholders. A successfully designed CSR strategy could also address problematic issues regarding informational democracy for equal access to decision making between global stakeholders, qualifying for highly impactful global collaborations.

Finally, future research could employ this novel design as a tool to reveal how firms successfully engage CSR values to innovative products and services. Another example of future research is the discovery of the necessary conditions under which firms are more or less likely to focus on IA based on this innovative design of a CSR strategy. This study could also motivate a further systematic examination of ontologically empowered value added managerial decisions that could reveal the sustainability and growth of the proposed CSR design.

References

Barjis, J. (2011). Enterprise process modelling complemented with business rules. *International Journal of Business Process Integration and Management, 5*(4), 276–286.

Bunge, M. (2012). *Treatise on basic philosophy: Ethics: The good and the right* (Vol. 8). Springer Science & Business Media.

Busch, T., Stinchfield, B. T., & Wood, M. S. (2011). *A triptych inquiry: Rethinking sustainability, innovation, and financial performance* (Tinbergen Institute Discussion Paper, No. 11-026/2/DSF 9).

Chesbrough, H., & Crowther, A. K. (2006). Beyond high tech: Early adopters of open innovation in other industries. *R&D Management, 36*(3), 229–236.

Clausen, T. H. (2014). The role of institutional arbitrage in the search for product innovation: Firm level evidence from Norway. *Industrial Marketing Management, 43*(3), 392–399.

Crane, A., Matten, D., & Laura, J. S. (2013). Corporate social responsibility: Readings and cases in a global context. In A. Crane, D. Matten, & J. L. Spence (Eds.), *Corporate social responsibility: Readings and cases in a global context* (2nd ed., pp. 3–20). London: Routledge.

Dietz J. L. G., & Hoogervorst, J. A. P. (2008). Enterprise ontology in enterprise engineering. In *Proceedings of the 2008 ACM symposium on applied computing*, pp. 572–579.

Dietz, J. L. G., Hoogervorst, J. A. P., Albani, A., Aveiro, D., Babkin, E., Barjis, J., Caetano, A., et al. (2013). The discipline of enterprise engineering. *International Journal of Organisational Design and Engineering, 3*(1), 86–114.

Du, S., Bhattacharya, C. B., & Sen, S. (2007). Reaping relational rewards from corporate social responsibility: The role of competitive positioning. *International Journal of Research in Marketing, 24*(3), 224–241.

Giovinco, S. W. (2007). Image reputation management: What it is, and why you should care. Retrieved March 10, 2016, from Medium.com.Medium

Girth, A. M. (2014). A closer look at contract accountability: Exploring the determinants of sanctions for unsatisfactory contract performance. *Journal of Public Administration Research and Theory, 24*(2), 317–348.

Grayson, D. (2004). *How CSR contribute to the competitiveness of Europe in a more sustainable world*. Netherlands: The World Bank Institute and The CSR Resource Centre.

Jackson, G., & Deeg, R. (2008). Comparing capitalisms: Understanding institutional diversity and its implications for international business. *Journal of International Business Studies, 39*(4), 540–561.

Kusyk, S. M., & Lozano, J. M. (2007). SME social performance: A four-cell typology of key drivers and barriers on social issues and their implications for stakeholder theory. *Corporate Governance: The International Journal of Business in Society, 7*(4), 502–515.

Love, P. E. D., Mistry, D., & Davis, P. R. (2010). Price competitive alliance projects: Identification of success factors for public clients. *Journal of Construction Engineering and Management, 136*, 947–956.

MacGregor, S. P., Fontrodona, J., & Hernandez, J. (2010). Towards a sustainable innovation model for small enterprises. In C. Louche, S. O. Idowu, & W. L. Filho (Eds.), *Innovative CSR: From risk management to value creation* (pp. 305–330). Sheffield: Greenleaf.

Marc, O., Schmidt, F. L., & Rynes, S. L. (2003). Corporate social and financial performance: A meta-analysis. *Organisational Studies, 24*, 403–441.

Marcus, A. A., & Anderson, M. H. (2006). A general dynamic capability: Does it propagate business social competencies in the retail food industry? *Journal of Management Studies, 43*, 19–46.

Margolis, J. D., Elfenbein, H. A., & Walsh, J. P. (2007). Does it pay to be good? A meta analysis and redirection of research on the relationship between corporate social and financial performance. *Ann Arbor, 1001*, 48109–41234.

Matten, D., & Crane, A. (2005). Corporate citizenship: Toward an extended theoretical conceptualization. *Academy of Management Review, 30*(1), 166–179.

Palazzo, G., & Richter, U. (2005). CSR business as usual? The case of the tobacco industry. *Journal of Business Ethics, 61*(4), 387–401.

Porter, M. E., & Kramer, M. R. (2011). Creating shared value. *Harvard Business Review, 89*(1/2), 62–77.

Porter, M.E., & Kramer, M. R. (2006). Strategy and Society. *Harverd Business Review, 84*(12), 42–56.

Powell, W. W., & Grodal, S. (2005). Networks of innovators. In J. Fagerberg, D. C. Mowery, & R. R. Nelson (Eds.), *The Oxford handbook of innovation* (pp. 56–85). Oxford: Oxford University Press.

Spence, L. J., Habisch, A., & Schmidpeter, R. (Eds.). (2004). *Responsibility and social capital: The world of small and medium sized enterprises*. New York: Palgrave Macmillan.

Spence, L. J., Schmidpeter, R., & Habisch, A. (2003). Assessing social capital: Small and medium sized enterprises in the UK and Germany. *Journal of Business Ethics, 47*(1), 17–29.

Steurer, R., Langer, M. E., Konrad, A., & Martinuzzi, A. (2005). Corporations, stakeholders and sustainable development I: A theoretical exploration of business-society relations. *Journal of Business Ethics, 61*(3), 263–281.

Story, V., O'Malley, L., & Hart, S. (2011). Roles, role performance and radical innovation competences. *Industrial Marketing Management, 40*(6), 952–966.

Part II

Corporate Responsibility in the "Post-Financial Crisis": A Need to Institutionalize

6

Who Is Ethical?: The Code of Business Ethics in Korean Workplaces

Kyungmin Baek

6.1 Introduction

Corporate social responsibility (CSR) is a form of corporate level self-regulation integrated into business strategies (Matten and Moon 2008). Corporations have adopted CSR as their future business strategies since the late twentieth century, at a time when many tragic corporate accidents, such as the notorious oil spill by British Petroleum (BP) in 2010, occurred. Many organizations in Korea have already adopted a variety of CSR practices—environmental management programs, diversity management programs, and codes of business ethics—to reorient their business strategies to sustainable business (Baek 2015). The Korean Workplace Panel Survey of 1768 Korean workplaces

K. Baek (✉)
Sociology, Nazarbayev University, Astana, Kazakhstan
e-mail: loveglory99@gmail.com

© The Author(s) 2017
A. Theofilou et al. (eds.), *Corporate Social Responsibility in the Post-Financial Crisis Era*, Palgrave Studies in Governance, Leadership and Responsibility, DOI 10.1007/978-3-319-40096-9_6

99

surveyed in 2011 shows that 66 percent of the sampled workplaces have a code of business ethics. Why do Korean workplaces have a code of business ethics?

This chapter extends the literature on CSR in the Korean context. Since CSR is a recent phenomenon in Korea, there is not much academic research on it. Only a few studies ask why and how Korean organizations conduct social responsibilities (Kang and Moon 2011; Baek 2015; Kim et al. 2013). Since the Asian financial crisis of 1997, governmental control and regulation over the Korean business and society have been significantly weaker, while the influence of corporations over the society has become stronger. Since then, CSR has begun to be considered a significant business strategy in Korea (Gond et al. 2011; Kang and Moon 2011). The previous studies suggest that CSR has replaced governmental control and regulations in Korea. As a result, the studies have focused on corporate outcomes of CSR in economic perspective.

However, this chapter claims that the Korean government has still strong influence over the business sector, and it has controlled the sector in an indirect way through facilitating CSR. Also, the previous studies of CSR in Korea have mainly focused on environmental management and work–family programs (Lee and Rhee 2007; Baek and Kelly 2014), and few studies have investigated how organizations coordinate and manage their business in ethical ways. This study is the first theoretically informed investigation into the reasons for a code of business ethics within Korean enterprise. The code of business ethics is a written set of guidelines that codify the values and principles of a corporation and specify the responsibilities, duties, and obligations that the members in the corporation are expected to have toward its stakeholders. Previous studies consider the code of business ethics a good indicator of CSR (Payne et al. 1997; Smeltzer and Jennings 1998).

Previous studies using samples from Western countries find that institutional contexts and economic motives are important factors impacting the organizational adoption of CSR programs (Matten and Moon 2008; Doh and Guay 2006; Gond et al. 2011). Other studies from the West, furthermore, claim that institutional environments and economic motives operate differently in Western and East Asian countries (Biggart 1991; Hamilton and Biggart 1988). Therefore, it is an open question as to whether those theories developed in Western countries explain the Korean case as well. In this chapter, I use the Korea Workplace Panel Survey of 2011 (a representative sample of Korean workplaces) to examine the presence of a code of business ethics in the Korean context.

6.2   Theory and Hypotheses

This chapter examines why the Korean workplaces have a code of business ethics. To investigate this question, it uses the Workplace Panel Survey of 2011 through neo-institutional theory and economic perspective. This section of the chapter describes how the institutional context impacts the adoption of a code of business ethics in Korea.

6.2.1   Neo-Institutional Theory

Neo-institutionalists suggest that organizational changes occur in response to institutional pressures if managers desire to enhance legitimacy (Meyer and Rowan 1977; DiMaggio and Powell 1983; Scott 2013). The institutional pressures originate from three identifiable sources: regulations, norms, and peers. Existing literature has shown that institutional pressures originate from these sources and promote organizational changes in different ways (Scott 2013; Meyer and Rowan 1977; Tolbert and Zucker 1983; Oliver 1991; Edelman 1990). Following this insight, this section starts by outlining how institutional pressures regarding CSR are created in the Korean context. Then, it describes how the institutional pressures encourage Korean workplaces to have a code of business ethics.

The Korean government has established a variety of laws to encourage CSR in business sectors. CSR is emphasized at three aspects in Korea: labor rights and gender, environment, and corporate transparency. For labor rights and gender, the Korean government established the Equal Employment Opportunity Act (EEOA) in 1987 and required employers to provide equal conditions for both men and women. The EEOA in Korea banned employment discrimination based on an employee's demographic characteristics such as gender. Also, this law intends to create a gender-neutral workplace culture by requiring benefits such as maternity and parental leave (Baek and Kelly 2014). These maternity benefits have gradually expanded over time. By 2010, the Korean government had revised the EEOA 20 times to reinforce equal opportunity and treatment in employment and promote a gender-neutral workplace culture (Baek et al. 2012).

For the environment, the Korean government established "The Promotion Act for Conversion to Environmental-Friendly Industry Structure (PACEFIS) in 1995." This law was legislated in response to the global request for improved environmental quality from United Nations Conference on Environment and Development (UNCED) in Rio de Janeiro in 1992 and General Agreement on Tariffs and Trade (GATT) Uruguay Round Ministerial Decision on Trade and the Environment in 1994. PACEFIS stipulates that both public and private sectors are expected to commit themselves to environmental protection and promote their act accordingly (Baek 2015).

Regarding corporate transparency, the Korean government established a number of laws to encourage corporations to be transparent in their business. For example, "The Act on Anti-Corruption (AAC)" was legislated to discourage public servants to be corrupt in 2001. In addition, "The Securities and Exchange Act (SEA)" was amended to create a sound corporate governance structure in Korean business in 2001. This law has been intensified over time (Lee et al. 2007).

Further, public and private research institutes in Korea notify corporations of the increasing legal risks, re-interpret legal compliance to improve awareness through using financial terms, and ask them to integrate CSR to their business strategies (Kelly and Dobbin 1998; Baek et al. 2012; Baek and Kelly 2014). For example, Korea Institute for Industrial Economics, Samsung Economic Research Institute, and LG Economic Research Institute have reported that CSR can be a source of corporate competiveness (Lee 2005). Therefore, they claim that CSR can reduce the possibility of legal liabilities, will help firms enhance their image, and eventually improve their financial performance.

Together with the intensifying legal pressures about CSR and re-orientation of corporate attention to CSR, press attention to CSR has been rapidly increasing. Figure 6.1 demonstrates that the number of newspaper articles using CSR as a key word has been increasing. The increasing legal pressures noted above and this press attention have been combined and created an emerging norm that corporations should

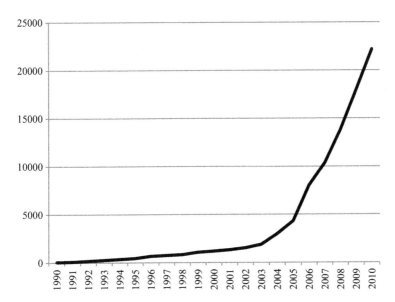

Fig. 6.1 The cumulative number of newspaper articles regarding CSR, 1996–2010.
Source: **Korea Press Foundation (http://www.kinds.or.kr)**

run their business in socially responsible ways. Many organizational studies have found that organizations are inclined to be sensitive to this institutional pressures if they have a high level of visibility to outsiders (e.g. Kalleberg and Van Buren 1996; Knoke 1994; Edelman 1992; Frumkin and Galaskiewicz 2004) and if they are vulnerable to social recognition (Baek 2015; Delmas and Montiel 2009; Haveman 1993).

Based on these ideas suggested from neo-institutional theory, the claim here is that large workplaces are highly visible to outsiders. Also, the visible workplaces are subject to high levels of scrutiny from external forces, such as press and governmental regulations, and are willing to respond to institutional pressures that promote organizations to be socially responsible. Therefore, it is expected that large workplaces are requested to run their businesses in responsible ways and that they end up having a code of business ethics to symbolize their compliance with the institutional pressures. Accordingly, the following hypothesis is suggested:

Hypothesis 1: *Large workplaces are more likely to have a code of business ethics.*

Public sector organizations are also likely to be sensitive to societal norms. They tend to embrace socially responsible policies or management practices because they are judged more by their intentions than by their financial performance (Dobbin and Sutton 1998). In addition, public sector organizations are often subjected to stronger public scrutiny than the private sector. Previous US-based research has found that public sector organizations are more likely to have affirmative action, due process and work-family programs which are examples of socially responsible policies (Baron et al. 1986; Kelly and Dobbin 1999; Kelly 2003; Dobbin et al. 1993). In recent studies in the Korean context, Baek et al. (2012) have also found that workplaces in public sector have high visibility and they are more likely to have work-family programs. Therefore, it is expected that workplaces in public sector are requested to behave in socially responsible ways and that they are more likely to have a code of business ethics to signal their commitment to the compliance with the institutional pressures regarding CSR. Accordingly, the following is predicted:

Hypothesis 2:   *Workplaces in the public sector are more likely to have a code of business ethics.*

Previous studies show that ownership structures affect corporate decision making (Jensen and Meckling 1976). In corporations where ownership separates from management, shareholders as corporate owners need a mechanism to monitor professional managers (such as CEOs) who actually engage in management. In one of the monitoring systems, owners appoint outside board directorates to protect shareholders' interests (Baysinger and Butler 1985). Under such monitoring systems, board members force professional managers to maximize shareholders' benefits. Also, they encourage the managers to engage in socially legitimate and desirable behavior (e.g. compliance with laws) because noncompliance with laws or social norms could hurt the image of the corporation, which would ultimately decrease organizational performance. Therefore, organizations run by professional managers are more likely to manage their business in socially responsible ways in order to enhance their company's image as well as avoid legal sanctions (Baek et al. 2012). In contrast, management may violate social norms and laws more easily in organizations without outside monitoring

(Baek and Kelly 2014). Therefore, I expect that corporations run by professional managers seek to be socially responsible in response to the institutional pressures, and workplaces associated with such corporations need to have a code of business ethics. Accordingly, the following hypothesis is suggested:

Hypothesis 3: *Workplaces belonging to a corporation run by professional managers are more likely to have a code of business ethics.*

Existing literature suggests that younger organizations are sensitive to institutional pressures because they are exposed to "liability of newness" (Haveman 1993). In other words, younger organizations are more inclined to be vulnerable to environmental uncertainty than older organizations. Their products or services might not be socially recognized and legitimized (Delmas and Montiel 2009; Baek 2015). To lessen this environmental uncertainty and obtain social legitimacy, the younger organizations strive to comply with societal norms. Therefore, it expects that if a workplace is newer, it is more likely to run its operation in responsible ways, and have a code of business ethics to conform to the normative pressures. Accordingly, it is predicted as follows:

Hypothesis 4: *Newer workplaces are more likely to have a code of business ethics.*

6.2.2 Economic Perspective

Above, the institutional factors associated with the presence of a code of business ethics across Korean organizations have been discussed. However, an economic perspective suggests alternative explanations concerning the presence of a code of business ethics. In particular, this perspective stresses that organizations are likely to use CSR to attempt to maximize their profits (Siegel and Vitaliano 2007; McWilliams and Siegel 2001; Porter and Kramer 2006). Based on this perspective, economists and management scholars claim that corporations with a higher level of demand for CSR are more likely to adopt various CSR practices to show off their active engagement in CSR, which can maximize corporate profits (Williamson 1981; Barney 1991).

According to the previous studies of CSR, economists and management scholars have considered CSR to be a form of investment for organizational innovation and product differentiation. They argue that CSR policies and programs can lead to the innovation of products and processes by means of social, environmental, or sustainable drivers that create new ideas of working, new products and services, all of which ultimately lead to new market demands (Porter and Kramer 2006; Porter and Van Der Linde 1995). In other words, innovation-oriented firms that invest in a certain level of CSR through embodying its products with CSR attributes or using CSR-related resources in its production process can be enabled to achieve product or process innovation (Baek 2013). For example, Ben & Jerry's has invested in CSR-related resources such as using high-quality ingredients and supporting the local community, and as a result they have succeeded in innovating their processes and distinguishing their products from other products in the market. Therefore, organizations using innovation strategies are likely to invest in CSR in order to differentiate their products and processes, which ultimately improves their market performance. Such organizations would accept and coordinate the powerful demands made by CSR. Therefore, the following hypothesis is suggested:

Hypothesis 5: *Workplaces using innovative management strategies are more likely to have a code of business ethics.*

Previous studies show that the level of demand for CSR can be different depending on the extent of information asymmetries between sellers and buyers concerning goods (Nelson 1974; McWilliams and Siegel 2001). The marketing literature distinguishes between two types of goods: "experience goods" and "search goods." Experience goods are products that must be consumed to be aware of their true value. For example, food and cars are representative examples of experience goods. Consumers cannot determine from simply viewing these goods how specific food will taste or how particular cars will function. Therefore, organizations producing experience goods are likely to use a variety of strategies to overcome the problems of such information asymmetries (Baek 2013). Association with brand names and images can be one of the popular means of reducing the level of information asymmetries. Such associations can provide consumers with information about the product quality through the image and reputation of the brand.

Based on this logic, organizational support of CSR can enhance the reputation of companies and improve brand image, because CSR activities encourage consumers to consider a particular firm to be reliable and honest and thus its product would be of high quality (Siegel and Vitaliano 2007). Therefore, organizations that produce experience goods are more likely to have a strong demand for CSR to enhance their brand image and reputation, and they would need to coordinate and control expected CSR activities to meet such demand (McWilliams and Siegel 2001).

In contrast to experience goods, search goods are products whose attributes and quality can be determined by means of examining the product before purchase. Also, search goods are easily exposed to price competition because consumers can verify the price information of alternatives very easily (Nelson 1974). For example, clothing and furniture are good examples of search goods. People are already aware of the function of such goods before purchasing them. Therefore, consumers are less likely to experience information asymmetries between sellers and buyers in purchasing search goods. Organizations in industries producing search goods, therefore, are less likely to need to associate their product with their reputation and brand image. Nelson (1974) suggested that clothing, furniture, footwear, carpets, and mattresses are representative search goods. Organizations in the industries producing products related to clothing, furniture, footwear, carpets, and mattresses would have less demand for CSR than those in other industries (Baek 2013). Therefore, the following hypothesis is suggested:

Hypothesis 6: *Workplaces belonging to industries that produce search goods are less likely to have a code of business ethics.*

6.3   Methods

6.3.1   Data

The data used here come from the 2011 Korea Workplace Panel Survey (hereafter KWPS) collected by the Korea Labor Institute, a government-funded policy research organization. This panel survey design is modeled on the Workplace Employee Relation Survey (WERS) of the UK and Workplace Employee Survey (WES) of Canada (Han and Koo 2010). Workplaces were sampled in 2005 and are to be surveyed biannually for several years. This survey aims to understand the contemporary employment structures and labor demands in Korean workplaces and to assess the Human Resources (HR) policies of workplaces in order to inform government policy.

The sample organizations were selected by the stratified sampling of all private and public sector workplaces with over 30 employees. Eligible organizations are private sector workplaces, listed on the "Workplace Demographics Survey" issued by Statistics Korea, with 30 or more employees, and public sector organizations including public institutions and local state-owned enterprises. These data were collected in 2005. The sample of 4275 workplaces consisted of 359 public workplaces and 3916 private workplaces. A total of 723 workplaces were excluded for various reasons. Of the remaining 3552 workplaces, the survey was completed in 1905 workplaces. The response rate is about 53.6 percent. Also, these surveys were conducted through face-to-face interviews with HR and industrial relation managers and worker representatives of the sample workplaces. The data included corporate profile information as well, including financial and employment data. In 2011, the fourth wave surveys (2011 KWPS) were completed in 1770 workplaces. The Korean Labor Institute limited their questions regarding CSR to workplaces with at least 300 employees. Given the constraints of all these data, the scope of data of the present analysis must be limited to organizations with at least 300 employees. Excluding workplaces with fewer than 300 employees, the number of remaining workplaces is 468.

6.3.2   Measures

6.3.2.1   Dependent Variable

My dependent variable is binary, whether or not each workplace has a code of business ethics. To measure the presence of this code, a question from the KWPS 2011 survey asking whether the workplace has a code of business ethics is used. The percentage of the presence of a code of business ethics in Korean workplaces in 2011 was about 66 percent. A logistic regression model is used to identify the predictors of the presence of a code of business ethics.

6.3.2.2   Independent Variables

Descriptive statistics are provided in Table 6.1. The measures associated with institutional factors are: the size of a workplace, whether the workplace belongs to public sector, whether the workplace belongs to a corporation managed by professional managers, and the age of a workplace. The workplace size is measured by the natural logarithm of the number of employees as of 2011 at the workplace. The survey sampling frame is used to measure whether the workplace belongs to public sector. In order to measure "management by professional managers," a survey question asking about the ownership structure of the firm to which the workplace belongs is used. This question included the following responses: (1) an ownership management system where the owner has the authority to make most decisions and directly oversees management activities; (2) an owner-centric management system where a professional manager is entrusted with management of the company but where very little authority is transferred to the manager; (3) a system where much of the management authority is transferred to a professional manager, but the owner still retains authority over major management decisions involving executive-level personnel management, new investment, and so on; and (4) a professional management system that is completely independent from the influence of the owner, and where ownership and management are completely separate. The fourth category is an indicator of the "management by professional managers" and others as a reference group. To calculate the age of a workplace, the workplace founding year is subtracted from 2011 (the survey year) and then natural logarithms is used to accommodate the left-skewed distribution of the variable.

Table 6.1 Descriptive statistics

Variable	Obs.	Mean	Std.Dev.	Min	Max
Code of business ethics	468	0.66	0.47	0	1
Workplace size	468	6.59	0.74	5.70	9.62
Public sector	468	0.11	0.32	0	1
Professional management	468	0.11	0.31	0	1
Workplace age	468	3.24	0.65	1.10	4.84
Experience good	468	0.09	0.28	0	1
Innovation strategy	468	0.56	0.50	0	1
Union	468	0.64	0.48	0	1

The measures associated with the economic perspective are innovation as a competitive strategy and industries producing search goods. To measure how much the workplace regards innovation as a competitive strategy, a question asking the types of innovation which the workplace employs is employed. This question included the following responses: (1) "Innovation is a key to our competitive strategy. Research and development are constantly carried out for the development of goods and services and for innovating processes. Other enterprises imitate our innovation"; (2) "Innovation is not a core activity, and research and development are carried out only when necessary. A large portion of research and development is carried out to introduce new technologies developed by other enterprises"; (3) "Existing goods, services, and processes are improved through other means than research and development. Manufacturing processes are improved through production engineering"; (4) "I don't invest in research and development, but I bring in innovation developed by other enterprises." The first category is used as an indicator of the "innovation as a competitive strategy," and others as a reference group. In order to measure whether the workplace belongs to the industries producing search goods, I followed the classification suggested by Nelson (1974). As noted above, he suggests that clothing, furniture, footwear, carpet, and mattress are representative search goods. Therefore, the industries producing products related to clothing, furniture, footwear, carpet were coded 1, and mattress into 1, otherwise 0. The KWPS 2011 data set provided only two-digit KSIC (Korea Standard Industry Code), equivalent to Standard Industry Code (SIC) in the USA. This can be only a proxy to measure whether the workplace produces search goods. The KWPS 2011 data set did not provide detailed product information of workplaces within the manufacturing industries.

6.3.2.3   Control Variables

The statistical models of the present analysis include two additional control variables: the presence of a union and head quarter status. For unionized workplaces, previous studies show that unionization push management for better employment, working conditions, and social responsibility (Matten and Moon 2008). To measure the presence of a union, the workplace was coded 1 for the unionized workplace, otherwise 0.

6.4   Result

The results of this analysis are presented in Table 6.2 with the model for the presence of a code of business ethics across the Korean workplaces. The results show that workplaces sensitive to institutional pressures are more likely to have a code of business ethics in Korea. Large organizations would be more likely to have a code of business ethics because they are highly visible to outsiders (Hannan and Freeman 1977). This evidence confirms H1. Also, the results show that workplaces in public sector are more likely to have a code of business ethics than those in private sector. This strongly supports H2. The expected odds of having a code of business ethics in the workplaces in public sector are around 24 times greater than in private sector ones. However, the remaining variables in institutional perspectives are not significant to explain the presence of a code of business ethics.

Table 6.2 Statistical results of the presence of a code of business ethics across workplaces in Korea

	Code of business ethics
Neo-institutional theory	
Workplace size	0.651***
	(0.172)
Public sector	1.216**
	(0.442)
Professional management	0.485
	(0.379)
Workplace age	−0.137
	(0.173)
Economic perspective	
Experience good	0.802
	(0.426)
Innovation strategy	0.778***
	(0.210)
Control variable	
Union	0.098
	(0.233)
Constant	−3.798**
	(1.155)
Observations	468

Standard errors in parentheses
***$p < 0.001$, **$p < 0.01$, *$p < 0.05$

For economic perspective, organizations using innovation strategies are more likely to have a code of business ethics. Those organizations are likely to use CSR as a business strategy to improve organizational profits, and they would need to adopt a code of business ethics. The expected odds of having a code of business ethics in those organizations are around 11 times greater than in organizations that do not use the innovation strategy. However, departing from my prediction, the statistical results do not strongly support other hypotheses based on economic perspective. As a control variable, unionized workplaces do not have any significant impact on the presence of a code of business ethics.

Conclusion

The statistical results obtained in this analysis show that large workplaces, workplaces in the public sectors, and workplaces using innovative management strategy are more likely to have a code of business ethics. This empirical evidence reflects that both institutional context and economic motivation are associated with the presence of a code of business ethics across Korean workplaces. The findings contribute to expanding of CSR studies in primarily two ways. First, this chapter shows why organizations have a *code of business ethics*. The results indicate that the change of legal context and public attention create a norm that corporations should operate in socially responsible ways, which results in diffusing a code of business ethics across Korean workplaces. In addition, the results indicate that Korean workplaces have a code of business ethics in an attempt to enhance their image and eventually improve their business profits.

Second, this chapter shows that *Korean* workplaces have been driven by institutional pressures to conduct CSR. Most CSR literature has focused on Western countries such as the USA and Europe, and it is very important to compare CSR programs and policies of East Asian countries with Western countries (Matten and Moon 2008). The organizational response to institutional pressures regarding CSR in East Asian countries may not exactly reflect Western countries such as the USA because institutional arrangements among business and society in two geographical regions are be very different (Kang and Moon

2011; Gond et al. 2011). Previous studies have found that the USA has regarded CSR as discretionary and voluntary contributions by businesses to society (Matten and Moon 2008).

This chapter reveals that CSR in Korea has been initiated by administrative guidance through law. This feature has suggested that institutional pressures that push organizations to conduct social responsibilities are state-oriented in Korea (Gond et al. 2011). This finding challenges the previous notion that governmental control and regulation over the Korean business and society have been significantly weaker since Asian financial crisis of 1997. Alternatively, the results confirm the notion that Korea still remains in the strong state tradition even after the financial crisis of 1997 (Kang and Moon 2011; Kim 1997).

In the strong state tradition, governments are able to mobilize organizations through regulations or incentives to behave in socially responsible ways. This could partially reflect that the demand for CSR in Korea has come from the institutional context unlike the case of the USA. More comparative studies about CSR (in particular, in other East Asian countries) would be needed to expand our understanding of CSR.

Although my research has the advantage of explaining the presence of a code of business ethics in the Korean context, these findings cannot address the causal relationship between the theoretical factors of my interest and the presence of a code of business ethics. Data collection for longitudinal analysis is required to examine why and how Korean workplaces adopt a code of business ethics.

References

Baek, K. (2013). Corporate social responsibility department in Korean organizations. *Survey Research, 14*, 191–211 (In Korean).

Baek, K. (2015). The diffusion of voluntary environmental programs: The case of ISO 14001 in Korea, 1996–2011. *Journal of Business Ethics,* 1–12. Retrieved November 24, 2015, from https://dx.doi.org/10.1007/s10551-015-2846-3

Baek, K., & Kelly, E. L. (2014). Noncompliance with parental leave provisions in Korea: Extending institutional research to a new legal context. *Law & Social Inquiry, 39*, 176–202.

Baek, K., Kelly, E. L., & Jang, Y. S. (2012). Work–family policies in Korean organizations: Human resources management and institutional explanations. *Asian Business & Management, 11*, 515–539.

Barney, J. (1991). Firm resources and sustained competitive advantage. *Journal of Management, 17*, 99–120.

Baron, J. N., Dobbin, F. R., & Devereaux Jennings, P. (1986). War and peace: The evolution of modern personnel administration in US industry. *American Journal of Sociology, 92*, 350–383.

Baysinger, B. D., & Butler, H. N. (1985). Corporate governance and the Board of Directors: Performance effects of changes in board composition. *Journal of Law, Economics, & Organization, 1*, 101–124.

Biggart, N. W. (1991). Explaining Asian economic organization. *Theory and Society, 20*, 199–232.

Delmas, M., & Montiel, I. (2009). Greening the supply chain: When is customer pressure effective? *Journal of Economics & Management Strategy, 18*, 171–201.

DiMaggio, P. J., & Powell, W. W. (1983). The iron cage revisited: Institutional isomorphism and collective rationality in organizational fields. *American Sociological Review, 48*, 147–160.

Dobbin, F., & Sutton, J. R. (1998). The strength of a weak state: The rights revolution and the rise of human resources management divisions. *American Journal of Sociology, 104*, 441–476.

Dobbin, F., Sutton, J. R., Meyer, J. W., & Scott, R. (1993). Equal Opportunity Law and the Construction of Internal Labor Markets. *American Journal of Sociology, 99*, 396–427.

Doh, J. P., & Guay, T. R. (2006). Corporate social responsibility, public policy, and NGO activism in Europe and the United States: An institutional-stakeholder perspective. *Journal of Management Studies, 43*, 47–73.

Edelman, L. B. (1990). Legal environments and organizational governance: The expansion of due process in the American workplace. *American Journal of Sociology, 95*, 1401–1440.

Edelman, L. B. (1992). Legal ambiguity and symbolic structures: Organizational mediation of civil rights law. *American Journal of Sociology, 97*, 1531–1576.

Frumkin, P., & Galaskiewicz, J. (2004). Institutional isomorphism and public sector organizations. *Journal of Public Administration Research and Theory, 14*, 283–307.

Gond, J.-P., Kang, N., & Moon, J. (2011). The government of self-regulation: On the comparative dynamics of corporate social responsibility. *Economy and Society, 40*, 640–671.

Hamilton, G. G., & Biggart, N. W. (1988). Market, culture, and authority: A comparative analysis of management and organization in the Far East. *American Journal of Sociology, 94*, 52–94.

Han, J., & Koo, J. (2010). Institutional isomorphism and decoupling among Korean firms: Adoption of performance compensation system. *Korean Journal of Sociology, 44*, 27–44.

Hannan, M. T., & Freeman, J. (1977). The population ecology of organizations. *American Journal of Sociology, 82*, 929–964.

Haveman, H. A. (1993). Follow the leader: Mimetic isomorphism and entry into new markets. *Administrative Science Quarterly, 38*, 593–627.

Jensen, M. C., & Meckling, W. H. (1976). Theory of the firm: Managerial behavior, agency costs and ownership structure. *Journal of Financial Economics, 3*, 305–360.

Kalleberg, A. L., & Van Buren, M. E. (1996). Is bigger better? Explaining the relationship between organization size and job rewards. *American Sociological Review, 61*, 47–66.

Kang, N., & Moon, J. (2011). Institutional complementarity between corporate governance and corporate social responsibility: A comparative institutional analysis of three capitalisms. *Socio-Economic Review, 10*, 85–108.

Kelly, E. (2003). The strange history of employer-sponsored child care: Interested actors, uncertainty, and the transformation of law in organizational fields. *American Journal of Sociology, 109*, 606–649.

Kelly, E., & Dobbin, F. (1998). How affirmative action became diversity management employer response to anti-discrimination law, 1961 to 1996. *American Behavioral Scientist, 41*, 960–984.

Kelly, E., & Dobbin, F. (1999). Civil rights law at work: Sex discrimination and the rise of maternity leave policies. *American Journal of Sociology, 105*, 455–492.

Kim, E. M. (1997). *Big business, strong state: Collusion and conflict in South Korean development, 1960–1990*. Albany: SUNY Press.

Kim, C. H., Amaeshi, K., Harris, S., & Suh, C.-J. (2013). CSR and the national institutional context: The case of South Korea. *Journal of Business Research, 66*, 2581–2591.

Knoke, D. (1994). Cui Bono? Employee benefit packages. *American Behavioral Scientist, 37*, 963–978.

Korea Press Foundation. *Article search*. Retrieved November 24, 2015, from http://www.kinds.or.kr

Lee, Wonjae. (2005). *The discover of strategic ethical management*. Seoul: Samsung Economic Research Institute (In Korean).

Lee, H. Y., Baek, K., & Jang, Y. S..(2007) The expansion of outside directorate in Korea: Agency control, resource dependency and neo-institutional perspective. *Korean Journal of Sociology, 41,* 27–66. (In Korean).

Lee, S. Y., & Rhee, S.-K. (2007). The change in corporate environmental strategies: A longitudinal empirical study. *Management Decision, 45,* 196–216.

Matten, D., & Moon, J. (2008). "Implicit" and "explicit" CSR: A conceptual framework for a comparative understanding of corporate social responsibility. *Academy of Management Review, 33,* 404–424.

McWilliams, A., & Siegel, D. (2001). Corporate social responsibility: A theory of the firm perspective. *Academy of Management Review, 26,* 117–127.

Meyer, J. W., & Rowan, B. (1977). Institutionalized organizations: Formal structure as myth and ceremony. *American Journal of Sociology, 83,* 340–363.

Nelson, P. (1974). Advertising as information. *The Journal of Political Economy, 82,* 729–754.

Oliver, C. (1991). Strategic responses to institutional processes. *Academy of Management Review, 16,* 145–179.

Payne, D., Raiborn, C., & Askvik, J. (1997). A global code of business ethics. *Journal of Business Ethics, 16,* 1727–1735.

Porter, M. E., & Kramer, M. R. (2006). The link between competitive advantage and corporate social responsibility. *Harvard Business Review, 84,* 78–92.

Porter, M. E., & Van der Linde, C. (1995). Toward a new conception of the environment-competitiveness relationship. *The Journal of Economic Perspectives, 9,* 97–118.

Scott, W. R. (2013). *Institutions and organizations: Ideas, interests, and identities.* Thousand Oaks: Sage Publications.

Siegel, D. S., & Vitaliano, D. F. (2007). An empirical analysis of the strategic use of corporate social responsibility. *Journal of Economics & Management Strategy, 16,* 773–792.

Smeltzer, L. R., & Jennings, M. M. (1998). Why an international code of business ethics would be good for business. *Journal of Business Ethics, 17,* 57–66.

Tolbert, P. S., & Zucker, L. G. (1983). Institutional sources of change in the formal structure of organizations: The diffusion of civil service reform, 1880–1935. *Administrative Science Quarterly, 28,* 22–39.

Williamson, O. E. (1981). The economics of organization: The transaction cost approach. *American Journal of Sociology, 87,* 548–577.

7

CSR and Banking Morals: On the Introduction of the Dutch Banker's Oath

7.1   Introduction

The National Dutch Statistics agency measures institutional trust on a yearly basis to report on the public trust in state, church and also banks. In their latest report (Centraal Bureau Statistiek 2015), it was shown that only 34 percent of the Dutch trust banks. These numbers can be compared to the Banking Confidence Monitor (Nederlandse Vereniging van Banken 2015a) which shows that 27 percent of Dutch bank customers have low to very low confidence in the banking sector. The banking crisis of 2008 hit the Netherlands particularly hard. At the height of the crisis, the Dutch government had to inject 40 billion euro into a number of financial institutions including ABN-AMRO, ING and SNS bank. By 2013, two of the four biggest (systemically important, too-big-

W.T. Popma (✉)
Brighton Business Schoool, University of Brighton, Brighton, East Sussex, UK
e-mail: wtp@brighton.ac.uk

© The Author(s) 2017
A. Theofilou et al. (eds.), *Corporate Social Responsibility in the Post-Financial Crisis Era*, Palgrave Studies in Governance, Leadership and Responsibility, DOI 10.1007/978-3-319-40096-9_7

to-fail) banks had effectively been nationalized (ABN-AMRO and SNS bank). Meanwhile, the economic crisis depressed economic growth and impacted real estate prices which on average dropped 20 percent between 2008 and 2014 (Centraal Bureau Statistiek 2016). The public image of banks was harmed particularly by the post-2008 remuneration of top managers which had traditionally been high (to Dutch standards) but now looked out of line when compared to the financial situation of banks which needed continuous financial support from the government to survive. In one particular case in 2011, the CEO of ING was to receive a 1.25 million euro bonus on top of his 1.35 million euro salary. The general public and politicians were outraged, particularly since ING still owed the public purse half of an earlier injection of 10 billion euro. Bank managers were seen as irresponsible and selfish. Public money had saved banks from certain bankruptcy, yet still banks and bank managers were behaving as if they owed nothing to the general public. In this climate, politicians voted in a legal requirement in 2012 for all senior managers (with a direct influence on corporate policies) in the financial sector to swear a so-called Banker's Oath. In this oath, they promised to take into account all stakeholders (and particularly customers) in order to grow public confidence in the financial sector. Despite opposition from the Council of State and the biggest finance-sector labor union (85 percent of its members voted against the oath), the Banker's Oath was expanded in 2015 to include all employees of banks (around 94,000 people) and all customer-facing employees of other financial institutions. With around 250,000 people working in the financial sector, a majority of them would have to swear the Banker's Oath by March 31, 2016, when it became required by law. The Dutch Banker's Oath is the first oath to be introduced worldwide where employees of private organizations are obliged to swear and sign an oath by law.

7.2   The Dutch Banker's Oath

The Dutch Banker's Oath must be taken by all directors as well as employees with direct customer contact and any employees who can impact the financial profile of the organization within the financial services industry. This includes for instance pension fund managers and independent mortgage consultants but also all front-office employees of organizations in the financial sector. The Banker's Oath has an even broader application specifically in the banking industry, where all employees of Dutch banks must swear the Banker's Oath within three months of starting their job at a bank. For new employees this regulation was applicable (by law) from March 31, 2015. For existing employees swearing the Banker's Oath became law on March 31, 2016. There are two identical versions of the Banker's Oath, one specifically for senior managers which omits the words "that I will inform the client to the best of my ability" and the (nearly identical) other version which is shown below:

I swear/promise that I will exercise my function properly and carefully.
I swear/promise that I will duly weigh all the interests involved in the enterprise, that is, those of the clients, the shareholders, the employees and the society in which the enterprise is active.
I swear/promise that in this weighing I will focus on the client's interest and that I will inform the client to the best of my ability.
I swear/promise that I will act in accordance with the laws, regulations and codes of conduct which apply to me.
I swear/promise that I will observe secrecy about anything to which I have been entrusted.
I swear/promise that I will not abuse my knowledge.
I swear/promise that I will maintain an open and verifiable attitude and I know my responsibility toward society.
I swear/promise that I will perform to the best of my abilities to maintain and promote confidence in the financial services sector.
So help me God!/This I declare and promise!

The law ("Article 4.15a Wft—Regeling Eed of Belofte Financiele Sector 2015") specifies that the oath has to be spoken out loud in front of a person of higher authority within the same organization. After that, the Banker's Oath form must be signed, again in attendance of a person of higher authority within the organization. The level of required ceremony is related to the formative and psychological role of the oath in addition to the normative value of its content, as will be clarified later. The signed document must be kept by the bank for the duration of the employment contract with the employee. Within the limitations stated above, banks can individually decide how to arrange the oath swearing ceremony. There is no requirement for the ceremony to be public, but many banks did invite the press to attend their early ceremonies in 2015.

7.3   The Political and Legal Framework

From a corporate social responsibility (CSR) perspective, the Banker's Oath is particularly interesting in terms of its legal embedding and the expected effects on employee morality. The financial services industry in the Netherlands is overseen by the "Authoriteit Financiele Markten" (Authority Financial Markets—AFM). In principle both the AFM and the Dutch National Bank could revoke the operating permit of a financial services organization if the Banker's Oath is not taken by all relevant employees as required. In addition all employees of Dutch banks are now (since 2015) subject to disciplinary law. An independent Bank Disciplinary Law Foundation ("Stichting Tuchtrecht Banken") is responsible for overseeing compliance at employee level. On an organizational level there is a code of conduct (a code of corporate governance called the Banking Code) which consists of a number of corporate governance requirements which would (at first sight) only apply to the way the bank is structured and how it reports its annual financial results. Responsibility for corporate governance will normally lie with the top management and board of directors of the bank. When the initial Banker's Oath was rolled out in 2012, it was only required to be taken by senior decision makers of banks, not by all employees. This was in line with the assumption that ethical corporate governance was enacted by the senior employees who held responsibility for structure and strategy of the firm. In 2015 the Banker's Oath was embedded in a disciplinary law framework for the banking sector where an independent committee consisting of a judge and independent members with banking expertise would rule on transgressions if they were reported. The outcome of such disciplinary law proceedings could range from an official reprimand and mandatory training through to a personal fine of 25,000 euro and in the most serious case a temporary occupational suspension from the banking industry. Opposition of the Banker's Oath has largely focused on these personal penalties that could come about when employees simply follow company orders (Consultation 2013). In 2015 the Banking Code was combined with a Social Charter and the Banker's Oath into a document called "Future Oriented Banking" by the NVB (Nederlandse Vereniging van Banken 2016). In this document the content of the Banker's Oath was specified in more detail so as to clarify and promote compliance by individual employees. The Banking Code part guides behavior at the senior level of banks, discussing issues such as integrity, risk management, auditing, remuneration and transparency. All banks with a permit from the Dutch National Bank fall under the Banking Code and are specifically required to report on the individual banks website about developments and improvements related to the Banking Code within the bank (using concrete examples) on a yearly basis. As the Banking Code indicates: "comply or explain".

Before the Banker's Oath was made mandatory the existing Banking Code already covered most of the elements that are now also included in the oath. Elements such as integrity, transparency and behaving according to the law were specifically addressed in the Banking Code and as such applied to senior directors of banks directly and also indirectly to employees of banks who were bound by internal codes of conduct specified by each bank based on the Banking Code. As such, the new Banker's Oath does not necessarily add any new legal expectations (Van Kranenburg-Hanspians and Jans 2013). Legal scholars as well as government bodies such as the Raad van State (Council of State—the highest advisory body of the Dutch government which particularly looks at the quality and feasibility of proposed new laws) therefore opposed the introduction of the Banker's Oath for all employees since the newly added elements in the oath (such as balancing stakeholder interests and focusing on client interest) are near impossible to weigh objectively in a legal framework and could never be the start of a disciplinary let alone civil legal case. From a practical perspective, it seems wrong to expect an employee to assume moral responsibility for actions which he/she may have initiated based on corporate requirements. The level of professional autonomy differs markedly between different functions within a bank. Many of the comments by union members included in the criticism of the Federatie Nederlandse Vakbeweging (FNV) financial labor union (Consultation 2013) indicate that employees expect senior executives to assume the responsibility as part of their role in the organization. The Raad van State opposed the introduction of a Banker's Oath for all employees because it did not see a legal justification (the oath would be a paper tiger), and it also feared that an oath sworn by so many people would lose its value as a symbolic tool. Despite initial opposition from banks, unions and the Raad van State, the Dutch parliament voted in the Banker's oath. In parliamentary discussions the then Minister of Finance, Mr. Dijsselbloem, explained that he saw two main reasons to broaden the oath to all employees of banks (Vaste Commissie voor Financien—September 8, 2014); first of all because it would be a symbolic appeal to all individuals working in banks to take their societal role into account and secondly (rather pragmatic) it would take away the difficulty for banks to determine who was or was not part of the initial group of employees who could impact the financial profile of the bank. From the discussion, it becomes clear that the idea to widen the oath to all employees was actually introduced by the banks themselves during a meeting with Dijsselbloem.

As such the Banker's Oath can be interpreted much more as public confirmation of existing legislation as well as a starting point for bank-internal discussions on ethics and integrity not just at the board level but throughout the organization.

7.4   Reasons Behind the Oath

Even though the Banker's Oath clearly has a symbolic function, if there were no direct legal reasons to introduce the Banker's Oath, why was it added to the existing legal frameworks? As can be seen from the Future Oriented Banking document (Nederlandse Vereniging van Banken 2016), the oath is presented as part of a broader package of measures which include a Social Charter and a Banking Code. As the NVB states: "The banks—individually and collectively—use this to show society what they stand for and what they can be held accountable for. It is part of accountable banking." This call for socially responsible practices in the banking system fitted in with an ongoing strengthening of corporate governance structures which was initiated in the early 2000s and further catalyzed by the financial crisis of 2008. In a Dutch document by the NVB, three reasons for the introduction of the oath are given: to codify the desired conduct of everyone working at a bank, to show society at large which rules of conduct bank employees must adhere to and to increase the trust of society in banks (Nederlandse Vereniging van Banken 2016c). The role of society and the opinion of society as a whole are clearly important considerations for the banking industry to publicize not only a Social Charter but also the Banking Code and the Banker's Oath in full. Clearly, the industry association is aware of the damaged public image of banks. The publication of the Banking Confidence Monitor in 2015 is another sign that customer confidence (which had been measured for a number of years by the NVB but always for internal use only) is high on the agenda. As is stated in the Monitor, the NVB intends to publish its results on a yearly basis from now on to measure improvement in public confidence in both banks in general and the biggest banks individually.

In order to understand the content and reasons behind the oath, it is interesting to look at the history of the Dutch Banker's Oath. The financial crisis of 2008 was certainly a catalyst, but in the Netherlands, there had already been a number of public scandals that had tainted the image of Dutch banks and insurers. One particular example was the "woekerpolis" (usury policy) scandal where banks had offered long-term insurance policies as a basis for paying mortgages and other debt in the future. The insurer/bank invested the monthly premiums in the stock market and customers were promised high returns at the end of the contract. In reality many customers found they had lost money at the end of the policy because of hidden management fees and inflated life insurance policies connected to the original policy. The so-called woekerpolis affair affected so many households that unethical behavior in the financial sector was a major focus of political and media attention in 2006 and 2007. Then in 2007 one of the biggest banks in the Netherlands, ABN-AMRO, was broken up and sold to three international banks after a shareholder vote lead by foreign hedge funds. As part of the break up (which would lead to thousands of job losses in the domestic market), the CEO of ABN-AMRO left the company with a 26 million euro bonus on top of his 4 million euro salary. In Calvinist Holland (where banking salaries were already considered extreme compared to other industries), this was not appreciated and comedians had a field day with caustic jokes about Rijkman Groenink (the CEO) whose surname translates to "Richman". In this environment of discontent, Hans van Mierlo published a book in which he proposed new ethical rules for bankers (Van Mierlo 2008) which became a bestseller after the economic crisis of 2008 hit the Dutch banking sector in full. Van Mierlo had a background as communications manager at banks including Rabobank and ING. Before that he had been head of communications for the Dutch House of Representatives and with relevant political connections he had recently worked for the Dutch Banking Association as a lobbyist. Based on the Hippocratic oath sworn by Dutch medical doctors, Van Mierlo formulated a "moral ethical statement" which grew into the Dutch Banker's Oath. Many elements of the Dutch Banker's Oath can be traced back to the Dutch Doctor's Oath (Artseneed 2009). Van Mierlo's "moral ethical statement" was adopted by the Dutch Banking Association in 2010, and at that time, it applied to around 17,000 bank directors and senior policy influencers in banks. At this point in time public outrage aimed at business and social inequality had reached its peak with movements such as Occupy Wall Street. In this atmosphere of public discontent, the change of government in 2012 led to a coalition agreement which stipulated that a banker's oath would become compulsory and involve strict ("strenge") sanctions if breached. This meant that by January 2013 the Banker's Oath received legal status and was not just an addition to an existing banking industry code of conduct. Not only did the Banker's Oath come into law (Wet Financieel Toezicht) but also a continuous political discussion came to the conclusion that all employees of banks should be obliged to take the oath, not just senior policy makers. This led to an amendment to the law (Wijzigingswet Wet Financieel Toezicht) in early 2015 which broadened the group to all 90,000 employees of banks in the Netherlands with a permit from the Dutch National Bank. In the explanatory memorandum published before the law change, the following reasons for the expansion of the oath to all employees of banks were given. The oath is expected to have three main functions: normative, formative and psychological. As a normative measure, the oath indicates what good financial service provision entails. As a formative measure, the oath invites employees to think about their actions and motivations. Finally as a psychological measure, the oath is a personal appeal and expected to be self-binding ("zelfbindend") in that taking and subscribing to the oath personally will make the employee feel personally directly bound to the content of the oath (Rijksoverheid 2014). The memorandum then adds that the oath being sworn by all employees is specifically important because of the role of public trust in the financial services industry. Much in this explanation points to the symbolic character of the Banker's Oath. At the same time the oath has potential legal consequences for the employee swearing it which makes it different from voluntary professional oaths such as the Hippocratic oath or oaths of office such as taken by newly elected members of parliament. As such the oath might encourage company-wide discussions about morals, ethics and the social responsibility of banks, but what were the exact consequences for corporate and individual morality? What kind of oath was this new Banker's Oath?

7.5   A Different Type of Oath

An oath can be defined as "a socio-linguistic act with a specific formula to provide the highest warranty for statements a person can give or is prepared to give in the specific circumstances according to his/her moral convictions and beliefs, that is accepted as such by the oath receiver and social community, that is accompanied by specific rituals, including specific gestures, and that is recorded" (Rutgers 2013). One of the earliest recorded oaths in relation to business activities was found in the Fayum region of Egypt. It is a papyrus document from 230 BC which states that one Semtheus ("I swear by King Ptolemy [...] and Isis and all the other gods and goddesses of the land, that I will perform my duties") swore and subscribed to perform his duties as banker's assistant accurately and justly (Austin 2006; Verboven et al. 2008). Even in this early example of an oath, all the typical elements of a Bankers Oath are included; a higher authority (the gods), duties which are expected to be performed (being truthful, delivering results accurately) and a reference to justice (doing the right thing). Interestingly this is the only known business oaths which remains from the Ptolemaic era. The limited number of recovered papyri from this region and era do include a number of labor contracts (Von Reden 2010); it is likely that the oath was taken in addition to a "normal" employment contract. A millennium later, business-related oaths were widely used by medieval merchant guilds. Guild members swore oaths when joining the guild to promise mutual assistance (particularly financially) within the guild in case of adversity such as shipwrecks or fire (Verhulst 1999). This would give members an advantage when doing business with other parties as their reputation and trustworthiness were bound to a larger guild with ample resources and an incentive to enforce dutiful behavior from all members of that guild (Ogilvie 2011). Comparing the Banker's Oath with some of these earlier business-related oaths shows many similarities. As in ancient Egypt, the oath must be both sworn and subscribed on paper. The oath is a guarantee of mutual assistance in the banking industry; by promising to improve confidence in the financial services sector as a whole, the oath is not just aimed at improving the image of the bank where the individual works. Although contractual relationships are now much more prevalent in the business environment, as a symbol of virtuous banking the oath seems to make sense.

These days oaths are mainly known from the medical and law professions where new doctors and lawyers swear an oath upon the start of their professional career. Similarly, public office oaths are still widespread where public servants are sworn into a specific public position. An oath is thus a promise (as Rutgers (2013) states: "the most powerful promise") that guarantees the expected behavior of the oath taker. In today's day and age, contracts are the business tool generally used to guarantee business agreements and economic interaction. The expected behavior of the other party is thus secured with a contract, and any unexpected or immoral behavior is avoided by reliance on mutual trust and reputation. In terms of expected behavior of banks (and its employees), it is interesting to compare the content of the Banker's Oath with the content of the ISO26000 social responsibility guidance introduced in 2010 (ISO26000 is not a certification, but can be used as a statement of intent). Of the seven principles of social responsibility, the first five are all applicable to the Banker's Oath. Accountability, transparency, ethical behavior, respect for stakeholder interests and respect for the rule of law are not difficult to recognize in the wording of the oath. The final two principles (respect for international norms of behavior and respect for human rights) would be of less relevance for banking employees operating mainly within their national context. As such the oath promises professional virtue in the area of social responsibility. The individual employee becomes the representative of the social conscience of the bank.

When the initial limited banker's oath was introduced, it only applied to the senior directors and employees who could have a material impact on the financial profile of the bank. This early oath (identical in content to the current oath sworn by all employees) could to some extent be compared to the Hippocratic Oath or similar professional oaths. As was mentioned before, the structure and content of the Dutch Banker's Oath resemble the Dutch Doctors Oath. However, although both professions are governed by a disciplinary law body, the Hippocratic Oath is not included in any official laws. Furthermore the Hippocratic Oath is taken voluntarily and not required by law as the Banker's Oath now is. This is one of the reasons the Council of State opposed the broadening of the oath to all employees, as it would risk making the oath "just another box to tick" as part of an employment contract in banking. Similar to professional oaths, the Banker's Oath is a promissory oath (such as the Hippocratic Oath) and so-called oaths of office. An oath of office is sworn by a public official upon entering a civil service role (Rutgers 2010). Examples include the oaths sworn publicly by US presidents and Supreme Court justices when starting their term of office. As Boatright (2013) points out, the Banker's Oath is neither an oath of office nor a professional oath. It does not award special privileges to the oath swearer apart from forming the required basis for an employment contract at the bank. As Blok (2013) points out, oaths have traditionally been regarded as a "performative speech act"; in professional oaths the swearing of the oath transforms the graduating student into a doctor, the paralegal into a lawyer. In that case the oath receivers are fellow doctors or lawyers who adopt the new professional into their community. Similarly in swearing an oath of office, the public (the oath receivers) accepts the oath swearer into their new (temporary) position. The Banker's Oath is different as the oath receiver is a senior employee in the same bank (who does not necessarily represent the public to whom several of the virtues in the oath are aimed). And the oath swearer is not accepting a specific (public) office, nor are they entering a profession which is ultimately aimed at the public good (as lawyers and doctors may claim). Of course from a CSR perspective, it can be claimed that banks have a public function and are highly relevant for the economic wellbeing of society, but the individual oath swearer (employee) is part of an organization which pays her salary and expects loyalty to the firm. Whether that bank as principal to the employee as agent has benign intentions for society is another matter; the employee does not get new powers from the oath, only new duties. Becoming a "banker" then does not seem a fair deal. No wonder then that so many bank employees objected to the introduction of the Banker's Oath.

To whom then is the oath taker beholden, the general public (state) or the company (private)? The answer is more or less both, which interestingly from a CSR perspective changes the way in which social responsibility is transferred in part from the legal corporation level to the individual employee level. By legally forcing all bank employees to take the Banker's Oath, moral responsibility is not just enforceable at the corporation level but also at any other level within the organization. To some extent this was the original intention of the widening of the oath to all bank employees when discussed in politics. It was too difficult to draw a line of moral responsibility, so forcing all employees to answer to disciplinary law and swear a Banker's Oath was a pragmatic solution. In terms of individual versus CSR, the Banker's Oath opens up some interesting legal and moral questions. Legal questions include the conflict between personal responsibilities and corporate role. What power does the employee have to fulfill the virtues of the oath? Can the employee be expected to understand the roles of all different stakeholders involved with the bank? Is the employee required to become a whistle blower if they detect behavior of superiors which appears to break the oath? As Van Kranenburg-Hanspians and Jans (2013) recommended, from a legal perspective it is crucial that banks should be required to provide detailed step-by-step plans to employees about actions to take when they perceive colleagues breaking the oath.

Although the Banker's Oath is specific focusing on the client's interests, the role that clients play in a typical bank can be quite diverse. If a client wishes to speculate on the stock market with money borrowed from the bank, is the bank employee only obliged to inform the client of possible risks or does the oath expect a more active role in terms of protecting the client from themselves? And what exactly is the role of the banker in terms of "responsibility towards society"? How can an individual employee balance the needs of all stakeholders including the shareholders? And what if this individual interpretation contradicts corporate policies? What then is the balance between individual legal and moral obligations?

7.6   Locus of Moral Responsibility

Gailey and Lee found that the attribution of responsibility for ethical wrongdoing in business as perceived by the general public depends on the level of perceived autonomy of the employee within the firm. If an employee has more autonomy, more responsibility is attributed to the employee and less to the organization as a whole. Similarly, when employees are perceived to have less autonomy, in the public eye they were attributed less responsibility individually and more responsibility was attributed to the organization as a whole (Gailey and Lee 2008). For the banking sector as a whole to be regarded as morally responsible, individual banks need to be regarded as responsible. As Ronnegard (2013) has argued, corporations themselves cannot act as moral agents. They are legal agents and carry legal responsibilities, but they should not be held responsible morally as long as they fulfill their legal duties. Individual moral agency of employees within a firm is difficult to establish. In the classic hierarchical structure of the firm, can an employee be held responsible for the actions with which they contributed to the collapse of the firm if those actions were sanctioned and even encouraged within the hierarchy of that firm? A strong push in the area of Corporate Governance regulations in the Netherlands in the early 2000s had made banks aware of their duties toward shareholders and society in terms of issues such as transparency and remuneration (Code Tabaksblat 2004). The so-called Code Tabaksblat was mainly aimed at improvements in corporate governance in relation to shareholders. Other stakeholders and society at large were not addressed, and labor unions complained that the Code even had adverse effects, for instance the required publication of detailed executive remuneration packages which was part of the new code appeared to lead to a sharp increase in executive salaries now that they could compare what they earned among themselves. Corporate governance regulation improved responsibility toward shareholders but not necessarily to society at large. Corporate governance structures and the existing code of conduct within the banking industry both were managed in a top-down fashion. The firm was given a number of legal responsibilities which were then distributed throughout the bank in the existing hierarchical structures. In terms of moral responsibility, virtues such as accuracy and transparency were translated into specific legal requirements which the firm could then manage internally as long as the annual report showed compliance. Within a typical bank organization it is not difficult to imagine how different legal requirements and moral expectations can be between for instance retail banking and investment banking. If expected individual morality is codified in legal requirements, which seem to increase based on rank in the organization (as would be the case in a typical corporate hierarchy), every employee will follow the rules and do what they are expected to do by their direct superior. The moral impact of daily decisions is then easily forgotten, and lack of autonomy lower in the organization will lead to employees following orders without questioning the larger impact of their actions on stakeholders other than the shareholders around which codes of conduct and corporate governance structures are designed. In contrast the Banker's Oath can be regarded as a method to infuse moral responsibility into the corporation by getting every single employee to swear an oath based on a mixture of both morally expected virtues and legally expected duties. The public outrage at banks was aimed at the behavior of bankers, who had profited from political deregulation. As Van Tulder (2011) formulates it, *"The trade-off between "risk" (creating uncertainty) and "responsibility" (managing uncertainty) became settled in favor of the risk takers."* In the 2012 Dutch government coalition accord there is specific mention of bankers. After emphasizing the importance of a healthy financial sector for the economy, it is argued that "but when bankers take outsized risks this can cause great damage to our economy. We have that experience and we do not want to experience that again". In this document a number of measures are introduced to reform the banking sector. The first measure on this list is the Banker's Oath and the second measure is related to extended screening of banking employees responsible for high-risk transactions. These two employee-related measures are then followed by a list of institution-based measures regarding issues such as capital requirements (Basel III) and a maximum percentage of flexible remuneration (bonuses) for executives. The wording of the coalition accord points toward a philosophy of act utilitarianism (Hare 1982); bankers need to be kept in line to avoid them making decisions which will harm the national economy and which will harm themselves ("A Banker's Oath will be introduced, with strict sanctions upon violation"). This would lead to the expectation that the content of the Banker's Oath would be utilitarian as well, a promise to perform certain actions in order to attain a preferential outcome. A promise to take less outsized risks so as not to endanger the viability of the bank and damage stakeholders, among them customers and the state. The main problem that still remains is that parts of the oath as it is worded now are open to multiple interpretations. The oath swearer promises to be a virtuous banker, honoring transparency, accuracy and considering clients and society in decision-making situations. However the meaning of these virtues must then be found in the internal bank code of conduct which is partly based on the Banking Code corporate governance rules which were never specified at the individual employee level. CSR is thus moved from a higher corporate level to a lower employee level without a clear legal framework which could clarify the exact expectations of the individual. The benefit of the Banker's Oath is then that it invites individual employees to more closely consider CSR within the firm and social responsibilities at the personal level. The drawback (at this point in time) is still that there is not enough guidance in terms of how this CSR can be enacted at the individual level. In that regard jurisprudence of the disciplinary legal framework which started in 2015 will be necessary to clarify which responsibilities employees of Dutch banks now have. As Wouter Keuning noted in a *Financieel Dagblad* article on April 1, 2016, in the first year of the existence of the Bank Disciplinary Law Foundation, no rulings have been made. A total of 57 possible offenses were reported of which 43 were not valid, mainly because customers complained against banks and not individual bankers. Clearly the division of social responsibility between the corporation and the employees of that corporation is an interesting discussion generated by the introduction of the Banker's Oath.

Conclusion

The Dutch Banker's Oath was introduced as a symbolic measure to foster a spirit of social responsibility within the banking sector. The initial oath was only taken by senior executives and employees with material impact on the financial situation of banks. Because of the difficulty in delineating who should and should not swear the oath, it was made compulsory for all bank employees in 2015. Because of the legal embedding of the oath, it raises questions about individual responsibilities of the employee in relation to corporate responsibilities codified along corporate governance standards. As such the Banker's Oath not only encourages bank-internal discussions about responsibilities toward stakeholders and society but may also be a first step in distributing legal responsibility down from the corporation level to the employee level. This could mean a paradigm shift in terms of accountability for moral behavior of the firm. Although no jurisprudence related to the Banker's Oath is available yet, the legal implementation of a moral oath in a private business setting opens up promising new interpretations of CSR.

References

Artseneed. (2009). *Nederlandse Artseneed.* Retrieved March 5, 2016, from http://www.nfu.nl/img/pdf/Artseneed2009.pdf

Austin, M. M. (2006). *The Hellenistic world from Alexander to the Roman conquest: A selection of ancient sources in translation.* Cambridge: Cambridge University Press.

Blok, V. (2013). The power of speech acts: Reflections on a performative concept of ethical oaths in economics and business. *Review of Social Economy, 71,* 187–208.

Boatright, J. R. (2013). Swearing to be virtuous: The prospects of a banker's oath. *Review of Social Economy, 71,* 140–165.

Centraal Bureau Statistiek. (2015). *Rapport Sociaal en Institutioneel Vertrouwen in Nederland.* Retrieved March 20, 2016, from http://www.cbs.nl/nl-NL/menu/themas/bevolking/publicaties/bevolkingstrends/archief/2015/2015-sociaal-en-institutioneel-vertrouwen-in-nederland-pub.htm

Centraal Bureau Statistiek. (2016). *Bestaande Koopwoningen; verkoopprijzen.* Retrieved March 12, 2016, from http://statline.cbs.nl/StatWeb/publication/?PA=81884NED

Code Tabaksblat. (2004). *Code Tabaksblat.* Retrieved March 24, 2016, from http://www.rijksoverheid.nl/bestanden/documenten-en-publicaties/richtlijnen/2003/12/09/code-tabaksblat/code-tabaksblat.pdf

Consultation. (2013). *Wijzigingsbesluit Financiele Markten 2013.* Retrieved March 10, 2016, from https://www.internetconsultatie.nl/wijzigingsbesluitfm2013/reacties/

Gailey, J. A., & Lee, M. T. (2008). Influences and the assignment of responsibility for wrongdoing in organizational settings. *Sociological Focus, 41*, 71–86.

Hare, R. M. (1982). *Moral thinking: It's levels, methods and point.* Oxford: Oxford University Press.

Keuning, W. (2016, April 1). Nog geen uitspraken vanwege schending bankierseed. *Financieel Dagblad.* Retrieved April 2, 2016, from http://fd.nl/ondernemen/1145733/jaar-na-invoering-bankierseed-nog-geen-uitspraken-door-tuchtcommissie

Nederlandse Vereniging van Banken. (2016). *Future oriented banking.* Retrieved March 20, 2016, from https://www.nvb.nl/media/document/002235_future-oriented-banking-q-a.pdf

Ogilvie, S. (2011). *Institutions and European trade: Merchant guilds, 1000–1800.* Cambridge: Cambridge University Press.

Rijksoverheid. (2014). *Memorie van Toelichting Wijzigingswet Financiele Markten.* Retrieved from https://www.rijksoverheid.nl/binaries/rijksoverheid/documenten/kamerstukken/2014/04/14/memorie-van-toelichting-wijzigingswet-financiele-markten-2015/pz0xhgg6.pdf

Ronnegard, D. (2013). How autonomy alone Debunks corporate moral agency. *Business and Professional Ethics Journal, 32*, 77–106.

Rutgers, M. R. (2010). The oath of office as public value guardian. *The American Review of Public Administration, 40*, 428–444.

Rutgers, M. R. (2013). Will the Phoenix fly again? *Review of Social Economy, 71*, 249–276.

Van Kranenburg-Hanspians, K., & Jans, J. A. (2013, September). De Bankierseed. *Tijdschrift voor Arbeid en Onderneming, 3*, 91–97.

Van Mierlo, H. L. (2008). *Gepast en ongepast geld.* Schiedam: Scriptum.

Van Tulder, R. (2011). Crisis ... what crisis? Exploring multinational enterprises' responsiveness to the financial crisis. In D. H. Claes & C. H. Knutsen (Eds.), *Governing the global economy* (pp. 247–276). New York: Routledge.

Verboven, K., VanDorpe, K., & Chankowski, V. (2008). *Pistoi Dia Ten Technen. Bankers, loans and archives in the ancient world* (p. 139). Leuven: Peeters.

Verhulst, A. (1999). *The rise of cities in north-west Europe.* Cambridge: Cambridge Univeristy Press.

Von Reden, S. (2010). *Money in Ptolemaic Egypt: From the Macedonian conquest to the end of the third century BC.* Cambridge: Cambridge University Press.

8

Private–Public Sector Interaction in Terms of Crisis Management for Maintaining Sustainability and Enhancing CSR

Christina Nizamidou and Fotis Vouzas

8.1 Introduction

Operations act and develop on a global level, within a constantly altering instable business environment. The business community, as well as the society in a wider scale, is vulnerable to various types of disorders, which may prove to be of enormous cost. Kemper and Martin (2010, p. 229) indicate that "as the size and shape of the financial and economic crises have become clearer, the relationship between firms and society has begun to shift markedly." The majority of businesses worldwide are still struggling to recover from the recent global financial crisis. In the aftermath of this crisis, organizations and humans experienced and captured that it is only through genuine interplay and interaction of a plethora of different type of organizations—private, public, Non-Governmental Organizations' (NGO) institutions, governmen-

C. Nizamidou (✉) • F. Vouzas
Department of Business Administration, University of Macedonia, Thessaloniki, Greece
e-mail: c.nizamidou@mail.com

© The Author(s) 2017
A. Theofilou et al. (eds.), *Corporate Social Responsibility in the Post-Financial Crisis Era*, Palgrave Studies in Governance, Leadership and Responsibility, DOI 10.1007/978-3-319-40096-9_8

tal agencies—and through the integration of diversified individuals can they survive; can society itself survive. According to Mintzberg (1983, p. 3) "in its purest form, social responsibility is supported for its own sake because that is the noble way for corporations to behave." Therefore, organizations have to enhance substantially their corporate social responsibility (CSR) in order to offer greater social value and an increased population awareness regarding their liabilities against themselves and the society.

This chapter makes an effort to accentuate the contribution of the principles of crisis management in relation to the collaboration and integration between different types of organizations, thus to be prepared to manage a crisis with the minimum losses, in terms of time and cost. The current financial crisis confirmed that businesses and societies can no longer afford the reoccurrence of a similar event. The uncertain business environment demands from all companies to be alert, being in a position to deal with unpredictable crisis situations, at any given time.

Events of great importance, such as an economic failure due to management mistakes or due to the lack of allocating financial resources, labor accidents, electronic crime, the early deterioration of a product, a strike of the trade union or even natural catastrophes such as an earthquake, may lead to substantial, unrepairable damages and losses, in economic terms and in human lives in some extreme cases.

Crisis management is not only a top priority for the organization, but for every party involved such as investors, employees, stakeholders, customers, suppliers and the community. Therefore, the collaboration and the integration between the private and the public sector involving firms, political actors and social constituents is an absolute necessity for every business, in order to manage a crisis successfully and achieve operational continuity.

8.2 Developing Private–Public Sector Interaction for Maintaining Operational Sustainability Under Crisis

By definition, crisis is "a major unpredictable event that likely is accompanied with potential negative effects. The event and its aftermath may significantly damage an organization and its employees, products, services, financial condition and reputation" (Barton 1993, p. 2).

Crisis is a multidimensional and complex notion that may affect any business. By any means, there are no standards in effects caused by crisis as the recent financial crisis indicated. Every business is obliged to develop its co-operational skills in interacting with the public sectors and vice versa, in a higher or lower level, according to the crisis type. However, this interactive relationship is essential in favor of the common wealth of the society. Karaibrahimoğlou (2010, p. 385) supports that "in order to cope with the financial and economic downturn, organizations need to focus on providing society's needs; therefore, transparent CSR projects could provide the social support needed by organizations and society to overcome the down turn". Adopting a hybrid model of interaction between the private and the public sectors, which can be adjusted accordingly, depending on the occasion and on the crisis type, may be a fundamental tool for any business, in order to ensure its operational sustainability under crisis. As Kolk and Pinkse (2006, p. 61) underline "the greater the number of ties between stakeholders, the greater their ability to collaborate and to influence organizational practices".

Fernández-Feijóo Souto (2008, p. 46) argues that "the new attitude, forms and perspectives should be the result of a deep internal reflection that will increase the core value of the firm. This core value will be favored by the innovation inherent in CSR". Peloza and Shang (2011, p. 119) support that "value is interactive because it can be created only when a firm and stakeholder come together". Additionally, according to Lin et al. (2011, p. 455) "CSR refers to the moral obligations that maximize the positive influence of the firm on its social environment (e.g., environmental protection, social charities, etc.) and minimize the negative influence".

8.3   The Process of Accomplishing an Integrated Relationship

The majority of theorists and experts of crisis management support the necessity and the utility of a crisis management plan. "Every business, large or small, public or private, should have a crisis management plan. Every division of every company, industrial or service business, should also have a crisis management plan" (Fink 1986, p. 54).

It is worth mentioning that in order for this bidirectional co-operation to be carried out and resolved between private and public sectors, under crisis, the development and existence of a feasible plan is presumed. It is impossible by any means to achieve a sufficient level of synchronization and co-ordination between two or more individual organizations, without having their roles and obligations predetermined.

Having as a cornering stone the planning principles of crisis management, companies may be more efficiently prepared to deal with unexpected, random or not, events, which in turn may result in serious damages. These losses may surpass the financial sense of a business loss. Realistically, in some cases they may cause irreparable catastrophes, which may trigger political anxiety and social disorder.

The article fulfills the literature related to the process by which an organization may collaborate and integrate with other organizations of the same sector or from other sectors, either private or public, in order to maximize its crisis awareness and preparedness. It illustrates how a new model can emerge from the interactive relationship developed between organizations, NGOs, public agencies, government and funding institutions in order to respond effectively to a wider range of human and social requirements which often rises under the shadow of a crisis that can be a potential threat for the society.

The need for enhancing co-operation with a diversity of organizations, in order to deal with a crisis, may contribute in alerting the consciousness for socialization, maximizing the level of awareness for greater corporate social responsibility. It also aims in determining a theoretical hybrid model of interplay of the private and public sectors that may challenge the interest of many for further research and study, since crisis is an integral piece of the modern business era and of the society.

Based on the actions performed individually by a company, in the three separate stages of crisis, a hybrid new model is quoted, focusing on the collaboration between private and public sectors. The role of the determination of this model is not only to enable a business to maintain its operational sustainability but to return to its weekday pace and business activity, with the lowest possible cost, not just for the company itself, but for all the involved parties, such as stakeholders, employees, suppliers and the wider social spectrum. An additional fundamental criterion is achieving the abovementioned, in the less possible time.

In this new co-operative form, apart from presenting the modus operandi of the cross-sector partnership, a thorough analysis is cited regarding the operations of the members of the crisis management team, including the methods of interaction followed by sectors of the company.

Many different models have been developed, throughout the years, to illustrate crisis management procedures. All of them have been outlined by a number of researchers and represent the most commonly followed paths for crisis analysis (Turner 1976; Fink 1986; Shrivastava et al. 1988; Pearson and Clair 1998; Pauchant and Mitroff 1992; Heath 1998; Ray 1999; Mitroff 2005). Turner (1976) first established a model comprising of six stages, which was adopted by Mitroff (2005) also. Pauchant and Mitroff (1992) developed a model consisting of five stages. Heath (1998) proposes a four-stage model, commonly known as the "4R's". The three-stage model (Seeger et al. 2003) was not developed or supported by theorists. It is perceived to have emerged from practical research attempts in an effort to be used as a general analytical framework (Coombs 1999; Ray 1999).

The following table, see "Table 8.1", represents a comprehensive presentation of the different theoretical models:

This chapter utilizes the three-stage model of crisis, based on the crisis time period: pre-crisis—crisis—post-crisis. The three-stage model combines the flexibility of adaptation with ease in various conditions conveniently by separating the process of every action, depending on each

Table 8.1 Models of Crisis Management

Three-stage Model of Crisis Management	Four-stage Model of Crisis Management (4R)	Five-stage Model of Crisis Management	Six-stage Model of Crisis Management
Pre-crisis	Reduction Readiness	Signal detection Preparation	Signal detection Probing/preparation
Crisis	Response	Containment/ damage limitation	Containment/damage limitation
Post-crisis	Recovery	Recovery Learning	Business recovery No fault learning Redesign

Source: Developed by authors

time phase. The three-stage crisis model was selected due to the simplified analysis it provides. This model can be understood by the majority of people, as the distinguishability between the stages is distinctive and offers a more explicit view to non-specialists.

8.3.1 The Pre-Crisis Stage

Crisis management is a topic of greater importance than many presume. Managers and leaders are obliged to take responsibility, since they are considered to be liable for the prosperity of the company, the well-being of their employees, the welfare of the outer environment and of the society it operates. The assurance of the company itself, in terms of operational existence and profitability, in relation to maintaining its development and growth, is on the top of the pyramid of priorities. Therefore, before each organization is challenged with a crisis, it has:

1. **To identify and prepare.** Every business has to have the ability of identifying beforehand a potential threatening crisis. The company may determine and acknowledge the exact organizations from the private and the public sector, in order to establish a co-operative relation at any given time when a crisis appears.

   A characteristic example of the above is quoted by Fink (1986, p. 56) regarding a sudden power failure which occurred in the Los Angeles Herald Examiner. The Herald Examiner had to face the incident, which caused a halt in printing from its own plant. In order to overcome the problems caused, as headlines were extremely pressing, the newspaper presses of Los Angeles Times were recruited and the paper was distributed on time. In this case, a crisis was contained due to a pre-arranged cross-sector partnership, between the two publishers. "Herald Examiner" as a proactive company was fortunate enough to be prepared and have an alternative operation plan in hand, if an unexpected crisis occurred. According to Burke and Logsdon (1996, p. 498) "one might argue that the firm may be motivated by the desire to save on future compliance costs. If so, the CSR behavior may be strategic in terms of proactivity." In this case, everything was preorganized in an orchestral level of performing every single action. This is an illustrative example of an efficient partnership, in terms of crisis management planning, between two organizations of the same operational activity.

Under the spectrum of even bigger crises, an extensively detailed, fully integrated preparation is crucial in conjunction with a harmonic co-ordination of a plethora of governmental organizations, institutions, businesses, volunteers, paramedics and non-governmental organizations.

2. **To provide appropriate training.** Within the framework of crisis management, it is commonly known that every company is obliged to train and educate accordingly all of its employees, including managers, assistants and production-line workers. The training scheme has to provide sufficient knowledge of the actions performed during a crisis. Training programs are being utilized throughout presentations, role-playing, distribution of informative material and table top exercises.

   The new hybrid model proposes that specially designed integrated seminars and realistic simulations with every single external and organizational entity have to be performed as predetermined by the former stage of planning.

3. **To develop a sufficient level of communication**. In terms of crisis management, a correct and sufficient level of communication is a prerequisite during all stages of crisis. At the pre-crisis stage, alternative communication channels have to be defined, which will be activated consecutively when crisis emerges.

   Prior to a crisis, all involved organizations, either public–private or cross-sector partnerships, must be fully aware with whom or how they have to communicate. Particularly, in relation to the inner business environment, crisis managers should have full acknowledgment of providing 24-7 easy access to communication and information means, to the company's employees (Mitroff and Pearson 1993; Kovoor-Misra 1996). Apart from businesses' privately owned network platform, emergency call-free phone numbers should be provided with easy and free access or even text messages, informing and advising employees, in emergency situations.

   Nevertheless, communication plans have certain limitations, when it comes to informing a large number of people. At that time, the media may undertake a fundamental role in providing information to the masses. No government emergency management institution can be compared to the speed and level of information that can be spread by the established "television, radio and newspaper outlets across the country" (Haddow et al. 2008).

4. **To detect the signals and interact.** Troubles usually emerge as insignificant, appearing with minor symptoms that can become easily unidentified. Unfortunately, they can be escalated radically, triggering incidents and metamorphose into the cause of major consequences. Many different variables must be taken under consideration, such as the value level given by people in developments on the premature stage of escalation, the level of knowledge they process in relation to the system's identification capabilities of allocating the first signs of a trouble and the level of support provided from the available resources given by the top management in dealing with the unexpected (Weick and Sutcliffe 2007).

   The ability of interaction between organizations may prove to be extremely cost-effective and even life-saving, whenever minor trouble signals are identified at their very early stage, avoiding crisis before it even occurs.

5. **To test and review.** In order for a plan to achieve maximum effectiveness, the perfect co-ordination and close co-operation of various different entities are required including the company's management team, the local authorities, the emergency services and others. In this case, crisis and emergency plans should be designed thoroughly, reviewed and prepared accordingly.

   In addition to testing, the retrospection of the model accompanied with all the necessary alterations that have to be implemented is very significant. There are incidents that do not allow any margin for mistake. There is no space for trial and error learning, as in many cases the first error may be simultaneously the last trial (Ramsay 1999). Review the already existing plan and its related procedures of the private–public co-ordination scheme, whenever it is necessary. Previous crises have to be reviewed, underlying any processing errors, problems, misunderstandings or false actions that may have emerged due to system failure or to its resources.

8.3.2 The Crisis Stage

The crisis stage is the most crucial stage of all. When a crisis is not fronted accordingly and effectively, a much longer period of time may be required, in order to re-establish a sufficient level of operational sustainability, or in some cases, it may even take years for the business to return to a normal operating status.

In terms of crisis management, the hybrid model described requires from organizations the following:

1. **To identify the crisis**. It is impossible to set forth any action, to select which application has to be implemented within the framework of the general hybrid model, if someone does not have the clearest possible view of what he has to deal with. It is commonly known that a crisis occurs, despite the level of preparedness, in any type of an organization. Panic emerges and spreads everywhere. Panic prevents the involving parties to acquire a clear view of the situation and its extent, thus creating a merely vague perception.

   It is critical to be able to identify, instantly, the crisis situation and mainly to clarify realistically its possible extent. Following this step, any organization has the ability to allocate the proper institutions, organizations or any third party, in order to co-operate and interact, so as to confront effectively the crisis. At this time exactly, the general hybrid model under crisis will be formed according to the circumstances. The action framework, consisting of all the activities for implementation, is determined at this stage.

2. **To isolate the crisis.** It is the immediate forthcoming step that has to be activated based on the hybrid planning. According to Fink (1986, p. 80) "there is no question that a crisis is a disease and should be treated as such. Moreover, it should be viewed and regarded as a communicable disease. And as any first-year medical student will tell you, communicable-disease patients should be quarantined or put into isolation, to prevent the disease from spreading." Accordingly, no one wants a crisis to spread, contaminating other entities. A crisis must be constantly monitored and restricted as much as possible. Until it is fully isolated, no operations can take place.

3. **To make decisions under pressure**. In order to accomplish a sufficient level of co-ordination for the operational efficiency of the hybrid model, it is essential to acknowledge the person in-charge who is responsible of synchronizing different parties together. One of the main responsibilities of this individual is to maintain the organization's credibility and simultaneously enhance the trust among every entity involved with the crisis. Depending on the nature of the crisis, the managerial team has to enhance by any means the organization in a productive and profitable state (Lockwood 2005, p. 3).

The aftermath of this stage is the arousing emotions, such as fear and anxiety (Smith and Ellsworth 1985). Wooten and James (2008) claim that the psychological influence of these emotions may affect severely the decision-making ability of a leader. Being able to perform and deliver under pressure, within a crisis, throughout wise and sound decisions, is a fundamental attribute.

The main issue is to allocate the individual who is charismatic in making decisions under pressure, coordinating the action framework of the existing model, integrating with all other involved entities and willing to undertake the burden of responsibilities. These people may drive a crisis challenge to success, adding social value, with a positive outcome for everyone.

4. **To achieve a sufficient communication level.** When dealing with a new status of private–public collaboration, crisis communication may have a wider perspective. It is not viable to establish any form of alignment and collaboration, when the involved parties cannot engage an efficient method of communication. Communication is not only the cornering stone within the integration of a business, but it is extended in every edge of the operational and social environment.

According to Dean (2004, p. 196) "corporate communications during a crisis should address issues of corporate control over the event and the processes and procedures for dealing with the event (to ensure fair treatment for all affected parties)." The communication factor and the level of efficiency in exchanging information, between all involving parties, as it can be perceived from real incidents, are extremely important (Wang and Hutchins 2010). It is not only time-

and cost-effective, but it can also save lives. The importance of this article is emphasized by the fact that the embracement of a co-operative synergy model can promote social value.

5. **To manage crisis.** The action that remained is to manage crisis having under main consideration to restrict and overcome all its negative attributes as quickly as possible in order to reach the post-crisis stage. The crisis stage reaches to an end, when the organization is able to operate in a state near normal. Crisis, despite being the shortest in chronicle terms, has the highest level of strain. It starts by sensing the crisis, through an event that triggers it, and does not have any constraints, till the crisis-management team's intervention. During this period and until the post-crisis stage, intense confusion, uncertainty and emotional arousal occur (Brockner and James 2008). At this point, a multiple process is required in order to resolve a crisis, including all the necessary actions that must be performed by every single member of the model, either as individuals or as an assembly, depending on the issues that have to be resolved, providing radical integrated solutions and maintaining the highest possible level of operational sustainability.

The crisis stage requires accurate, precise and strategically designed interventions, which will focus in minimizing the harm and the losses, confining the impact of the crisis. By applying similar tactics, the organizations can move into the post-crisis stage efficiently.

8.3.3 The Post-Crisis Stage

As researchers have shown, the cost of a crisis does not end simultaneously when the crisis ends, particularly for the human factor such as employees, their families and the community. According to Shrivastava (1995, p. 222) "the last and longest phase is the post-crisis long-term recovery. It takes months and sometimes years for crisis-affected communities and environments to recover from direct and indirect impacts. This is the period of economic, ecologic, social, political, and cultural normalization." Moreover, the mode of action during the last stage will be cited, after the successful outcome of the organizational crisis. The actions to be taken are as follows:

1. **To restore for achieving recovery.** Primarily, as soon as the crisis incident has reached its ending, all the losses and damages have to be precisely recorded. Every party involved in the hybrid model has to identify the nature and size of each loss, assessing the required activities for the purpose of restoring and reconstructing the operational scheme, using and exchanging all available info.

2. **To monitor the safety and mental health of people.** Organizations are obliged to intensify their attention to the impact of the crisis on employees, their families and the community as well. As Lockwood states: "Business recovery and operational sustainability cannot occur without employees" (Lockwood 2005). Managers tend to turn their greater attention toward systems, operation, infrastructure and public relation, instead of the human factor.

   Although crisis is permanently terminated, the morale of the employees is low and emotions such as fear, psychological stress and uncertainty capture their state of mind, affecting their mental health (Wang and Hutchins 2010). Considering that post-trauma issues may emerge in the near future, due to the nature of human psychology and mentality, organizations and top-level managers, including the HR Department, must ensure the fine physical and mental health of the employees, contributing in maintaining a high morale state and helping them extensively in returning back to a normal productive state. Most of the times, external collaboration is required in the form of expert psychological counseling.

   The process of the participation of consulting agencies, psychologists, academics and others, led by experts in trauma management, is now more essential than ever. People, that are in a post-trauma state, in case of not receiving proper and immediate attention, tend to have a vast decrease of their productive performance and most importantly, can be extremely vulnerable to any future crisis.

3. **To learn.** Despite the fact that the majority of organizations are in a state of continuous self-analysis, post-crisis situations impose an increased awareness period (Ahmed 2009). The organization, within

its external communication strategy and public announcements, describes corrective actions, for the purpose of restoring primarily its image and regaining its lost trust. These changes have to be applied in reality, being constantly monitored for their effectiveness and evaluated for their positive results.

Moreover, during this stage all the involved parties are obliged to separately study thoroughly, what they have obtained from the crisis event, identify any mistakes and how these mistakes can be avoided at the next similar crucial incident. Sharing their knowledge and organizing a coordinated study as an entity is the next step, throughout interaction, focusing on the mistakes the group has made. After performing this team study and having a clear view regarding every issue, the group should allocate the methods-tools, proceeding in reviewing and revising, if necessary, their common crisis management plan and provide knowledge, not only for the purpose of maintaining operational sustainability, but for the purpose of increasing the Corporate Social Responsibility (CSR).

4. **To redesign and re-evaluate.** The absolute necessity of intervention of the public–private sectors and of the cross-sectors partnerships is fundamental in contributing in any emergency and crisis situation. Unfortunately, learning, evaluating and rethinking emergency plans are always done after a major catastrophe occurs. Only after a major crisis, organizations go through three stages' defensiveness, openness and forgetfulness (Premeaux and Breaux 2007). All individual organizations, part of the proposed model, have to learn from their mistakes, interact and co-ordinate effectively in order to re-evaluate and redesign the crisis management plan wherever it is necessary.

5. **To remember.** It is commonly known that the majority of the organizations and societies tend to forget crisis incidents over time. This is a characteristic behavior and a basic attribute of the human brain. The brain mechanism deletes any unpleasant memories, replacing them with memories of euphoria (Payne 1989). Organizations seek to reframe the crisis, in order to have a positive or optimistic reference point. Survivors and victims of crisis are perceived and honored as heroes, who suffered for the survival of the organization or of the community (Seeger et al. 2003). These ceremonies inspire society with feelings of bravery, persistence resourcefulness and sacrifice.

The actions implied within the post-crisis stage may lead in turning a crisis into a lifetime opportunity for improvement and renewal. The positive outcome from the recovery of a crisis depends solely on the organization's ability to gain knowledge from it, including all the parties participating in the hybrid collaboration model. Ceremonies and memorials are often actions of retrieving self-confidence and assurance in communities that endured a crisis.

8.4   The New Hybrid Model

The general form of the New Hybrid Model, as depicted on the following figure, may set the basis or even constitute a primary tool which can be modified or applied depending on the circumstances, in order to become an additional aid in planning, managing or even avoiding potentially emerging crisis. Eventually, it may trigger the interest and attract the attention of researchers and scholars for further examination analysis and research. At this stage it is essential to underline that certain restrictions apply, regarding the development of the model, due to the fact that it was selected to be analyzed and developed according to the general theoretical framework of crisis management, separated in three different stages.

The following figure illustrates the model as analyzed beforehand:

Figure 8.1 represents the methods by which all the necessary co-operation and co-ordination activities are to be accomplished between various forms of organizations, based on the crisis management plan. Additionally, a clear view of the interactive relation between them can be identified in all three stages of a crisis (pre-crisis—crisis—post-crisis). Undoubtedly, some may become interested in developing a similar form in a different stage model.

8.5   Private–Public Integration Under Crisis

The past years, risk has been on the first page of every organization's agenda, particularly due to the globalized business environment. Information is spread and distributed instantly nowadays, as it can be

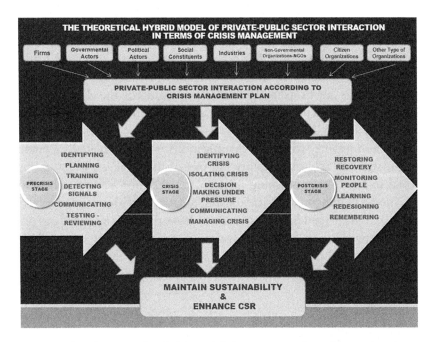

Fig. 8.1 The Theoretical Hybrid Model. (*Source*: Developed by authors)

accessed by the majority of the planet's population (Parrett 2007). Present facts have indicated that a crisis is not restricted on the boundaries of an organization, but it can be extended on an enormous wide social range, enforcing the establishment of public–private sector co-ordinations, in order to return to normalcy and restore not only the business itself, but the society as well.

An illustrative example of the above model between private and public sector co-operation and integration is the case of Schwan's food-borne illness that took place in 1994. Schwan is a company that trades different type of frozen foods and juice drinks, but it is commonly known for its ice cream products. "In 1994, Schwan's experienced the largest outbreak of illness caused by the food-borne bacteria Salmonella in U.S. history" (Seeger et al. 2003, p. 134). Schwan could not prevent the crisis from taking place despite doing everything within its power to restrict it.

During the crisis stage, Schwan co-operated and interacted with numerous different organizations. This included public health inspectors, to whom Schwan granted full access to their central plant for further investigations, federal and state investigators, the majority of its suppliers, numerous law firms in order to settle voluntarily the claims of thousands of its customers and the media, so as to keep all of its stakeholders constantly updated.

In the outcome, when the investigations were completed, it proved that it was not Schwan's liability but one of its suppliers, who was supposed to have their incoming mixes pasteurized for Schwan. However, this model of honest collaboration and integration with abundant diverse organizations helped Schwan to recover from the crisis as quickly as possible. Schwan's high level of conscious for CSR and its responsibility toward its stakeholders and mainly its customers is an exemplar of how the proposed hybrid model may be implemented even when the crisis cannot be averted.

Conclusion

In the modern era, the private sector contributes to the economic growth and to the social progress greater than ever in the history of humanity. The global business community and its stakeholders can no longer rely on governments, in terms of safeguarding people from catastrophic threats (Parrett 2007); the global financial crisis has confirmed it. Businesses and communities have to co-ordinate together, emphasizing in reaching perfect synchronization.

The present article has made an approach to enlighten and enhance an integrated form of collaboration and interaction between the public–private sector and cross-sector partnership, in terms of crisis management. A general theoretical framework was given, which can be modified and adopted, depending on the circumstances and on the crisis type, for every organization.

Throughout crisis management plan, collaborations and partnerships are determined, in relation to the attributes of each crisis. The roles and responsibilities in every stage were analyzed in order to manage crisis successfully. By using actual facts, the importance between partnerships was illustrated, emphasizing in maintaining operational sustainability, contributing to the economic growth and providing effective solutions in raising public welfare concern.

Lastly, the current article, apart from triggering the researcher's interest for further study, may become a useful tool, enabling businesses to broaden their horizons, when preparing a crisis management plan. Crisis management procedures may expand the ability of organizations to integrate with a plethora of other type of organizations. The repercussion of the recent financial crisis has demonstrated that only through alert CSR, conscientious and ethical co-operation can organizations overcome difficult and critical situations.

References

Ahmed, A. (2009). Creating opportunity from crisis: Taking a strategic and learning-focused perspective. *Development and Learning in Organizations: An International Journal, 23*(5), 4–6.

Barton, L. (1993). *Crisis in organizations: Managing and communicating in the heat of chaos*. Cincinnati, OH: South Western Publishing Co.

Brockner, J., & James, E. H. (2008). Toward an understanding of when executives see opportunity in crisis. *Journal of Applied Behavioral Science, 44*(7), 94–115.

Burke, L., & Logsdon, J. M. (1996). How corporate social responsibility pays off. *Long Range Planning, 29*(4), 495–502.

Coombs, W. T. (1999). *Ongoing crisis communication: Planning, managing and responding*. Thousand Oaks, CA: Sage.

Dean, D. H. (2004). Consumer reaction to negative publicity: Effects of corporate reputation, response, and responsibility for a crisis event. *Journal of Business Communication, 41*(2), 192–111.

Fernández-Feijóo Souto, B. (2008). Crisis and corporate social responsibility: Threat or opportunity? *International Journal of Economic Sciences and Applied Research, 2*(1), 36–50.

Fink, S. (1986). *Crisis management: Planning for the inevitable*. New York: AMACOM.

Haddow, G. D., Bullock, J. A., & Coppola, D. P. (2008). *Introduction to emergency management* (3rd ed.). Oxford: Butterworth-Heinemann.

Heath, R. (1998). *Crisis management for managers and executives: Business crises—The definitive handbook to reduction, readiness, responses and recovery.* Harlow, UK: Pearson Education Ltd.

Karaibrahimoğlou, Y. Z. (2010). Corporate social responsibility in times of financial crisis. *African Journal of Business Management, 4*(4), 382–389.

Kemper, A., & Martin, R. L. (2010). After the fall: The global financial crisis as a test of corporate social responsibility theories. *European Management Review, 7*, 229–239.

Kolk, A., & Pinkse, J. (2006). Stakeholder mismanagement and corporate social responsibility crises. *European Management Journal, 24*(1), 59–72.

Kovoor-Misra, S. (1996). Moving toward crisis preparedness: Factors that motivate organizations. *Technological Forecasting and Social Change, 53*, 169–183.

Lin, C.-P., Chen, S.-C., Chiu, C.-K., & Lee, W.-Y. (2011). Understanding purchase intention during product-harm crises: Moderating effects of perceived corporate ability and corporate social responsibility. *Journal of Business Ethics, 102*, 455–471.

Lockwood, N. R. (2005). *Crisis management in today's business environment: HR's strategic role.* 2005 SHRM Research Quarterly. Retrieved June 19, 2014, from http://www.shrm.org/research/articles/articles/documents/1205rquartpdf.pdf

Mintzberg, H. (1983). The case for corporate social responsibility. *Journal of Business Strategy, 4*(2), 3–15.

Mitroff, I. I. (2005). *Why some companies emerge stronger and better from a crisis. Seven essential lessons for surviving disaster.* New York: AMACOM.

Mitroff, I. I., & Pearson, C. M. (1993). *Crisis management: A diagnostic guide for improving your organization's crisis-preparedness.* San Francisco, CA: Jossey-Bass.

Parrett, W. G. (2007). *The Sentinel CEO. Perspectives on security, risk, and leadership in a post—9/11 world.* Hoboken, NJ: John Wiley & Sons, Inc.

Pauchant, T. C., & Mitroff, I. I. (1992). *Transforming the crisis-prone organization.* San Francisco: Jossey-Bass.

Payne, D. (1989). *Copying with failure: The therapeutic uses of rhetoric.* Columbia: University of South Carolina Press.

Pearson, C. M., & Clair, J. A. (1998). Reframing crisis management. *Academy of Management Review, 23*(1), 59–76.

Peloza, J., & Shang, J. (2011). How can corporate social responsibility activities create value for stakeholders? A systematic review. *Journal of the Academy of Marketing Science, 39*, 117–135.

Premeaux, S. F., & Breaux, D. (2007). Crisis management of human resources: Lessons from Hurricanes Katrina and Rita. *Human Resource Planning, 30*(3), 39–47.

Ramsay, C. G. (1999). Protecting your business: From emergency planning to crisis management. *Journal of Hazardous Materials, 65*, 131–149.

Ray, S. J. (1999). *Strategic communication in crisis management: Lessons from the airline industry.* Westport, CT: Quorum Books.

Seeger, M. W., Sellnow, T. L., & Ulmer, R. R. (2003). *Communication and organizational crisis.* Westport, CT: Praeger Publishers.

Shrivastava, P. (1995). Industrial/environmental crises and corporate social resposibility. *The Journal of Socio-Economics, 24*(1), 211–227.

Shrivastava, P., Mitroff, I. I., Miller, D., & Miclani, A. (1988). Understanding industrial crises. *Journal of Management Studies, 25*(4), 285–203.

Smith, C. A., & Ellsworth, P. C. (1985). Patterns of cognitive appraisals in emotions. *Journal of Personality and Social Psychology, 48*, 813–838.

Turner, B. A. (1976). The organizational and interorganizational development of disasters. *Administrative Science Quaterly, 21*, 378–397.

Wang, J., & Hutchins, H. M. (2010). Crisis management in higher education: What have we learned from Virginia Tech? *Advances in Developing Human Resources, 12*(5), 552–572.

Weick, K. E., & Sutcliffe, K. M. (2007). *Managing the unexpected: Resilient performance in age of uncertainty* (2nd ed.). San Francisco: Jossey-Bass.

Wooten, L. P., & James, E. H. (2008). Linking crisis management and leadership competencies: The role of human resource development. *Advances in Developing Human Resources, 10*(3), 352–379.

9

The Need for a Responsible Public Administration

Athanasios Chymis, Paolo D'Anselmi,
and Christos Triantopoulos

9.1 Introduction

The literature addressing corporate social responsibility (CSR) has made great strides since its emergence, and has established itself as an important field of research in the general area of management. As the very term denotes, CSR is the study of the social responsibility of corporations or, broadly speaking, of business or the private sector of the economy. Interestingly, CSR scholars have implicitly excluded the public sector from the investigations despite the fact that the greater discussion being generated around the social responsibility of organizations recently, especially after the financial crisis, does not focus only on the private sector. For example, the theme of the annual meeting of the Academy of Management (AOM) in 2015 was "Opening Governance", which does

A. Chymis (✉) • C. Triantopoulos
Centre for Planning and Economic Research, KEPE, Athens, Greece

P. D'Anselmi
University of Rome Tor Vergata, Rome, Italy

© The Author(s) 2017   **155**
A. Theofilou et al. (eds.), *Corporate Social Responsibility in the Post-Financial Crisis Era*, Palgrave Studies in Governance, Leadership and Responsibility, DOI 10.1007/978-3-319-40096-9_9

not necessarily refer only to private organizations. Even better, the theme of the last AOM meeting (2016) "Making Organizations Meaningful" definitely does not exclude public organizations. These are occasions that offer an opportunity to those contributing to the literature on CSR to broaden its concept and include public organizations in their research agenda.

The chapter is particularly relevant to the theme of this book, namely, CSR in the post financial crisis. The recent economic and debt crisis that hit many countries raised questions about the behavior of public organizations and public administration,[1] since their irresponsible behavior is partly to be blamed for the economic downturn that still bedevils the world economy. The public sector is too major a pillar of socioeconomic activity to be left out of the scope of CSR. The Weberian view of the benevolent bureaucrat cannot explain the irresponsible actions observed within public administration management (Chymis et al. 2015). Principal–agent theory explains how public administration managers and employees face dilemmas similar to those being faced by firm managers and employees. Moreover, public administration is largely unaffected by the elections that take place, on average, every four years. These are some of the reasons for which public administration needs to increase its accountability, transparency and integrity, and become more socially responsible.

At the same time, some recent strands of CSR literature have increasingly dealt with country comparisons and investigated factors that affect CSR at the national level, thus recognizing some important driving forces behind the socially responsible behavior of firms. The main proposition of this chapter is that, first, we need to address the issue of social responsibility at the public sector level and, second, that this presents an opportunity and a challenge for the literature regarding social responsibility to take the lead in this discussion. Most economics scholars and

---

[1] For the needs of this chapter the terms public administration, public organizations and public sector are used interchangeably. Although there are differences among the three groups, for example, a state-owned enterprise is not part of public administration, but it is a public organization and part of the public sector, the terms are used in parallel in order to stress the need for an extension of the social responsibility literature toward the public sphere of the socioeconomic life.

international organizations talk about the effectiveness and efficiency of public administration, inherently referring to its social responsibility; however, nobody says so explicitly and this is where social responsibility scholars can make a contribution.

This chapter presents the perspective of economics and international organizations concerning the impact of institutions on the economy and how they shape incentives for firms to behave in a socially responsible fashion, thus revealing the need to address the social responsibility of organizations that engender public institutions. The CSR perspective is then presented, and the recent developments related to the chapter's topic are succinctly described. The presentation of the proposition that social responsibility literature could include in its research agenda the social responsibilities of public organizations is posited and, finally, the chapter focuses on the important role of competition in increasing incentives for socially responsible behavior.

9.2 The Perspective of Economics and International Organizations

According to the perspective of New Institutional Economics (NIE), firms—that is, the private sector—do not operate in a vacuum (North 2005). They operate in a more or less developed institutional environment. This environment is the result and the responsibility of public organizations such as governments (at a national or local level), licensing authorities, tax authorities, judicial authorities and so on. These organizations are part of public administration.

Public administration crafts the "rules of the game" to use Williamson's words for institutions (Williamson 2000). Williamson explains that there are four levels of social analysis. The first, namely the social embeddedness level, refers to informal institutions such as customs, traditions, norms and religion. This is the level which is mainly studied by economic historians as well as sociologists, psychologists, ethnologists and other social scientists. Changes at this level do not occur very often and take any time between tens and hundreds of years. The second level is the institutional environment. This includes the formal rules of the game and especially property (polity, judiciary, bureaucracy). Changes at this level occur more often compared to the previous one; that is, within decades. The third level is governance. It refers to aligning governance structures with transactions. Here, change takes place even more often, within a few years. Finally, the last level comprises everyday economic life; that is, resource allocation and employment. This refers to prices and quantities. Changes at this level are continuous as the market is the main forum for constantly aligning incentives at this level (Williamson 2000).

Williamson argues that NIE deals mostly with the second and third levels of analysis, that is, institutional environment and governance. The purpose of these levels is, respectively, to "get the institutional environment right" and to "get the governance structures right" (Williamson 2000, p. 597). From Williamson it becomes clear that the last level of analysis depends heavily on the previous ones. For an economy to work properly and fulfill its purpose, which is to increase the level of well-being (i.e. wealth, satisfaction, happiness) of its citizens, we need the "right" institutions to be in place so that they shape incentives and drive socioeconomic development. As Williamson notes, this is the key role of the polity, judiciary and bureaucracy. All three are part of public administration.

The discussion presented above and developed over the last few decades by the NIE has been addressed more fervently in the aftermath of the credit financial crisis of 2007–2008, which in many countries evolved into a severe economic crisis and, more specifically, a debt crisis, bringing the global economy to its knees and raising questions about the management of public organizations. International organizations such as the OECD (2010), the World Bank (WB) (2015), the World Economic Forum (WEF) (2012) and the United Nations (UN), in their publications, stress the importance of incorporating integrity, transparency, accountability and trust into the mandate of public sector organizations worldwide in order to enhance economic performance and the efficient use of tax payers' money. In a similar vein, the IMF (2012) produces several series of policy analyses and informs public authorities how they can reduce the waste of valuable resources and increase the efficacy and efficiency of public sector organizations.

Scholars have long recognized the importance of institutions and their impact on country development and economic growth (Acemoglu and Robinson 2012; North 1990, 2005; Olson 1982). Well managed (i.e. responsibly managed) public organizations can make the difference between a wealthy nation and a poor one. Specifically, the literature argues that institutions are more important for development than the physical endowment of each country. It is more important to have a stable political environment that reduces uncertainty; stable tax laws which do not change frequently; rule of law and law enforcement; effective and time efficient justice; a high degree of meritocracy and property rights protection—all without unnecessary bureaucracy (Acemoglu et al. 2002; Acemoglu and Robinson 2012; De Soto 2000; Easterly and Levine 1997; North 1990, 2005; Olson 1982; Rodrik et al. 2004; Sala-i-Martín and Subramanian 2003; Williamson 1985, 2000).

The quality of institutions determines the level of a country's competitiveness (WEF 2015). According to the 2015 report of the Global Competitiveness Index (GCI) of the WEF, institutions include (1) formal and legally binding constraints as well as enforcement mechanisms, and (2) informal constraints, namely, behavior, conventions and codes of conduct such as business ethics and norms of corporate governance (WEF 2015). Their quality is directly related to the existence of transparency as well as checks and balances, and public sector efficiency. The public sector (public administration) or the state has, according to the WEF, fundamental roles to play. Protecting property rights is one; guaranteeing the security of the citizens is another. The public sector is also responsible for minimizing corruption and undue influence from special interest groups (WEF 2015).

Principal–agent theory (Grossman and Hart 1983) as well as public choice theory (Buchanan and Tullock 1962; Lapiccirella 2015; Niskanen 1968, 1975, 2001) has shown that, much like the managers of corporations, the officials of government and public organizations have incentives to maximize their own utility function, which does not necessarily coincide with their principal's (i.e. the citizens') utility function. This means that public organization managers are tempted to misuse public resources for private gain (e.g. by extorting bribes). Responsible (i.e. effective and efficient) public administration also entails reducing unnecessary red tape and providing effective and efficient public services and a stable policy environment (WEF 2015). Ultimately, responsible public administration increases the level of trust citizens have toward their government, public administration and public organizations overall.

It is relevant to note that the level of trust citizens have for their public organizations is very low and has worsened in the aftermath of the recent economic crises. An online survey by Edelman (2015), which included 33,000 respondents in 27 countries, measured the trust level of citizens regarding four major institutions, namely, Government, Business, Media and non-governmental organizations (NGOs). The survey showed that Government came last among the four institutions; specifically, only 48 percent of respondents said they trust Government, while NGOs were first, for 63 percent. Business followed with 57 percent and the Media, 51 percent.

The OECD conducts surveys and every two years publishes a report called *Government at a glance*. In the 2015 report, OECD researchers recognize that culture plays a significant role in the level of trust, and influences differences across countries. However, when controlling for cultural factor by comparing changes in the level of trust over time, they find a consistent decline—specifically between 2007 and 2014, that is, the period of the economic crisis, during which confidence in national governments across OECD countries decreased by 3.3 percentage points, from 45.2 to 41.8 percent. The OECD report notes that the misuse (i.e. irresponsible use) of public resources negatively affects public opinion not only toward government in general but public service providers in particular, such as the judicial system, local police, the educational system and health care.

Prior to the financial and economic crisis, it was commonly believed that it was mostly developing countries that needed to improve the institutional environment. However, the crisis showed that developed counties are also in need of better and more responsible public organization management. The crisis reminded us that problems like poverty and social exclusion, mostly attributed to developing countries, are also present in the affluent societies of the developed world. According to Eurostat (2014), in 2013, 122.6 million people (24.5 percent of the European Union [EU] population) were at risk of poverty or social exclusion. Averages, of course, vary significantly and range between 14.6 and 48 percent among the 28 countries. Before the crisis, in 2005, according to Eurostat the population at risk of poverty and social exclusion comprised 78 million people, or 16 percent of the EU population. This is a significant increase, which raises questions regarding the responsible use of public resources, that is, tax payers' money (Chymis et al. 2016). In most European countries, the crisis was a public debt crisis caused not by the irresponsible behavior of some greedy corporation managers but the irresponsible behavior of public organizations and public administration—the public sector in general—which funnels over 30, 40 or even 50 percent of a country's gross domestic product (GDP) (Di Bitetto et al. 2015).

9.3   The CSR Perspective

CSR literature has expanded considerably over the last few decades, and the concept has gained scholarly recognition in the social sciences (Wood 2010; Chymis and Skouloudis 2014). Although mainstream CSR focuses on a firm-level analysis, there is a nascent strand of research focusing on country comparisons. Pioneering work in this area includes Chymis and Skouloudis (2014), Gjølberg (2009a, b), Ioannou and Serafeim (2012), Jackson and Apostolakou (2010), Midttun et al. (2006), Ringov and Zollo (2007) and Skouloudis and Evangelinos (2012). Gjølberg (2009a, b) constructed a composite national CSR index. She included nine international indicators, such as the Dow Jones Sustainability Index, FTSE4Good, Global 100, UN Global Compact, the Global Report Initiative and others, and examined firms across 20 developed countries in order to compare and identify factors affecting CSR levels across them.

Chymis and Skouloudis (2014) extended Gjølberg's work by creating a composite national CSR index composed of 16 international indicators, and applied it across 86 countries, both developed and developing. They also looked at the issue from a different perspective. Based on the conceptual article by Campbell (2007), they tested some of Campbell's propositions (hypotheses). Campbell offered important insights on the institutional factors that affect the socially responsible behavior of firms. Although the focus remains on the level of the firm, Campbell recognizes that the general public sector is a catalyst for the socially responsible behavior of individual firms and corporations. He posits several institutional and macroeconomic factors, such as "strong and well-enforced state regulations" (p. 955), healthy economic environment, level of market competition as well as civic activism ("independent organizations, including NGOs, social movement organizations, institutional investors and the press", p. 958).

Results from the research conducted by Chymis & Skouloudis confirm Campbell's propositions. Specifically, civic activism, public institutions and the level of competition significantly affect CSR at the country level. This is in accordance with prior research (in the social sciences in general and management and economics in particular), which has stressed the role of institutions (Brinton and Nee 1998; Furubotn and Richter 2005; Powell and Di Maggio 2012). Moving from the firm-level analysis to cross-country comparisons and investigating factors that affect CSR is a step forward. One major factor affecting CSR across countries is the policies and management of public institutions, which could represent the next step forward for literature concerning social responsibility.

9.4   Taking Social Responsibility a Step Forward

Responsibility is not often considered in economics. Many international organizations strive to increase public sector efficiency and effectiveness but seldom have they used the term "responsibility". However, it is obvious that this term is implicit throughout the literature on economics. When the IMF, the OECD, the UN, the WEF or the WB publish reports advising public administrations worldwide on how to increase their level of transparency, accountability and integrity, the similarities with CSR jargon are obvious.

This chapter's thesis is that the literature addressing social responsibility has an opportunity to expand its field of research and include public sector organizations. There is a gap in the ethics literature which needs to be filled. It is time for CSR scholars to deal with the responsibilities not only of the private but also the public sector. CSR has, so far, done some tremendous work on the responsibilities of business. These very same tools can be used to apply CSR concepts to public organizations since they are, like private entities, composed of human beings. Concepts of ethics and social responsibility should apply to both sectors, especially when considering that, as mentioned above, the public sector in some countries accounts for more than 50 percent of the GDP (Di Bitetto et al. 2015). This is a very large part of the socioeconomic reality to be ignored by the literature on social responsibility.

As Chymis et al. (2016) argue, it was the irresponsible spending of tax payers' contributions that partly caused the debt crisis in some European countries. According to Gudić et al. (2016), when public administration is not effective, it is not socially responsible (it does not deliver what society has been promised); when it is not efficient, it is not economically responsible (delivering at a higher cost). It would be valuable if the literature concerning social responsibility backed the work of international organizations as they strive to increase the effectiveness and efficiency (i.e. responsibility) of public administration across countries.

It should be noted here that public administration does not refer only to the higher echelon managers. While there is no doubt that public management has to implement the basic social responsibility concepts of accountability and transparency, this refers to the millions employed therein and, as agency theory postulates (described above), there are incentives for a public employee to follow his/her own utility function maximization to the detriment of public resources. Papadopoulos and Triantopoulos (2014) describe a situation they call a "unionistic" type of corporate governance, referring to the state-owned enterprises (SOEs) where unions are strong enough to go on strike to demand higher salaries for employees without connecting them to any increase in productivity or quality of service provided. This peculiar, irresponsible situation plays out in the following fashion: the top managers of SOEs are often appointed by political officials. Consequently, they are not subject to market competition. It follows that they have low incentives to operate the firm efficiently. At the same time, strong trade unions (hence the term "unionistic") go on strike in order to put pressure on the government to increase employee wages. Due to the lack of transparency and accountability, it is easier for managers, as well as political officials, to raise wages rather than dissatisfy their potential clientele. Papadopoulos and Triantopoulos describe this situation as a win-win-lose game. The winners are the special interest groups of unions, top managers and politicians. The losers are the constituents, that is, the rest of society. Ultimately, the whole economy crumbles under the weight of deficits and accumulated debt, as happened in the case of Greece (Papadopoulos and Triantopoulos 2014).

9.5   The Role of Competition

At this point, it is relevant to elaborate briefly on the issue of competition. As noted earlier, competition plays a significant role in social responsibility. It is a key driver for social performance (Berman et al. 2005; Campbell 2007; Chymis 2008; Chymis et al. 2015; D'Anselmi 2011). As Campbell (2007) and Chymis et al. (2015) explain, the more we move toward competitive market conditions, the less opaque the market becomes. Transparency increases, as do the flow of information and the awareness of citizens/consumers. International organizations are very keen on competitive market conditions. Figure 9.1 shows market competition as measured by a group of WEF indicators on goods market efficiency and the ethical behavior of firms. There is evidence of a strong relation between the two variables.

It should be noted that WEF captures the efficacy of public institutions in creating competitive conditions at the goods market, through the effectiveness of anti-monopoly policy, the intensity of local competition, the extent and effect of taxation and the number of procedures required to start a business.[2] As WEF states in its 2015 report, the efficiency of goods and services markets can be undermined by (1) the lack of competition and (2) distortionary (i.e. irresponsible) fiscal policies and regulations. Barriers to entry, such as licensing—especially of professional or public services—and public monopolies create environments where few people benefit to the detriment of many. This is an important issue with significant ethical ramifications that the literature on social responsibility could tackle. From an ethical perspective, another critical

---

[2] For more information regarding WEF indicators, see here: http://www3.weforum.org/docs/gcr/2015-2016/Global_Competitiveness_Report_2015-2016.pdf (page 35 and following).

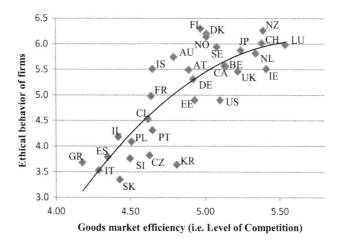

Fig. 9.1 Relation between competition and the ethical behavior of firms
Source: WEF 2015. The graph depicts the group of the OECD 31 high-income countries.

issue is that of fiscal policies based on political selection, which may favor specific sectors of the economy while harming others.

A major issue in the public sector is that most public services are less subject to competition. The literature on social responsibility could provide important input on ways to decrease the monopolistic nature of public administration and infuse more competition. There are ways to increase competition in public administration and the public provision of goods and services. These may include rotating employees within public administration to reduce the possibility of fief-type monopolies, avoiding the consolidation of bureaus as well as limiting the economies of scale in services (though this may run against the dominant logic of Spending Reviews), instituting a multiplicity of bureaus (which does not necessarily mean privatization), and introducing yardstick competition and benchmarking. The purpose here is not to fully develop these potential solutions but simply provide a broad idea of the possibilities the literature on social responsibility can entertain if this subject is considered.

9.5.1   Some Indicative Data

Comparing the wages between employees in the public and private sectors is very interesting as it reveals significant differences among countries. Table 9.1 presents the wages of public versus private sector employees in three European countries (France, Italy and the UK). In Italy, public sector employees are paid considerably higher (49 percent more) than their private sector counterparts. In France, public employees earn 7 percent more, while in the UK, it is the reverse—employees in the private sector earn almost 12 percent more than public sector employees.

Now, taking into consideration the indicators from international organizations regarding public sector efficiency (either measured directly, such as cost per unit of produced good or service—quite difficult to capture—or, indirectly, such as levels of citizen satisfaction and trust) in the UK (where public employees earn much less compared to their colleagues in Italy and France, controlling for the level of remuneration of the private sector), the public sector performs significantly better. Table 9.2 presents two different measures of public sector performance: (1) OECD levels of

Table 9.1 Average compensation (euro/year) 2013

Country	Public sector (A)	Private sector (B)	Ratio (A/B)
Italy	34,851	23,406	1.49
France	35,984	33,574	1.07
UK	34,093	38,047	0.90

Source: Forum PA 2013

Table 9.2 Public sector efficiency

Country	Trust (percent of respondents)[a]					Government efficiency[b]
	Government	Judicial	Police	Education	Health	
France	44 %	50 %	74 %	67 %	78 %	50
Italy	28 %	38 %	76 %	62 %	55 %	53
UK	47 %	62 %	76 %	78 %	92 %	19

Source: OECD 2015; IMD 2015
[a]Larger numbers denote higher trust
[b]Number denotes ranking over 61 countries. The larger the number the lower the ranking

trust toward different areas of the public sector and (2) the IMD world competitiveness yearbook indicator of government efficiency.

Even though many questions could be asked, and observations made, regarding the level of education across sectors and countries, as well as methodological and measurement issues, the tables are quite eloquent. Admittedly, these data should be taken with a grain of salt, yet, how to explain the poor performance of the public sector in Italy despite the fact that public sector employees earn so much more than their private sector colleagues? Similar questions can be asked for France. Inversely, how can it be explained that in the UK, where public sector performance is higher and people trust public service providers much more than in Italy or France, public employees earn considerably less than their Italian or French colleagues?

The analysis so far indicates that competition (or the lack of it) may provide some answers to these questions. It may be the case that in the UK, public goods providers compete at a much higher level than in Italy or France. D'Anselmi (2011) refers to a study in Italy which shows that although employees in the private sector comprise 75 percent of the total workforce, their earnings are only 65 percent of total salary earnings. It seems public sector employees earn a premium due to the restricted competition they face. This is an important issue from an ethical point of view. Is it socially responsible that people working in a sector shielded from competition and enjoying the perks of a public sector job (work stability, guaranteed salary, etc.) earn considerably more than their private sector colleagues even though their productivity may be significantly lower?

While the above tables do *not* prove that people working in public administration are less productive, the data provide evidence that there might be some inconsistencies, and that social responsibility and ethical issues need to be taken into consideration. These questions loom large and beg for answers. The literature on social responsibility cannot and should not avoid asking them since they are not only within the scope of social responsibility but at the core of social justice, fairness and ethics.

A final point concerns the tools that can be used to address the above questions. International organizations can play a significant role by creating more accurate indicators, resolving measurement problems and trying to tackle the thorny issue of directly measuring the productivity of public goods and services providers, as well as their efficacy and efficiency. In other words, using similar methodology as that applied to the social performance of business, social responsibility scholars could start investigating social responsibilities and performance of public organizations. The major social responsibility of public service providers mostly lies within their core business, the very reason they exist, their raison d'être, rather than within the issues that are usually considered when addressing private business.

The economic responsibility of business is usually taken for granted and, rightly so, given that if a firm is not economically responsible, it will drop out of the market. However, this is not the case for public administration, which can operate at a deficit that can backfire, as discussed earlier. Another critical issue for public administration is efficacy. Do public administrations produce what they are supposed to? The levels of citizen trust toward multiple public sectors are not satisfying, to say the least. In some cases they may be worrying. The recent economic and debt crisis revealed some of these ethical issues and dilemmas that modern society needs to address.

9.6   Concluding Remarks

CSR has the tools that can be used to address issues of the social responsibility of public organizations. CSR can inform and be informed by the international organizations regarding crafting ways to effectively measure economic and social responsibility in the public sector. In the post financial crisis (to echo the theme of this book)—an era of fervent discussions regarding economizing, reducing public resource wastefulness, boosting sustainable development, making the public sector sustainable and helping it to meet its citizens' expectations—social responsibility and ethics scholars cannot remain silent. It is an opportunity and, at the same time, a challenge to incorporate in their research agenda the second pillar of the socioeconomic reality, namely, the public sector.

This is an opportunity for CSR scholars to take a look beyond (and at the same time, behind) business, private organizations and corporations;

to take a step back and look at what lies behind the operation of everyday business. Institutions and public administrations that engender these organizations play an important role in shaping incentives for private firms to behave in a specific way. Examining the social responsibility of such public organizations may shed more light on mainstream CSR literature. CSR research that investigates factors affecting CSR at a national level is moving in this direction. It seems there is another, brand new line of research—the responsibility of the country-level public policies, institutions and administrations that support an environment more or less conducive to the socially responsible behavior of firms.

At the same time, this is also a challenge. Public organizations differ from private ones in the sense that the economic level of responsibility in private organizations does not necessarily call for extensive research. The funding of private business is clearer, and production assessment (quantity and quality) is much more specific than in the public sector, where funding is quasi mandatory (through taxes) and an evaluation of the quantity and quality of goods and services more elusive. It is this mandatory nature of funding for public organizations that calls for the socially responsible use of these scarce resources. In private business, the talk is mostly about responsibilities beyond the bottom line, toward employees, the natural environment, suppliers, consumers, stockholders, the local community and so on. In the case of public organizations, the major question to be answered is directly related to the bottom line—before jumping into a discussion about how all the stakeholders are affected and treated. To what extent does a public organization responsibly use tax payer money? To what extent is the production and provision of goods or services done effectively and efficiently? Once these not-so-easy-to-answer questions have been addressed, then it will be easier to move toward considering the rest of the stakeholders.

Authors' Note

Athanasios Chymis is a research fellow at the Centre of Planning and Economic Research, (KEPE) in Athens, Greece. He holds a Ph.D. from the University of Missouri-Columbia in Agricultural Economics. He is interested in the connection between Ethics and Economics and, currently, his research is focused on how social responsibility could be infused in the public administration sector as well as in all organizations both of the private and the public sectors.

Paolo D'Anslelmi is a practitioner of management consultancy and policy analysis. He teaches CSR at the University of Rome Tor Vergata, Italy. He is a graduate in Engineering (Sapienza, Rome) and in Public Policy (Harvard). He is currently working on extending CSR to Public Administration.

Christos Triantopoulos is a research fellow at the Centre of Planning and Economic Research, (KEPE) in Athens, Greece. He holds a Ph.D. from Athens University of Economics and Business. His interests lie in the area of Political Economy and Financial System. He also does research on Financial Supervision, Institutions and Economy and Public Finance, and he regularly does consulting at the Ministry of Finance.

References

Acemoglu, D., Johnson, S., & Robinson, J. (2002). Reversal of fortune: Geography and institutions in the making of the modern world distribution of income. *Quarterly Journal of Economics, 117*(4), 1231–1294.

Acemoglu, D., & Robinson, J. (2012). *Why nations fail: The origins of power, prosperity, and poverty*. New York: Crown Publishers.

Berman, S. L., Phillips, R. A., & Wicks, A. C. (2005). *Resource dependence, managerial discretion and stakeholder performance*. Paper presented in the Academy of Management Meetings, August 5–10, Honolulu, Hawaii.

Brinton, M. C., & Nee, V. (Eds.). (1998). *The new institutionalism in sociology*. Stanford: Stanford University Press.

Buchanan, J. M., & Tullock, G. (1962). *The calculus of consent*. Ann Arbor: University of Michigan Press.

Campbell, J. L. (2007). Why would corporations behave in socially responsible ways? An institutional theory of corporate social responsibility. *Academy of Management Review, 32*, 946–967.

Chymis, A. (2008). *Reconciling Friedman with corporate social responsibility: How market competition affects corporate social performance*. Saarbrücken, Germany: VDM Verlag Dr. Muller.

Chymis, A., Di Bitetto, M., & D'Anselmi, P. (2015). Corporate social performance needs more competition not less: An idea for a paradigm shift. In A. Stachowicz-Stanusch (Ed.), *Corporate social performance: Paradoxes, pitfalls and pathways to the better world* (pp. 37–56). Charlotte, NC: Information Age Publishing.

Chymis, A., Di Bitetto, M., D'Anselmi, P., & Skouloudis, A. (2016). The importance of responsible public management in addressing the challenge of poverty. In M. Gudić, C. Parkes, & A. Rosenbloom (Eds.), *Responsible management education and the challenge of poverty: A teaching perspective* (pp. 222–235). Sheffield: Greenleaf Publishing.

Chymis, A., & Skouloudis, A. 2014. *National CSR and institutional conditions: An exploratory study* (Discussion Paper No. 193). Athens: KEPE.

D'Anselmi, P. (2011). *Values and stakeholders in an era of social responsibility: Cut-throat competition?* Basingstoke: Palgrave Macmillan.

De Soto, H. (2000). *The mystery of capital: Why capitalism triumphs in the west and fails everywhere else.* New York: Basic Books.

Di Bitetto, M., Chymis, A., & D'Anselmi, P. (Eds.). (2015). *Public management as corporate social responsibility: The economic bottom line of government.* Heidelberg: Springer International Publishing.

Easterly, W., & Levine, R. (1997). Africa's growth tragedy: Policies and ethnic divisions. *Quarterly Journal of Economics CXII*, 1203–1250.

Edelman Trust Barometer Global Results. (2015). *Online survey.* Retrieved November 15, 2015, from http://www.slideshare.net/EdelmanInsights/2015-edelman-trust-barometer-global-results

Eurostat. (2014). *People at risk of poverty or social exclusion.* Retrieved November 15, 2015, from http://ec.europa.eu/eurostat/statistics-explained/index.php/People_at_risk_of_poverty_or_social_exclusion

Forum PA. (2013). *Are public employees in Italy too many?* Retrieved November 15, 2015, from http://www.forumpa.it/lavoro-e-welfare/i-dipendenti-pubblici-in-italia-sono-troppi (In Italian).

Furubotn, E. G., & Richter, R. (2005). *Institutions and economic theory: The contribution of the new institutional economics.* Ann Arbor, MI: University of Michigan Press.

Gjølberg, M. (2009a). Measuring the immeasurable? Constructing an index of CSR practices and performance in 20 countries. *Scandinavian Journal of Management, 25*, 10–22.

Gjølberg, M. (2009b). The origin of corporate social responsibility: Global forces or national legacies? *Socio-Economic Review, 7*, 605–637.

Grossman, S. J., & Hart, O. D. (1983). An analysis of the principal-agent problem. *Econometrica: Journal of the Econometric Society, 51*(1), 7–45.

Gudić, M., Parkes, C., & Rosenbloom, A. L. (Eds.) (2016). *Responsible management education and the challenge of poverty: A teaching perspective.* Sheffield: Greenleaf Publishing.

IMD World Competitiveness Center. (2015). *IMD world competitiveness yearbook.* Retrieved November 15, 2015, from http://www.imd.org/uupload/imd.website/wcc/Factor_sample.pdf

International Monetary Fund (IMF). (2012). *Fiscal transparency, accountability and risk.* Retrieved November 15, 2015, from http://www.imf.org/external/np/pp/eng/2012/080712.pdf

Ioannou, I., & Serafeim, G. (2012). What drives corporate social performance? The role of nation-level institutions. *Journal of International Business Studies, 43,* 834–864.

Jackson, G., & Apostolakou, A. (2010). Corporate social responsibility in Western Europe: An institutional mirror or substitute? *Journal of Business Ethics, 94*(3), 371–394.

Lapiccirella, A. (2015). On bureaucratic behavior. In M. Di Bitetto, A. Chymis, & P. D'Anselmi (Eds.), *Public management as corporate social responsibility: The economic bottom line of government* (pp. 103–118). Heidelberg: Springer International Publishing.

Midttun, A., Gautesen, K., & Gjølberg, M. (2006). The political economy of CSR in Western Europe. *Corporate Governance, 6*(4), 369–385.

Niskanen, W. A. (1968). The peculiar economics of bureaucracy. *The American Economic Review, 58*(2), 293–305.

Niskanen, W. A. (1975). Bureaucrats and politicians. *Journal of Law and Economics, 18*(3), 617–644.

Niskanen, W. A. (2001). Bureaucracy: A final perspective. In W. A. Shughart & R. Laura (Eds.), *The Elgar companion of public choice.* Cheltenham: Edward Elgar.

North, D. C. (1990). *Institutions, institutional change and economic performance.* Cambridge: Cambridge University Press.

North, D. C. (2005). *Understanding the process of economic change.* Princeton, NJ: Princeton University Press.

OECD. (2010). *Accountability and transparency: A guide for state ownership.* Retrieved November 15, 2015, from http://www.oecd.org/daf/ca/accountabilityandtransparencyaguideforstateownership.htm

OECD. (2015). Trust in government. In *Government at a glance.* Retrieved November15,2015,fromhttp://www.oecd-ilibrary.org/docserver/download/

4215081ec050.pdf?expires=1449011416&id=id&accname=guest&checksu m=CB945617E6DFC3948D883F8CB7E82618

Olson, M. (1982). *The rise and decline of nations: Economic growth, stagflation, and social rigidities*. New Haven, CT: Yale University Press.

Papadopoulos, T., & Triantopoulos, C. (2014). Dealing with 'unionistic' corporate governance in Greece. *Journal of Computational Optimization in Economics and Finance, 6*(1), 1–16.

Powell, W. W., & DiMaggio, P. J. (Eds.) (2012). *The new institutionalism in organizational analysis*. Chicago, IL: University of Chicago Press.

Ringov, D., & Zollo, M. (2007). The impact of national culture on corporate social performance. *Corporate Governance, 7*(4), 476–485.

Rodrik, D., Subramanian, A., & Trebbi, F. (2004). Institutions rule: The primacy of institutions over geography and integration in economic development. *Journal of Economic Growth, 9*(2), 131–165.

Sala-i-Martín, X., & Subramanian, A. (2003, June). *Addressing the natural resources curse: An illustration from Nigeria* (NBER Working Paper No. 9804). Cambridge, MA: National Bureau of Economic Research.

Skouloudis, A., & Evangelinos, K. (2012). A research design for mapping national CSR terrains. *International Journal of Sustainable Development & World Ecology, 19*(2), 130–143.

United Nations (UN). *Public administration and development management*. Department of Economic and Social Affairs. Retrieved November 15, 2015, from https://publicadministration.un.org/en/externalaudit

WEF. (2012). *Transparency for inclusive governance: An assessment of India*. Retrieved November 15, 2015, from http://www.weforum.org/reports/ transparency-inclusive-governance-assessment-india

Williamson, O. E. (1985). *Economic institutions of capitalism*. New York: Free Press.

Williamson, O. E. (2000). The new institutional economics: Taking stock, looking ahead. *Journal of Economic Literature, 38*, 595–613.

Wood, D. J. (2010). Measuring corporate social performance: A review. *International Journal of Management Reviews, 12*(1): 50–84.

World Bank (WB). (2015). *Accountability, transparency & integrity program*. Ongoing Project, Retrieved November 15, 2015, from http://www.world-bank.org/projects/P070544/accountability-transparency-integrity-program?lang=en

World Economic Forum (WEF). (2015). *Global competitiveness report 2015–2016*. Retrieved November 15, 2015, from http://www3.weforum. org/docs/gcr/2015-2016/Global_Competitiveness_Report_2015-2016.pdf

Part III

Corporate Responsibility in the "Post-Financial Crisis": Case Studies As discussed in previous cases

10

Exploring Post-Financial Crisis CSR Digital Communications by MNEs in Mexico

María Castillo and Virginie Vial

10.1 Introduction

The 2008 global financial meltdown has had direct economic consequences on resources available to companies, while painfully underlining the societal responsibilities borne by large financial institutions and MNEs in terms of the causes and consequences of the crisis, heightening society's expectations. In the face of this double constraint, companies' choices range from pure economic rationality of cutting costs by disregarding corporate social responsibility (CSR) issues to an increased awareness and engagement in CSR so as to deal with the causes and consequences of the crisis and consolidate a competitive advantage.

In both choices, corporate communication to restore, maintain, and improve trust, transparency, accountability, and stakeholder engagement become essential drivers of value and legitimacy, and are thus vital for

M. Castillo (✉) • V. Vial
Strategy Department, Kedge Business School, Marseille, France
e-mail: maria.castillo@kedgebs.com

© The Author(s) 2017
A. Theofilou et al. (eds.), *Corporate Social Responsibility in the Post-Financial Crisis Era*, Palgrave Studies in Governance, Leadership and Responsibility, DOI 10.1007/978-3-319-40096-9_10

177

corporate survival (Cornelissen 2014; Fernandez-Feijoo 2009; Jacob 2012, p. 259).

As an umbrella term *CSR* is defined as "actions that appear to further some social good, beyond the interests of the firm and that which is required by law" (McWilliams and Siegel 2001) and varies in the ways it is perceived, implemented, and communicated (Crane et al. 2008) according to the institutional context (Brammer et al. 2012). Context-specific social, economic, cultural, and historical elements can lead to a variety of communication styles dependent on the MNE's country of operations (Gjolberg 2009).

CSR communication (CSRC) augments corporate value through the enhancement of image and reputation (Schneider et al. 2007), establishing legitimacy (Schneider et al. 2007). CSRC reinforces stakeholder relations, potentially forming a "psychological bond" (Korschun et al. 2014, p. 21) between parties, addressing concerns through constructive reactions (Morsing and Schultz 2006) based on shared values. Finding the appropriate channels and messages to reach stakeholders therefore becomes central (Wanderley et al. 2008). CSR reports, corporate websites, and social media are the most commonly used CSRC channels. Providing more widespread and cost-effective ways to communicate, digital channels are trending, and, in a context of cost cutting and the necessity of a broader outreach, should dominate a firm's communications plan.

In addition to conventional periodical CSRC, social media enable companies to establish more informal conversations with their stakeholders and have changed the way business interacts with society. The rapid growth of tools such as Twitter and Facebook enables companies to increase awareness about their activities (Kaplan and Haenlein 2010) and engage a broader stakeholder base on a recurrent instant basis. By acquiring "followers" or "fans," companies create intimate bonds that enable more casual—but extremely powerful—ways to communicate. This bond enables a dialogue with stakeholders that was previously nonexistent, supporting the rapid propagation of messages (Qualman 2010), and providing instant feedback from the market (Lee et al. 2013).

The case of Mexico is interesting in two important aspects. First, Mexico is one of the emerging countries that is most directly affected by the global crisis through its tight economic and social relationships with the USA, where the crisis ignited. Second, although there is an increased interest in the study of CSR in emerging countries, few studies have looked at the way MNEs operating in such countries communicate CSR through digital channels.

This chapter is organized as follows. We first theoretically position the characteristics of CSR communication in a post-crisis era. We then describe the use of social media in Mexico. Third, we expose the methodological approach adopted to analyze the types of channels and messages through which the 50 largest MNEs in Mexico (CNN Expansion 2014) communicate CSR, comparing and contrasting traditional proprietary channels with the use of social media during the post-crisis period. We then present the main findings. Finally, we discuss the theoretical and practical implications.

10.2   Literature Review and Background

10.2.1 Corporate Social Responsibility

The field of CSR has evolved over the last decades and scholars have addressed issues such as CSR measurement, disclosure, performance, and strategy, among others. Even with such a diversity of research topics, the essence of CSR rests on the idea that "it reflects the social imperatives and the social consequences of business success" (Matten and Moon 2008, p. 2) and thus requires clearly communicating the CSR ideals and practices of companies to its wider stakeholder network (Matten and Moon 2008).

Globalization and technological advances have been the main drivers in the evolution of CSR (Jamali and Mirshak 2006; Scherer and Palazzo 2008). The growth of business and its increasing complexity have led to heightened expectations on transparency (Jamali and Mirshak 2006), and stakeholders seek to engage in dialogues with companies. Thus, studying the way companies communicate their CSR efforts in order to satisfy this need for transparency is of relevance.

10.2.2 Corporate Social Responsibility Communication

CSRC "is designed and distributed by the company itself about its CSR efforts" (Morsing and Schultz 2006) and is an essential element to coordinate social interaction with stakeholders that define the CSR practices of a company (Sorsa 2008). The importance of communicating CSR has become of interest both in academia and in practice (Golob et al. 2013), as more companies publish information on their CSR practices (Schmeltz 2012) through different communication channels.

Today, digital channels are preferred, enabling companies to publish information faster, cheaper, and reach a larger audience (Podnar 2008). Digital channel use also enables retrieving documents more easily, accessing up-to-date information from a variety of devices, and increasing and adapting interaction with stakeholders (Wanderley et al. 2008).

Companies have increased their CSRC efforts (Beckmann et al. 2006, pp. 11–36) to match the increased expectations of stakeholders regarding companies' engagement with society and the transparency of their actions. Because these expectations have increased in the post-financial crisis period, one should expect CSRC to escalate and that companies should take full advantage of social media channels.

Consumers desire to be informed about CSR practices and companies' compliance compared with their own expectations (Podnar 2008). However, stakeholder awareness tends to be relatively low (Lee et al. 2013). Companies' self-declarations regarding CSR activities are perceived as publicity, so society remains skeptical about their actual reach (Du et al. 2010; Lyon and Maxwell 2011), thus challenging companies to strike the right balance between awareness and suspicion (Lee et al. 2013). The use of social media amplifies messages in both directions, and corporations ought to proceed with caution in a context where public confidence has already been eroded.

Social media offer a comprehensive, cost-effective, broad-reach way to communicate about CSR and engage with stakeholders. However, those advantages represent a double-edge sword in cases of errors in communication. The distribution of CSRC between traditional digital means and social media therefore becomes an empirical issue to be explored.

10.2.3 Conventional CSR Communication: Corporate Websites and Annual Reports

The bulk of the literature focuses on corporate websites and annual reports, which represent the official vehicles for CSR (Wanderley et al. 2008). A study covering listed Spanish companies (Capriotti and Moreno 2007) finds that, although CSR is prominent on websites, the information focus is limited to corporate social and environmental actions. An analysis of 100 company websites in the United Kingdom, Germany, and Australia shows how websites serve CSR communication and engagement with stakeholders (Adams and Frost 2006). A survey of 127 company websites in eight emerging countries concludes that CSR web disclosure is dependent on country of origin and the specific industry (Wanderley et al. 2008).

10.2.4 Social Media Communication

Social media tools promote and facilitate instant and direct social interaction and engagement (Sweetser 2010). These include Facebook, Instagram, Twitter, LinkedIn, Google+, and YouTube. Social media attract millions of users daily and provide a massive communication platform, facilitating instant information, news, entertainment, socializing, and engaging with companies (He et al. 2013; Kaplan and Haenlein 2010).

For companies, it provides for an inexpensive, broad-range, powerful, and credible communication outlet. Increasing "social presence" (Short et al. 1976), or the perception that companies are accessible, has become essential. It contributes to business value creation by increasing customer loyalty and gaining competitive advantage (Porter and Kramer 2006). It supports and improves reputation and legitimacy through the establishment of a dialogue with society—in which parties engage in a conversation and both genuinely care about each other (De Bussy et al. 2003). Finally, social media use channels' responses to external expectations (Culnan et al. 2010; He et al. 2013; Kietzmann et al. 2011; Lee et al. 2013).

Because CSR has become important in the global business agenda, and as society members become more aware of the impact of business activities in their daily lives (Du et al. 2010), social media has developed into a central instrument for companies to communicate and directly engage with stakeholders on issues pertaining to the CSR domain (Fieseler et al. 2010).

10.2.5 CSR and CSR Communication in Mexico

Considering CSR as a "dynamic continuum of competing communicatively negotiated meanings" (Golob et al. 2013, p. 12), the understanding of contextual factors that determine and shape those meanings and interpretations of CSR is thus relevant. In the case of Mexico, the scarce literature on CSR in Mexico agrees that CSR is influenced by Catholic values, has been mostly based on philanthropy (de Oliveira 2006), and mainly addresses social issues (Casanova and Dumas 2010). Research has focused on different aspects of CSR, such as reporting, awareness, or local versus global norms, and shows that the Mexican CSR culture has evolved and moved away from its traditional philanthropic tendency and that social awareness is increasing (Weyzig 2006).

Reporting in Mexico has evolved from practices based on local norms to reporting that combines local and global norms (Meyskens and Paul 2010). In the early 2000s, CSR communication was embryonic—only two companies issued annual CSR reports, and only one of them followed Global Reporting Initiative (GRI) standards (Paul et al. 2006). A decade later, most large companies communicate CSR through their websites and annual reports, and they present economic gain as their main motivation (Amezaga et al. 2013).

The comparative analysis of traditional digital communication and social media proposed here aims to refine current knowledge about CSRC practices in Mexico and use it to illustrate the pattern of post-crisis CSRC.

10.2.6 The Use of Social Media in Mexico

With an estimated base of 53.9 million Internet users, the use of social media in Mexico is growing rapidly, from 17.5 million in 2013 to a forecasted 63.5 million in 2018 (Global Web Index 2015). In 2014, 94 percent of Mexican Internet users had at least one social media account, and 96 percent used social media daily (CIU 2015). Sixty-five percent of social media users are younger than 35 years old, with 33.2 percent falling in the 15–24 age range, and 22.3 percent in the 25–34 age range (ComScore 2015). Today, 22,799,780 people are connected to Facebook in Mexico (Facebook 2015).

Currently, Facebook and Twitter are two of the most used social media platforms around the world. In 2014, 51 million registered Mexican Facebook users represented 98 percent of Internet users (CIU 2015), and predictions set the number of Facebook users at 65.9 million by 2018 (Global Web Index 2015). The number of Twitter users in Mexico grew by 19 percent between 2014 and 2015, reaching 8.1 million, and is forecasted to attain 10.7 million users by 2018 (Global Web Index 2015).

10.3 Data and Methodology

In order to investigate the digital CSR communication practices of MNEs in the post-financial crisis period, and in line with the literature, we did a content analysis of the websites, online CSR reports, and social media content of the 50 largest MNEs in Mexico, as described in Table 10.1.

The sample was distributed across 16 industries, each comprising from one to nine companies. We selected these companies for their higher likelihood of attracting a larger audience because of their size, reputation, and greater resources devoted to communication.

Content analysis is a useful way to classify large amounts of textual data, enabling the data to be reduced into meaningful and smaller units, identifying major themes, and making inferences easy (Weber 1990, p. 5). Previous research suggests that content analysis is particularly well suited to researching CSR and sustainability reporting trends, because it permits a comprehensive evaluation of the disclosure items (Guthrie and Farneti 2008).

For each company, we first retrieved the official websites, analyzed them manually, and recorded the presence of the following items: CSR communication on website; dedicated CSR/sustainability report, CSR in integrated report, GRI guidelines compliance, and audit; and CSR communication through social media (Twitter and Facebook). This enabled us to obtain a first glance at the general digital CSRC pattern of the companies in the sample.

Table 10.1 List of the 50 largest MNEs in Mexico

Company name	Industry	Company name	Industry
12 General Motors de México	Automotive	5 CEMEX	Cement
13 Volkswagen de México		34 Mabe	Consumer goods
14 Nissan Mexicana		4 Grupo Carso	
17 Ford Motor Company México		10 Grupo Alfa	
20 Chrysler México		16 Grupo BAL	Holding
29 Flextronic Manufacturing Mexico	Electonics	22 Grupo Salinas	
41 Jabil Circuit Mexico		19 Infonavit	Housing
27 Grupo Televisa	Entertainment	44 Empresas ICA	Infrastructure
49 Cinepolis		46 Grupo Casa Saba	Medicine
50 Kidzania		36 Ternium México	Metals
7 BBVA Bancomer	Financial services	35 Industrias Peñoles	Mining
11 Banamex		1 PEMEX	
21 Santander de México		26 Alpek	Oil and related
23 Grupo Banorte		45 Mexichem	
33 HSBC México		3 Walmart de México	
42 MetLife México		15 Organización Soriana	
6 FEMSA	Food and beverages	25 Comercial Mexicana	
9 Grupo Bimbo		30 Chedraui	
			Retail
18 Grupo Modelo		31 El puerto de Liverpool	
24 Lala		38 Elektra	
28 Gruma		39 Grupo Coppel	
32 Cervecería Cuahutemoc Moctezuma		43 Grupo Sanborns	
37 Pepsico de México		2 América Móvil	
40 Nestlé México		8 Telmex	Telecommuni-cations
47 Grupo Sigma		48 Telefónica de México	

Source: CNN Expansion 2014 ranking

CSR/sustainability and integrated reports for 2014 were then downloaded for a first round of computerized content analysis using the NVivo software. We did not impose any specific CSR definitions and allowed key terms to emerge naturally from the data (Chapple and Moon 2005). We ranked the key terms results by occurrences, retaining all CSR-related terms appearing 100 times or more, and then regrouped them manually into the four broader CSR-related categories. This enabled us to produce a thesaurus of CSR-related terms that was specific to the companies in our sample, providing an overview of the dominant CSR themes communicated in the reports.

Finally, CSR-related tweets and Facebook posts from the Mexican MNEs' official accounts were retrieved. We extracted all tweets and Facebook posts issued between January 1 and August 31, 2015, that contained at least one of the key terms identified by the CSR/sustainability and integrated reports content analysis. We used Twitter's advanced search tool for tweets and extracted Facebook posts manually. Posts were subsequently classified into the four CSR-related categories identified during the integrated reports content analysis. Each post can only fall into one single category that corresponds to the key issue discussed.

Although all textual data were originally in Spanish, we present the results in English to provide an overview of the dominant CSR themes communicated through social media.

10.4 Results

10.4.1 Global Overview of Digital CSR/Sustainability Communication

We first depict in Fig. 10.1 the digital CSR communication distribution of the 50 largest MNEs in Mexico in the post-financial crisis period.

Corporate websites represent the preferred digital communication channel (44 companies, or 88 percent), with 39 of them referring to CSR on their main website, and five pointing to their philanthropic foundation website. Second, reports dealing with CSR/sustainability practices have been adopted by 37 companies (74 percent). Out of these, 31 companies publish specific CSR annual reports, and six include CSR reporting into their corporate annual report. It is important to highlight

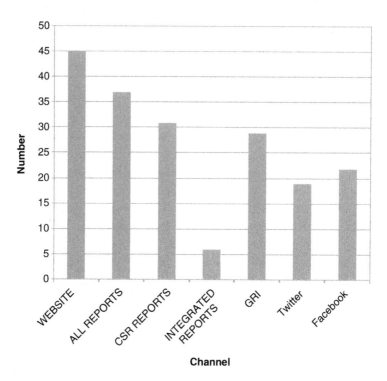

Fig. 10.1 Digital CSR communication distribution of the 50 largest MNEs in Mexico

that 78 percent of reports follow GRI guidelines and have been validated by external GRI auditors. Social media is the least used to communicate about CSR, with only 26 companies (52 percent) using at least one of the two selected platforms. An equal number of companies use Facebook (19, or 38 percent) and/or Twitter (19, or 38 percent).

Only 12 companies (24 percent) use both Twitter and Facebook.

10.4.2 CSR/Sustainability Reporting

The unconstrained computerized analysis of the CSR and integrated reports provided us with a list of CSR/sustainability-related key terms that we dispatched into four main categories: generic, social, environmental, and philanthropic (Table 10.2). When available, each company's report content

Table 10.2 Most recurrent CSR key terms in CSR and integrated reports grouped by category

Category (number of occurrences/percentage of total)	Key terms
Generic (1616/15 %)	Awards, recognitions, Distintivo ESR (firm award for social responsibility), CEMEFI, code of conduct, citizenship, stakeholder, human rights, CSR
Social (3166/29 %)	Community, volunteering, infrastructure development, literacy campaigns, health, nutrition, education, sports, social engagement, society, socially responsible
Environmental (5198/48 %)	Environment, energy reduction, water, pollution, recycling, waste, biodiversity, CO_2 emissions, sustainability
Philanthropic (861/8 %)	Foundations, philanthropy, donations, partnerships with philanthropic NGOs

covers the four main categories, although the scope of key terms and the presentation and depth of published information vary across the sample.

The *generic* category includes any CSR-related term that is generic enough to cover any of the subsequent three categories, which themselves depict specific areas of CSR. The *social* category refers to the social engagement of a company through mitigation of social problems in communities and the improvement of quality of life in society. The *environmental* category includes all information pertaining to environmental issues as well as the term *sustainability*. The *philanthropic* category includes information that refers to programs that companies fund through donations to a third party or their own foundations or NGOs. We note that our results coincide and complement the list of key terms found in the literature on CSR in Mexico (Meyskens and Paul 2010).

10.4.3 Social Media

Using the CSR key terms identified in the company reports, we collected a total of 283 Twitter and 373 Facebook CSR-related posts, for a total of 656 posts for the period covering January to August 2015, distributed among companies as shown in Table 10.3.

Table 10.3 Number of CSR posts and tweets by company (January–August 2015)

	Facebook		Twitter		Social media (total)		
Rank	Company	Posts	Company	Posts	Company	Posts	Rank
1	Bimbo	45	Bimbo	146	Bimbo	191	
2	Ternium	41	Femsa	47	Femsa	60	
3	Sigma	38	Telefonica	18	Telefónica	42	
4	Gruma Cervecería	28	Pepsi	13	Sigma	41	
5	Cuahutemoc Moctezuma	28	Gruma	11	Ternium	41	
6	Lala	25	Grupo Salinas	10	Gruma	39	
7	Telefónica	24	Nestle	6	Grupo Salinas	34	
8	Grupo Salinas	24	Santander	5	Lala Cervecría	30	
9	Pemex	21	Lala	5	Cuahutemoc Moctezuma	28	
10	General Motors	20	Banamex	4	Nestle	26	
11	Nestle	20	Cemex	4	Pemex	23	
12	Femsa	13	Sigma	3	General Motors	21	
13	Telmex	12	Kidzania	2	Pepsis	13	
14	Santander	8	Volkswagen	2	Santander	13	
15	Infonavit	8	Pemex	2	Telmex	12	
16	Cemex	6	Walmart	2	Cemex	10	
17	Bancomer	6	General Motors	1	Infonavit	8	
18	HSBC	5	MetLife	1	Bancomer	6	
19	Cinepolis	1	Ford	1	HSBC	5	
					Banamex	4	20
					Kidzania	2	21
					Volkswagen	2	22
					Walmart	2	23
					Cinepolis	1	24
					Ford	1	25
					MetLife	1	26
Total		373		283		656	

(continued)

Table 10.3 (continued)

| | Facebook | | Twitter | | Social media (total) | | |
| | Company | Posts | Company | Posts | Company | Posts | Rank |
Rank							
Average		19.6		14.9		25.2	
Median		20		4		13	
Min.		1		1		1	
Max.		45		146		191	
Sd Dev.		10.3		17.5		21.5	

Table 10.4 Posts by social media categories and by social network

Total %	Generic	Social	Environmental	Philanthropic
Facebook	12	43	37	8
Twitter	10	64	18	8
Social media (total)	11	52	29	8

Companies favor Facebook over Twitter in terms of numbers of posts. Basic summary statistics show that Facebook posts are relatively more homogeneously distributed across companies (with an average of 19.6 and a median of 20 posts) than Twitter posts (with an average of 14.9 and a median of 4 posts), further showing the dominance of Facebook over Twitter.

We then classify post content according to the four previously identified categories (generic, social, environmental, and philanthropic). Results are provided in Table 10.4.

Social media chiefly communicated messages in the *social* (52 percent) and *environmental* categories (29 percent), less so in the *generic* (11 percent) and *philanthropic* (8 percent) groups.

The *social* category was represented in 64 percent of all tweets, and 43 percent of Facebook posts. Common messages communicated social engagement initiatives in the areas of volunteering, infrastructure, sports, and health.

The *environmental* category appeared in 37 percent of Facebook posts and 18 percent of all tweets, communicating issues related to energy, water, paper consumption, ecology, and reforestation.

The *generic* category was present in 12 percent of Facebook posts and 10 percent of Twitter messages and mostly communicated about awards or certifications acquired by the companies, indicators, and promotion of social innovation and entrepreneurship contests.

Surprisingly, only 8 percent of tweets and Facebook posts fell into the *philanthropic* category. They mostly conveyed the work of the companies' foundations or donations made to other foundations.

The following chart summarizes our findings and put them into context (Fig. 10.2).

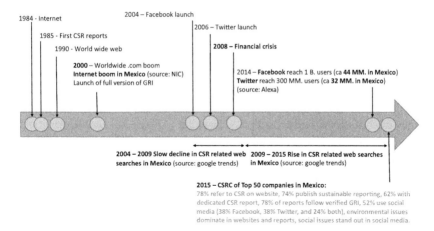

Fig. 10.2 Digital CSR communication of the top 50 largest companies in Mexico in context

10.5 Discussion and Conclusion

The results obtained through this exploration of CSR communication trends in Mexico show that there is a sort of bipolarity in the way the top MNEs communicate. On the one side, companies are actively engaged in conventional digital communication, publishing CSR information on their websites and providing CSR reports that are easily accessible and downloadable online. These results are consistent with Amezaga et al.'s (2013) findings showing that CSR communications in Mexico are "highly present" and concur with Meyskens and Paul's (2010) findings suggesting that large companies in Mexico are moving toward global standards in their communication and practices. Current conventional digital CSR communication practices also confirm that companies look to gain legitimacy by conforming to social expectations and by adopting institutionalized best practices and standards.

An explanation for this bipolarity could be the degree of maturity of CSR in Mexico. As was shown in Paul et al.'s (2006) study, in the early 2000s, most of the largest companies in Mexico were not communicating

CSR through conventional means, such as websites and annual reports. This, however, has clearly changed in the last 10–15 years, as our results show that 88 percent of the firms studied use their corporate website to communicate CSR, 74 percent of them publish CSR information through an annual CSR report or through its integrated annual report, and 78 percent of the companies that publish reports follow GRI guidelines and are externally verified. Thus, we can see an evolution in this specific communication segment, because this type of communication is not new and has existed for decades in developed countries, and because of globalization, competition, and heightened transparency expectations, particularly after the 2008 financial crisis, companies in an emerging country such as Mexico have progressively moved toward complying with global standards. Following this same line of thought, we could then predict that CSR social media communication is only at its early stages in Mexico, and thus, we could expect higher use in the next decade, once this type of CSR communication is well established in developed countries and CSR in Mexico reaches a higher degree of maturity.

Two different aspects might explain this lower percentage (Facebook and Twitter were used by 38 percent of companies, although not necessarily the same ones). The first is that CSR topics do not seem to be a communication priority when using social media to engage with stakeholders, because companies use their social media accounts as a platform for client service and a vehicle for product or service promotion. Also, some of the companies that do not communicate CSR through their official corporate account focus all of their CSR-related messages through their foundation social media account. However, these accounts only talk about the philanthropic work done by their foundation and were therefore not included in the analysis.

However, when looking at the use of social media to communicate CSR, results show a different picture, because only 52 percent of companies have used social media for this reason. Also, the social media use within companies for CSR is highly asymmetric in Mexico because some companies, such as Grupo Bimbo and FEMSA, are strongly engaged in communicating CSR through these platforms, whereas more than half of the companies rarely use these tools to communicate about CSR.

The potential to increase the use of social media to communicate CSR in Mexico exists because there is an impressive penetration of Facebook and Twitter. The audience is there and we know that CSR awareness exists (Muller and Kolk 2010); however, the generally low number of tweets and posts per company could also mean that interest in CSR issues from the company and the general public's perspectives is still low. This could be a consequence of a number of antecedents or processes that lead to the construction of messages (Riff et al. 2014) because company selection of information and judgment of what is demanded by its audience can be based on different conditions, shareholder expectations, or corporate strategies. Thus, the use of social media as an effective channel to communicate CSR needs to be further studied.

Future studies could include studying the engagement rate of CSR social media messages by looking at the numbers of retweets, shares, and likes that each post or tweet has in order to analyze the impact of CSR messages on the company stakeholders. Studying the interest of stakeholders in reading CSR tweets from companies could reveal if the low number of social media messages is a result of the company's strategy or the lack of general interest in the CSR topic.

This higher percentage of social messages could be explained by the fact that companies in Mexico still feel the need to act as facilitators of social and economic development. Furthermore, the institutional pressures and social expectations tend to determine the way companies respond and take action (Jackson and Apostolakou 2010), thus looking for initiatives that are socially acceptable and to gain legitimacy. Given that the literature classifies Mexico's CSR as mostly oriented toward philanthropy, this result was surprisingly low. This, however, could also be explained by the fact that official foundation accounts were not included in the analysis in order to provide an equal basis for analysis, because not all companies have Foundations.

References

Adams, C., & Frost, G. (2006). Accessibility and functionality of the corporate web site: Implications for sustainability reporting. *Business Strategy and the Environment, 15*(4), 275–287.

Amezaga, T., Wendlandt, R., Yan, H., & Cuervo, A. V. (2013). Socially responsible corporate communications in Mexico: Evidence of the large companies by their operational levels. *International Journal of Business and Management,* *8*(10), 144.

Beckmann, S., Morsing, M., & Reisch, L. (2006). *Strategic CSR communication: An emerging field.* Copenhagen: DJOF.

Brammer, S., Jackson, G., & Matten, D. (2012). Corporate social responsibility and institutional theory: New perspectives on private governance. *Socio-Economic Review, 10*(1), 3–28.

Capriotti, P., & Moreno, A. (2007). Communicating corporate responsibility through corporate web sites in Spain. *Corporate Communications: An International Journal, 12*(3), 221–237.

Casanova, L., & Dumas, A. (2010). Corporate social responsibility and Latin American multinationals: Is poverty a business issue? *Universia Business Review, 25,* 132–145.

Chapple, W., & Moon, J. (2005). Corporate social responsibility (CSR) in asia a seven-country study of CSR web site reporting. *Business & society, 44*(4), 415–441.

CIU. (2015). *Press release January 23, 2015.* Retrieved August 10, 2015, from http://www.the-ciu.net

CNN Expansion. (2014). Las 500 empresas mas importantes de Mexico. Retrieved May 2015, from www.cnnexpansion.com

ComScore. (2015). *State of social media in Mexico.* Retrieved August 20, 2015, from www.comscore.com

Cornelissen, J. (2014). *Corporate communication: A guide to theory and practice.* London: Sage Publications.

Crane, A., McWilliams, A., Matten, D., Moon, J., & Siegel, D. (Eds.) (2008). *The Oxford handbook of corporate social responsibility.* Oxford: Oxford University Press.

Culnan, M., McHugh, P., & Zubillaga, J. (2010). How large US companies can use twitter and other social media to gain business value. *MIS Quarterly Executive, 9*(4), 243–259.

de Oliveira, J. (2006). Corporate citizenship in Latin America: New challenges for business. *Journal of Corporate Citizenship, 21*(2), 17–20.

De Bussy, N., Ewing, M., & Pitt, L. (2003). Stakeholder theory and internal marketing communications: A framework for analyzing the influence of new media. *Journal of Marketing Communications, 9*(3), 147–161.

Du, S., Battacharya, C., & Sen, S. (2010). Maximizing business returns to corporate social responsibility (CSR): The role of CSR communication. *International Journal of Management Reviews, 12*(1), 8–19.

Facebook Ad Builder. (2015). Retrieved June 2015, from https://www.facebook.com/business/a/online-sales/ads-info

Fernandez-Feijoo, S. (2009). Crisis and corporate social responsibility: Threat or opportunity? *International Journal of Economic Sciences and Applied Research, 2*(1), 259.

Fieseler, C., Fleck, M., & Meckel, M. (2010). Corporate social responsibility in the blogosphere. *Journal of Business Ethics, 91*(4), 599–614.

Gjolberg, M. (2009). The origin of corporate social responsibility: Global forces or national legacies? *Socio-Economic Review, 7,* 605–637.

Global Web Index. (2015). *GlobalWebIndex's quarterly report on the latest trends in social networking.* Retrieved August 13, 2015, from https://www.globalwebindex.net

Golob, U., Podnar, K., Elving, W., Nielsen, A. E., Thomsen, C., & Schultz, F. (2013). CSR communication: Quo vadis? *Corporate Communications: An International Journal, 18*(2), 176–192.

Guthrie, J., & Farneti, F. (2008). GRI sustainability reporting by Australian public sector organizations. *Public Money Management, 28*(6), 361–366.

He, W., Zha, S., & Li, L. (2013). Social media competitive analysis and text mining: A case study in the pizza industry. *International Journal of Information Management, 33*(3), 464–472.

Jackson, G., & Apostolakou, A. (2010). Corporate social responsibility in Western Europe: An institutional mirror or substitute? *Journal of Business Ethics, 94*(3), 371–394.

Jacob, C. (2012). The impact of the financial crisis on corporate social responsibility and its implications for reputation risk management. *Journal of Management and Sustainability, 2*(2), 259.

Jamali, D., & Mirshak, R. (2006). Corporate social responsibility: Theory and practice in a developing country context. *Journal of Business Ethics, 72,* 243–262.

Kaplan, A., & Haenlein, M. (2010). Users of the world, unite! The challenges and opportunities of social media. *Business Horizons, 53*(1), 59–68.

Kietzmann, J., Hermkens, K., McCarthy, I., & Silvestre, B. (2011). Social media? Get serious! Understanding the functional building blocks of social media. *Business Horizons, 54*(3), 241–251.

Klement, P. (2008). Guest editorial: Communicating corporate social responsibility. *Journal of Marketing Communications, 14*(2), 75–81.

Korschun, D., Battacharya, C., & Swain, S. (2014). Corporate social responsibility, customer orientation, and the job performance of frontline employees. *Journal of Marketing, 78*(3), 20–37.

Lee, K., Won-Yong, O., & Kim, N. (2013). Social media for socially responsible firms: Analysis of fortune 500's Twitter profiles and their CSR/CSIR ratings. *Journal of Business Ethics, 118*(4), 791–806.

Lillian, W., Lucian, R., Farache, F., & Filho, J. (2008). CSR information disclosure on the web: A context-based approach analysing the influence of country of origin and industry sector. *Journal of Business Ethics, 22*(3), 369–378.

Lyon, T., & Maxwell, J. (2011). Greenwash: Corporate environmental disclosure under threat of audit. *Journal of Economics & Management Strategy, 20*(1), 3–41.

Matten, D., & Moon, J. (2008). "Implicit" and "explicit" CSR: a conceptual framework for a comparative understanding of corporate social responsibility. *Academy of management Review, 33*(2), 404–424.

McWilliams, A., & Siegel, D. (2001). Corporate social responsibility: A theory of the firm perspective. *Academy of Management Review, 26*(1), 117–127.

Meyskens, M., & Paul, K. (2010). The evolution of corporate social reporting practices in Mexico. *Journal of Business Ethics, 91*(2), 211–227.

Morsing, M., & Schultz, M. (2006). Corporate social responsibility communication: Stakeholder information, response and involvement strategies. *Business Ethics: A European Review, 15*(4), 323–338.

Muller, A., & Kolk, A. (2010). Extrinsic and intrinsic drivers of corporate social performance: Evidence from foreign and domestic firms in Mexico. *Journal of Management Studies, 47*(1), 1–26.

Paul, K., Cobas, E., Raul, C., Frithiof, M., Maas, A., Navarro, I., et al. (2006). Corporate social reporting in Mexico. *Journal of Corporate Citizenship, 22*, 67–80.

Podnar, K. (2008). Guest editorial: communicating corporate social responsibility. *Journal of Marketing Communications, 14*(2), 75–81.

Porter, M., & Kramer, M. (2006). The link between competitive advantage and corporate social responsibility. *Harvard Business Review, 84*(12), 78–92.

Qualman, E. (2010). *Socialnomics: How social media transforms the way we live and do business.* New York: John Wiley & Sons.

Riff, D., Lacy, S., & Fico, F. (2014). *Analyzing media messages: Using quantitative content analysis in research* (3rd ed.). New York: Routledge.

Scherer, A., & Palazzo, G. (2008). Globalization and corporate social responsibility. In A. Crane, A. McWilliams, D. Matten, J. Moon, & D. Siegel (Eds.), *The Oxford handbook of corporate social responsibility* (pp. 413–481). Oxford: Oxford University Press.

Schmeltz, L. (2012). Consumer-oriented CSR communication: Focusing on ability or morality? *Corporate Communications: An International Journal, 48*(2), 29–49.

Schneider, A. M., Stieglitzand, S., & Lattemann, C. (2007). Social software as an instrument of CSR. *Proceedings of ICT, Transparency and Social Responsibility*, Lisbon, Portugal.

Short, J., Williams, E., & Christie, B. (1976). *The social psychology of telecommunications*. New York: Wiley.

Sorsa, V. P. (2008). How to explain socially responsible corporate actions institutionally: Theoretical and methodological critique. *Electronic Journal of Business Ethics and Organization Studies, 13*(1), 32–41.

Sweetser, K. (2010). A losing strategy: The impact of nondisclosure in social media on relationships. *Journal of Public Relations Research, 22*(3), 288–312.

Wanderley, L. S. O., Lucian, R., Farache, F., & de Sousa Filho, J. M. (2008). CSR information disclosure on the web: a context-based approach analysing the influence of country of origin and industry sector. *Journal of Business Ethics, 82*(2), 369–378.

Weber, R. (1990). *Basic content analysis*. Newbury Park: Sage Publications.

Weyzig, F. (2006). Local and global dimensions of corporate social responsibility in Mexico. *Journal of Corporate Citizenship, 24*, 69–81.

11

Value Chain and CSR of Global Pharmaceutical Companies: *A Framework to Define Practices*

Nathalie Gimenes and Marielle A. Payaud

11.1 Introduction

The pharmaceutical industry is situated at the crossroads of humanitarian problems, ethical requirements, regulatory constraints, and major economies. Healthcare, defined as a human need recognized as a right by the United Nations (Turcotte and Pasquero 2007, p. 200), is considered as a public good under the responsibility of governments. However, the fact that medical innovation is the product of private R&D rather than public (Mills 2002) makes global pharmaceutical companies the central performer of humanitarian and economic development (Boidin and Lesaffre 2011). Although this industry is recognized as a leader in

N. Gimenes (✉) • M.A. Payaud
IAE Lyon—Université Jean Moulin Lyon 3, Centre de Recherche Magellan, Lyon cedex 08, France

© The Author(s) 2017
A. Theofilou et al. (eds.), *Corporate Social Responsibility in the Post-Financial Crisis Era*, Palgrave Studies in Governance, Leadership and Responsibility, DOI 10.1007/978-3-319-40096-9_11

"industrial sustainability" (Schneider et al. 2010, p. 421), it is still the object of numerous criticisms and controversies putting on the front page its corporate social responsibility (CSR). As such, investigating the manner in which global pharmaceutical companies contribute to a better society appears significant.

How can we define the responsible behaviors and practices in the pharmaceutical industry? Given the underlying question, how do these pharmaceutical companies carry out their activities in order to produce a positive impact on society? (Jenkins 2009). This chapter offers some insights into these questions. For this purpose, the authors constructed a framework. This framework is an extension of the taxonomy of the CSR strategies of Martinet and Payaud (2008), which, when looking at the value chain, identifies the dominant logics used by firms, in order to meet social expectations. During a financial crisis, societal awareness intensifies, inviting companies to deploy more CSR practices. The taxonomy of Martinet and Payaud enables forms of CSR exercises to be identified in this context. This framework fits in the CSR sociocognitive approach according to the classification of Gond (2011). It offers a heuristic reasoning to facilitate the understanding of the cooperative strategies used by firms and to qualify and characterize the socially responsible behavior of companies. The first section explains this demonstration. The second section presents the framework's results obtained through an exploratory study for the ten biggest global pharmaceutical companies. They offer examples from these companies to describe their CSR projects. At the end, the chapter derives a bigger picture of the responsible behaviors and practices deployed by global pharmaceutical companies toward society. The financial crisis has had an impact on public health budgets; the chapter studies implicitly the manner in which global pharmaceutical companies develop their CSR approach in order to meet societal challenges including innovation, access of care for everyone, and the protection of the patients.

11.2 How Can We Define the Responsible Behaviors and Practices in the Pharmaceutical Industry? A Framework to Identify Practices along the Value Chain

How far does the responsibility of the company extend? The justification of the implementation of CSR within the company matches the representation that managers have about the role and the raison d'être of his own company (Capron and Quairel-Lanoizelée 2004). Tackling the question of CSR for a company thus implies consulting the main purpose of the activities themselves (Hoffmann and Saulquin 2009). From this point, the authors propose in this section some elements which defend the idea that the engagement of a company in a real CSR entails taking into consideration the challenges throughout the value chain. This approach takes into account the society as an influencing participant of CSR theory formation (Acquier et al. 2011). Firstly, they will show how this vision leads us in a CSR sociocognitive approach (Gond 2011).

11.2.1 Theoretical Scope: CSR as a Sociocognitive Construction

Companies evolve in society and not only in a market (Martinet 1984). By being situated at the company–society interface, CSR raises the question of the role of the company in society and the level of its social engagement beyond the legal frame (Turcotte and Pasquero 2007, p. 220). It deals with the relations between various actors which have more or less interests in common. The analysis of this interface explains the complex and multiform character of CSR and that is why its conceptualization is an ongoing construction. Academic publications underline that CSR is suffering from the lack of consensus on its definitions (Gond 2011, p. 38). For certain authors, if the notion of CSR was always vague, it is due to a lack of analysis of its "pluralist character inherited by its sociological version" (Gond 2011, p. 39). This is because, intrinsically, "the notion of CSR spreads not only the representation of the company, but also the representation of the society" (Gond 2011, p. 39). Gond (2011, p. 44) proposes to adapt the sociological lecture grid of Burell and Morgan (1979) to the field of management, in order to place a framework to the analysis of the theories in the work of CSR when the latter is designed by the prism of the company–society interface (Gond and Igalens 2014, pp. 44–59). The theoretical frame of Burell and Morgan (1979) aims to structure and sort the theories of the social world, derived from their political origins (Gond 2011) to the approaches of the theory of the organizations (Lewis and Grimes 1999). This graph consists of two axes. The first epistemological and methodological axis allows making a choice by which the investigators conceive the observed reality. Through a positivist and objectivist approach, the social reality exists independently from the observer. On the other hand, from a subjectivist approach, the social reality is dependent on the observer and the very fact that to seek understanding participates in its construction. The second axis of the graph specifies two research orientations, studies which aim to analyze the mechanisms of the social regulation, and those which aim to reflect on social change. It is due to this that Gond (2011, p. 45) defines four perspectives on the company–society interface, allowing the establishment of four different visions: Functionalist, Sociopolitical, Culturalist, and Constructivist. The author identifies research questions for each perspective (see Table 11.1).

How can we define the responsible behaviors and practices in the pharmaceutical industry? This research question justifies a position in the studies which propose a sociocognitive vision of CSR. According to this perspective, CSR defines itself as "a product which is temporarily stable from a negotiation between the company and society, putting into play the identities, the values and the social problems" (Gond and Igalens 2014, p. 55). The companies and the stakeholders constantly negotiate the challenges brought by the concept of CSR in accordance with a *negotiated order*, with the possibility to reevaluate according to the strategies of all parties (Gond and Igalens 2014, p. 56). In this vision, the parties are free to propose new solutions of CSR, recalling the *voluntary* character of the concept, defended by the European Commission (EC). The EC indeed defines CSR as a concept in which the companies integrate the social, environmental, and economic preoccupations in their activities

Table 11.1 Research questions per form of CSR prospect (Adapted from Gond 2011)

CSR prospect	Illustrative research questions
Functionalist	• How does CSR benefit society? • How can we improve corporate profitability and social welfare simultaneously?
Sociopolitical	• How does the company influence society through CSR policies? • What are the limits of corporate power in the societal choices?
Culturalist	• How can the organizational culture facilitate CSR development? • How do societal values disseminate and circulate within the organization?
Constructivist	• What are the strategies of the actors to fit the definition of CSR? • How does a social group become cognitively a stakeholder?

and their interactions with their stakeholders on a voluntary basis (Gond and Igalens 2014, p. 23). The EC invites all the involved parties to collaborate around the projects, allowing the deployment of a policy of CSR to be favored for the general interest. It also proposes to conceive the company as a *partner* which accepts to share the responsibilities with other involved parties. This multi-stakeholder partnership between the private, public, commercial, and non-commercial parties can become a solution for the general interest. Consequently, the way to define the responsible behaviors and practices of a company could be predicted through the relations and the projects deployed with stakeholders. The taxonomy of Martinet and Payaud (2008) offers this possibility, because the taxonomy allows the ways and means of cooperation adopted by the companies with the various stakeholders to be established.

11.2.2 Evolution of a Taxonomy of CSR Strategies: A Framework

The taxonomy of CSR strategies proposed by Martinet and Payaud (2008, p. 200) is intended to identify "ways and means of cooperation with various partners" while providing a priority of CSR practices (see

Table 11.2 Taxonomy of CSR' strategies of Martinet and Payaud (2008)

| Stakeholders | Friedman' enterprise (profit for profit) | Make up CSR | | | | |
		Cosmetic CSR	Peripheral CSR	Integrated CSR	BOP CSR	Social enterprise
Principal company and/ or its subsidiaries						
Business partners						
Social(s) enterprise						
No-Profit organization						
Population shopkeepers						
Government and/or local authorities						

Table 11.2). The taxonomy can be used to classify the CSR practices of a plurality of firms (Martinet and Payaud 2008, p. 201). The authors locate four levels of strategic commitment to CSR, from the weakest to the most intense: cosmetic CSR, peripheral, integrated and the CSR-BOP Bottom of The Pyramid. These four columns show six types of stakeholders within which the company can build co-responsible partnerships: The principal company and/or its subsidiaries; Business partners; Social Enterprise; No-Profit organization; Population shopkeepers, and Government and/or local authorities. This taxonomy reveals a minimum of 24 possibilities of collaborative situations resulting in dispersions of the CSR strategy practices.

The actions which come from the base of a cosmetic CSR are the actions qualified as being light, that aim only to fulfill the legal conditions, without a permanent project using the stakeholders. The so-called peripheral CSR describes the actions of the involved CSR but without a direct connection with the activities of the company. Gifts to charities supporting a particular societal project come into this category. The integrated CSR thus concerns the implicated actions in relation to the activities of the company. They, therefore, impact its performance. These are measurable actions on the piloting chart on the balance score-card or the sustainability score-card in the KPMG office (Klynved Main Goerdeler, KMG; Peat Marwick International, PMI) (Martinet and Payaud 2008, p. 203). The CSR-BOP, bottom of the pyramid, concerns the actions which apply to people living off less than two dollars per day. The companies willing to help such people choose to put in place radical innovation policies which affect prices, the product, and the methods of management at the same time, enabling them to create an economically viable environment (Martinet and Payaud 2008, p. 203). A large number of responsible practices were developed over the last ten years due to the multi-stakeholder partnerships, integrating in a more operational manner the companies with local issues (Martinet and Payaud 2009, 2010). The analysis of the partnerships that the company will build is essential for the evaluation of the responsible practices work (Martinet 2006, pp. 9–18). Identifying these partnerships along the value chain allows researchers to understand how its relations contribute to a better society. In this reflection, the value chain allows the company to select the CSR challenges at each stage. A number of stakeholders intervene along the value chain it is, thus, the occasion for the company to create partnerships to solve sustainable issues identified. The taxonomy of Martinet and Payaud (2008, p. 201) allows the "form of the CSR exercises" to be defined. The taxonomy does not seek to qualify one company or one industry in particular. With the aim of defining the responsible practices deployed by global pharmaceutical companies, the authors propose to develop the taxonomy in order to have it in direct view of the value chain (see Table 11.3). They propose to add another column, to inform about CSR issues in which companies have chosen to be involved. Issues identify steps of the value chain that projects impact. The number of projects that were identified with the implementation of the taxonomy is reported per form of CSR along the value chain. The stakeholders are mentioned in the framework to visualize to what extent the maintained relations with them contribute to the social, environmental, and economic issues. The scope of the analysis proposes a heuristic method allowing response to questions such as: What level of the value chain do companies get involved in? (column Value Chain) In response to what challenge of CSR? (column CSR Issues)

Table 11.3 A framework to define CSR along the value chain

Value Chain	CSR issues	Stakeholders	Number of CSR projects					Distribution of the number of projects/ value chain in %
			cosmetic CSR	peripheral CSR	integrated CSR	BOP CSR	TOTAL CSR projects	
		TOTAL						
Projects outside the value chain								
		TOTAL projects						
		Distribution of the number of projects /Forms of CSR in%						

What responsibilities do companies think it must assume towards the society?

Values contribution of companies towards the society?

Forms of CSR exercises?

With what kind of partners? (column Stakeholders) For which projects and for which practices? (column Number of CSR projects).

The proposed reasoning translates the companies' willingness to consider the repercussions of its activities on society and reflects the obligations which they think it must assume toward it. The authors consider this approach pertinent for the global pharmaceutical companies because the CSR investigation is complex as it covers the product, management practices, and the mission which holds the industry together all at the same time (Turcotte and Pasquero 2007, p. 199).

11.3   An Exploratory Study in the Pharmaceutical Industry

11.3.1 Methodology

This qualitative study is based on the analysis of websites and CSR reports from 2013 of the top ten global pharmaceutical firms in terms of turnover, representing 39.7 percent of the world market (IMS-Health): Novartis, Pfizer, Sanofi, Merck&Co, Roche, GSK: GlaxoSmithKline, Johnson & Johnson, AstraZeneca, Teva, and Lilly. The CSR reports take into consideration the interests of the different stakeholders and take part in a process of negotiation and transaction (Hoffmann and Saulquin 2009, p. 44). In that, they represent the relevant secondary data to analyze with the goal of a constructivist approach. The authors complete this collection of secondary data with the observational and various expert reports. "The type of information which was researched does not require deepening by the data collection from the primary source" (Martinet and Payaud 2008, p. 201) due to their objective character. The CSR reports from global pharmaceutical companies clearly describe the projects for which they were engaged. It is, therefore, possible to find the goal of the action, the partners associated with the projects, the time taken, and the expected and/or obtained results. Each project is the object of an analysis, thus enabling the study to proceed with several mini-cases. These projects fit into issues which are well defined by pharmaceutical managers. The authors identified 12 of these (see Table 11.4).

Table 11.4 Main CSR issues defined by pharmaceutical companies

	CSR issues—What challenges?
1	Access to drugs and care
2	Innovation
3	Ethical business
4	Patient safety, quality of life, information and medical training, the "good use" of the drug
5	Education
6	Environmental protection
7	Health development
8	Protecting employees—Professional equalities—Diversity
9	Ethical research
10	Governance
11	Economic responsibility
12	Purchasing and responsible production

To specify these major issues for which pharmaceutical managers claim to base their projects is an important step since they implicitly interpret the challenges related to the CSR sector along the value chain. Three hundred and thirty projects have been identified.

The researchers first employed the taxonomy on the strategies of CSR of Martinet and Payaud (2008) for each of the ten pharmaceutical groups as recommended by the authors. They counted the number of projects per form of CSR and along the value chain, and they reported the number of projects in their framework.

11.4   Results

11.4.1 On What Stages of the Value Chain Is the Pharmaceutical Industry Engaged? To Respond to Which Challenges?

Table 11.5 structures the analysis. It shows that the commitments of CSR in the pharmaceutical companies' studied rest on all the stages of the value chain. They, therefore, revolve around their job, their mission, and the peripheral actions representing only 4 percent of the total actions which were gathered in the study. The pharmaceutical industry is an

Table 11.5 Defining CSR at the top ten biggest pharmaceutical companies

| Drug value chain | CSR issues | Stakeholders | Number of CSR projects | | | | | | Distribution of the number of projects/value chain in % |
			Cosmetic CSR	Peripheral CSR	Integrated CSR	BOP CSR	TOTAL projects	
Raw material	Purchasing and responsible production (12)	The focal companies and/ or their subsidiaries, business partners, (suppliers); Authorities	10		10		20	6 %
R&D	Innovation (2) Ethical research (9)	Business partners (Biotech); Academic research, Hospitals, Social organization; No-Profit organization	10		35	17	62	19 %

(continued)

Table 11.5 (continued)

Drug value chain	CSR issues	Stakeholders	Number of CSR projects					Distribution of the number of projects/value chain in %
			Cosmetic CSR	Peripheral CSR	Integrated CSR	BOP CSR	TOTAL projects	
Drug approval manufacturing and distribution	Access to care (1) Economic responsibility (11) Governance (10)	Authorities; No-Profit organization. Social organization; Business partners, Hospitals	12		43	32	87	27 %
Sales	Ethical business (3) Protecting employees— Professional equalities— Diversity (8)	The focal companies and/or their subsidiaries, Authorities, Business partners	10		24		34	11 %
Drug use by patients	Patient safety, quality of life, information and medical training, the "good use" of the drug, proximology (4) Healthcare development (7)	Business partners, Social organization. Hospitals, population, shopkeepers, No-Profit organization	10		38	24	72	23 %

Drug value chain	CSR issues	Stakeholders	Number of CSR projects					
			Cosmetic CSR	Peripheral CSR	Integrated CSR	BOP CSR	TOTAL projects	Distribution of the number of projects/value chain in %
Management post drug use	Environmental protection (6)	Authorities. Business partners, Social organization. No-Profit organization	6		35	2	43	14 %
		TOTAL	58		185	75	318	
Projects outside the value chain	Education (5)			6			6	
	Environmental protection not related to drug (6)			6			6	
		TOTAL projects	58	12	185	75	330	
		Distribution of the number of projects/Forms of CSR in %	18 %	4 %	56 %	23 %		

engaged sector, 56 percent of the actions are integrated and 23 percent of these are at the service of the poorer population across the BOP programs. These first results corroborate other studies which prove that the pharmaceutical sector is recognized as a leader in industrial sustainability (Gateaux and Heitz 2008; Schneider et al. 2010; PWC 2013).

The innovation, the access to care for everyone, and the protection of the patients are three major issues which account for statistically 19, 27, and 23 percent of the total projects that were studied. They specify the challenges that the global pharmaceutical laboratories want to assume toward the society in particular. Therein, the authors will focus the analysis of this communication on them.

The CSR challenges identified along the value chain aim to respect the implied contract which links the pharmaceutical companies to society. For a number of authors, the establishment of the license to the protection of the intellectual property forms the basis of this contract. On the one hand, society protects the companies by guaranteeing the return of the investments, on the other hand, society expects laboratories that they financially invest in the research of revolutionary molecules to respond to the medical needs which are still unsatisfied, while being in a position of responsibility (Turcotte and Pasquero 2007, p. 214).

11.4.2 With Which Partners? For Which Practices and with Which Projects?

The stakeholders with whom the global pharmaceutical companies negotiate and put in place its responsible projects are public, private, commercial, and non-commercial partners.

Innovation. Investing in research of medications to respond to the medical needs which are still unsatisfied, such as certain types of cancer, orphan diseases, and tropical diseases affecting third-world countries, is the responsible behavior which is expected by society.

Pharmaceutical manufacturers have understood the challenge of responsible innovation by registering it in an efficient restructuring of their R&D and for better productivity. The nature of the diseases targeted by new drugs is more complex and scarcer, and many molecules are being tested and many of them fail in clinical trials in humans

(Cavazzana-Calvo and Debiais 2011). In order to provide more upstream potential impact of a molecule and thus improve their productivity, the laboratories are developing new public and private multidisciplinary collaborations (Boidin and Lesaffre 2011, p. 332) with the goal of a better understanding of the physiopathology of diseases. For example, "Roche Partnering signed 73 new agreements in 2013, including eight product transactions, 54 research and technology collaborations and 11 products out licensing agreements" (Roche 2013a, p. 45) and AstraZeneca: "We are creating a more porous research environment that will help us Achieve Scientific Leadership by fostering collaboration between scientists both within and outside AstraZeneca" (AstraZeneca 2013, p. 37). These alliances are sealed under the form of licenses or R&D contracts (Belis Bergouignan et al. 2014). These rational expert partnerships transform the clinic research procedure and contribute to the progressive emergence of the biotechnological medications. These offer new therapeutically hope in treating more or less long-term, serious pathologies not benefiting hitherto an efficient treatment (Cavazzana-Calvo and Debiais 2011). The research on biotechnological medications targets a particular patient to the singular genomic profile: it demands an ethical, cultural, and environmental adaptation (Boidin and Lesaffre 2011). This is why certain pharmaceutical firms choose to create research facilities in emerging and developing countries, meeting thereby the societal needs of the latter in terms of public health policies. For example, "The Novartis Institutes for BioMedical Research (NIBR) is the innovation engine of Novartis. Its goal is to change the practice of medicine and it is achieving this primarily by discovering novel medicines that address unmet patient needs" (Novartis 2013, p. 26).

Access to treatments for everyone. The health authorities are the privileged partners at the core of discussions about the access to treatments. The financial resources are very unbalanced from one state to the other. The lack of harmonization of practices between countries obliges the laboratories to adapt their CSR strategies according to the local needs and the social expectations which are more or less wide. The pharmaceutical laboratories aware of these societal and economic stakes have gradually transformed their market access approach. With their subsidiaries, these companies create real operational structures entirely dedicated to access to medicines. Building the most efficient project with authorities to make drugs available to patients is the mission of these Market Access departments. Currently, these new governance standards allow the pharmaceutical industry to fully play its role in access to medicines in poor countries. To illustrate: "Johnson & Johnson strives to provide leadership in advancing a world in which all people have access to affordable, innovative and sustainable solutions for healthy living. Market access is determined by Policy and Regulatory constructs we must navigate to ensure our products and services can be accessed health by patients" (Johnson and Johnson 2013a, p. 26).

The access to care for everyone and the relocation of the facilities of R&D enter also in the biggest scope of development of the multi-stakeholder partnerships, which are at the core of the BOP programs in health. However, beyond the financial constraints that require innovation and access to medication, developing countries lack medical structure to ensure a delivery of care and products in the appropriate sanitary conditions. The necessity of a global and collaborative approach progressively imposed itself (Mills 2002). Thereby, the compromises which seal the cooperative strategies permit the raising of funds, competence, and expertise from R&D (Mills 2002). The partnership between Sanofi and the Drugs for Neglected Initiative permitted the development of the ASAQ, a combined medication to fight against malaria at a fixed dosage making it easier to use (Sanofi 2013, p. 23). GSK and the Bill & Melinda Gates Foundations (BMGF) are working jointly in order to develop vaccinations which are more resistant to heat, thus reducing the need for refrigeration. GSK and BMGF are dedicating a combined sum of 1.8 million dollars (GSK 2013a). The donation programs of Mectizan* and of albendazole including respectively that Merck&Co and GSK aim to eradicate river blindness and lymphatic filariasis. They rest on the long-term partnerships between World Health Organization (WHO), the World Bank, Task Force for Global Health, African Program for Onchocerciasis Control, Onchocerciasis Elimination Program for the Americas, health authorities, development organizations, and local communities in the countries concerned (WHO 2013; Donation Mectizan* Program 2013). Since 1987, in the fight against river blindness, Merk&Co have donated nearly USD 5.1 billion, that is 1 billion doses of Mectizan* to more than 117,000 communities in 36 equatorial African and Latin American countries as well as Yemen (Merck&Co 2014). GSK "commits itself to supply albendazole to treat one billion people in more than 80 countries. GSK equally provides subsidies and personal expertise to support the formation activities and communication with the World Alliance for the elimination of lymphatic filariasis" (GSK 2013b, p. 52). Since 2003, "the Lilly group through its "Lilly MDR-TB" carries the ambition to stop the spread of multi-drug resistant tuberculosis (MDR-TB). This program is done in collaboration with WHO. It is based on a transfer of technology and expertise in the production of antibiotics, but also in the establishment of health monitoring and implementation of training programs on prevention for nursing staff. MDR-TB kills more than 150,000 people each year. Lilly group has already contributed $ 135 million for this program" (Lilly 2013, p. 14).

A number of other examples of BOP projects could have been cited confirming the commitment of the pharmaceutical companies at their partners' side, to respond to a major societal issue which is the access to treatments in poorer countries.

The protection of the patients. The global pharmaceutical companies integrate the challenge of the protection of the patients at the core of its value propositions. Collaboration with private enterprises, associations of patients, NGOs, hospitals and authorities allows them to develop a global services approach around this medication. These are aid programs for the proper use of the drug, medical training and teaching tools to accompany patients to better understand their disease and their treatments. Concretely, the laboratories propose Support Programs to Patients. For example, the program of Sanofi, developed alongside the Mezzanine society, offers to new patients suffering from diabetes an educational and nurse-escort program and a monitoring by SMS (Sanofi 2013, p. 19).

11.4.3 Values Contribution of the Pharmaceutical Industry Toward the Society

Social contributions from industrialists take several forms:

1. Recurring and controlled medication donations using the example of Johnson and Johnson, through its Foundation, offers patients undergoing financial difficulty access to its medications for free and com-

pletes this process via an assisted program from Janssen, its pharmaceutic subsidiary. The program guides patients through the administrative process, while directing them toward humanitarian aid that would eventually accompany them through their period of illness. Between 2011 and 2013, the Foundation provided more than two million medications to over 300,000 patients in the USA (Johnson and Johnson 2013a, b). Pfizer proposes the same type of program under the name RxPathways™ (Pfizer 2013).

2. Laboratories adopt strategies of varying prices in order to adapt to circumstances in local sanitary facilities. They propose price reductions and discounts for NGOs, national organizations as well as bringing an end to exploitation rights (to allow firms that produce generic medications to sell them at a lower price). Thus, Roche committed themselves not to file intellectual protection patents within the poorest countries (Gateaux and Heitz 2008, p. 11).

3. They enrich their proposal of value aimed at health care professionals, patients and their families as well as supporting authorities developing sanitary structures. In certain countries, the contribution could become a technological transfer, integrating industrial expertise of R&D, training in medical services on the consequences when misused, patient protection and reinforcing the sanitary systems. In return, the laboratories can benefit from tax credits or be insured in advance by the purchase of their medical innovations that come at a certain price, a certain quantity, and within a specific time frame (Palazzo and Wentland 2011).

11.5   Discussion and Main Limitation

How can we then characterize the socially responsible behavior of the pharmaceutical industry? The analysis confirms that the implementation of responsible actions is strongly linked to respecting the implicit contract which links it to society. This is why strategies are driven by the parent company. The social expectations are integrated along the value chain, impacting business models. According to Teva "Our Corporate Social Responsibility program is a natural complement to our core business activities" (Teva 2013, p. 6), for Novartis "Responsibility is a core part of our business strategy" (Novartis 2015) and Roche "Sustainability is an integral part of the way we do business—now and in the future" (Roche 2013b). This final idea offers some prospects of research to provide insights into the role of CSR in transforming business.

It appears that global pharmaceutical companies do not evoke a particular change CSR management after the financial crisis and they adopt the same CSR strategy. This industry seems to have, therefore, taken the decision to work together for common good. Does the generalization of these practices in the developing countries, through behavioral mimicry in this industry contribute to the emergence of what Vogel calls "The Market for Virtue"? (Vogel 2006).

The main limitation is related to the data collection during the exploratory study. The authors needed to identify responsible projects according to the definition proposed by Martinet and Payaud (2008). The identification of the socially responsible projects also appears difficult because there are not any homogeneous guidelines in the structure of CSR reports. This mass of information requires a lot of time for deciphering, not to mention the possibility of a qualitative and/or quantitative error during the collection. Studying a significant quantity of responsible projects, here 330, allows the potential margin of error to be limited.

11.6 Conclusion

The goal of this chapter was to look at the manner in which global pharmaceutical companies carry out their activities in order to produce a positive impact on society. To answer this, the authors constructed a framework that allows responsible practices deployed by the global pharmaceutical companies to be detected along the value chain. Therefore, the authors initially showed that being at a company–society interface, CSR deals with relations between varying partners having more or less interests in common. Thus, CSR appears as an opportunity for dialogue and negotiations. In that role, it appears almost like a negotiated mandate, establishing itself as much in the construction of the company's practices as in the resulting dynamics within society. This is why the analysis of partnerships which the company can create proves to be essential to define the responsible practices (Martinet 2006, pp. 9–18). In this purpose, the contribution of the taxonomy of Martinet and Payaud (2008) is very important because it allows cooperative strategies used by firms to be established. Identifying the implementation of these cooperative strategies along the value chain enables CSR to be placed as a business opportunity contributing to social, environmental, and economic needs of stakeholders. The framework allows for a descriptive analysis into this idea. In the pharmaceutical industry, partnerships seem to have allowed divergences of interest to be transcended for global common good. Partnerships may be a serious strategy in order to meet societal challenges in the post-financial crisis.

References

Acquier, A., Daudigeos, T., & Valiorgue, B. (2011). Corporate social responsibility as an organizational and managerial challenge: The forgotten legacy of the corporate social responsiveness movement. *M@ N@ Gement, 14*(4), 222–250.

AstraZeneca. (2013). *AstraZeneca CSR Report.* Retrieved September 15, 2014, from http://astrazeneca-annualsreport.com/2013/

Bergouignan, B., Claude, M., Montalban, M., Sakinç, M. E., & Smith, A. (2014). *L'industrie pharmaceutique Régles, acteurs et pouvoir.* Paris: La ducumentation Française.

Boidin, B., & Lesaffre, L. (2011). L'accès Des Pays Pauvres Aux Médicaments et La Propriété Intellectuelle: Quel Apport Des Partenariats Multiacteurs? *Revue Internationale de Droit économique, 24*(3), 325–350.

Burell, G., & Morgan, G. (1979). *Sociological Paradigms and Organization Analysis. Elements of Sociology of Corporate Life.* Newcastle: Athenaeum Press.

Capron, M., & Quairel-Lanoizelée, F. (2004). *Mythes et réalités de L'entreprise responsable.* Paris: La Découverte.

Cavazzana-Calvo, M., & Debiais, D. (2011). *Biomédicament, économie et innovation.* Paris: Presses universitaires de France.

Donation Mectizan˙ Program. (2013). *Donation Mectizan˙ Program 2013.* Retrieved July 14, 2015, from http://www.mectizan.org/

Gateaux, V., & Heitz, J.-M. (2008). L'accès Aux Médicaments: Un Défi Pour L'industrie Pharmaceutique. *Humanisme et Entreprise, 286*(1), 13–28.

Gond, J.-P. (2011). La Responsabilité Sociale de L'entreprise Au-Delà Du Fonctionnalisme: Un Cadre D'analyse Pluraliste de L'interface Entreprise-Société. *Revue Finance Contrôle Stratégie, 14*(2), 37–66.

Gond, J.-P., & Igalens, J. (2014). *La Responsabilité Sociale de L'entreprise*. Paris: Presses universitaires de France.

GSK. (2013a). *New partnership between GSK and the Bill & Melinda Gates Foundation*. Retrieved July 28, 2015, from http://us.gsk.com/en-us/media/press-releases/2013/new-partnership-between-gsk-and-the-bill-andamp-melinda-gates-foundation-to-accelerate-research-into-vaccines-for-global-health-needs/

GSK. (2013b). *GSK CSR report*. Retrieved September 15, 2014, from http://www.gsk.com/media/325156/annual-report-2013.pdf

Hoffmann, G., & Saulquin, J.-Y. (2009). Quand La RSE Revisite La Chaîne de Valeur. *Management & Avenir, 28*, 37–55.

Jenkins, H. (2009). A "business opportunity" model of corporate social responsibility for small-and medium-sized enterprises. *Business Ethics: A European Review, 18*(1), 21–36.

Johnson and Johnson. (2013a). *Johnson and Johnson CSR report*. Retrieved July 13, 2014, from http://www.jnj.com/sites/default/files/pdf/cs/2013-JNJ-Citizenship-Sustainability-Report-FINAL061914.pdf

Johnson and Johnson. (2013b). *The patient assistance program JNJ*. Retrieved July 13, 2014, from http://www.jjpaf.org/

Lewis, M. W., & Grimes, A. I. (1999). Metatriangulation: Building theory from multiple paradigms. *Academy of Management Review, 24*(4), 672–690.

Lilly. (2013). *Lilly CSR report*. Retrieved October 13, 2014, from http://www.lilly.com/Documents/Lilly_2012_2013_CRreport.pdf

Martinet, A. C. (1984). *Management Stratégique: Organisation et Politique*. Paris: McGraw-Hill.

Martinet, A. C. (2006). Parties Prenantes, Management Stratégique et Politique. In M. Bonnafous-Boucher & Y. Pesqueux (Eds.), *Décider Avec Les Parties Prenantes* (pp. 9–18). Paris: La Découverte.

Martinet, A. C., & Payaud, M. A. (2008). Formes de RSE et Entreprises Sociales. Une Hybridation Des Stratégies. *Revue Française de Gestion, 180*, 199–214.

Martinet, A. C., & Payaud, M. A. (2009). Un Cadre Théorique Intégrateur Pour Le Management Stratégique «BOP». *Revue de l'Organisation Responsable, 4*, 19–30.

Martinet, A. C., & Payaud, M. A. (2010). La Stratégie BOP à L'épreuve Des Pauvretés. Une Modélisation Dialogique. *Revue Française de Gestion, 36*(208–209), 63–81.

Merck & Co. 2014. Merck & Co website. Retrieved September 15, from http://www.merck.com

Mills, A. (2002). La Science et La Technologie En Tant Que Biens Publics Mondiaux: S'attaquer Aux Maladies Prioritaires Des Pays Pauvres. *Revue D'économie Du Développement, 16*(1), 117–139.

Novartis. (2013). *Novartis CSR report*. Retrieved January 28, 2014, from https://www.novartis.com/corporate-responsibility/metrics-and-reporting/cr-performance-report.shtml

Novartis. (2015). *Novartis website*. Retrieved July 15, from https://www.novartis.com/about-us/corporate-responsibility

Palazzo, G., & Wentland, M. (2011). *Evaluation de la performance sociale et environnementale des entreprises*. Retrieved July 15, 2015, from http://www.unil.ch/files/live//sites/unicom/files/shared/pdfs/etude.pdf

Pfizer. (2013). *ProgramRxPathways^{TM}*. Retrieved September 20, 2014, from http://www.pfizerrxpathways.com

PWC. (2013). *Rapport 686*. Développement Durable Pharmaceutique. Retrieved July 15, 2015, from http://developpement-durable.pwc.fr/fr/approche-par-secteur-d-activite/secteur-pharmaceutique/

Roche. (2013a). *Roche CSR report*. Retrieved July 30, 2014, from http://www.roche.com/gb13e.pdf

Roche. (2013b). *Roche website*. Retrieved December 22, from http://www.roche.com/sustainability.htm

Sanofi. (2013). *Sanofi CSR report*. Retrieved May 6, 2014, from http://www.sanofi.com/Images/36400_Rapport_RSE_2013.pdf

Schneider, J. L., Wilson, A., & Rosenbeck, J. M. (2010). Pharmaceutical companies and sustainability: An analysis of corporate reporting. *Benchmarking: An International Journal, 17*(3), 421–434.

Teva. (2013). *Teva CSR report*. Retrieved April 14, 2014, from http://www.teva-csr-report-2013.com/

Turcotte, M.-F. B., & Pasquero, J. (2007). L'industrie Pharmaceutique et Ses Responsabilités Sociales. In J. J. Levy & C. Garnier (Eds.), *La Chaine Des Medicaments: Perspectives Pluridisciplinaires* (pp. 200–257). Quebec: Presses de l'Université du Quebec.

Vogel, D. (2006). *The market for virtue: The potential and limits of corporate social responsibility*. Virginia: Brookings Institution Press.

WHO. (2013). *Global programme to eliminate lymphatic filariasis*. Retrieved July 15, 2015, from http://www.who.int/lymphatic_filariasis/en/

12

Fear, Loathing and Shale Gas. The Introduction of Fracking to the UK: A Case Study

David McQueen

12.1 Introduction

Energy, whether from oil, gas, coal, nuclear or renewables, has become one of the most controversial areas of public policy in recent years, generating intense debate and disagreement about the related economic, social and environmental choices faced by nation states in an era of global insecurity. Politically divisive arguments around which energy sources should be prioritised, invested in and supported have flared up in countries around the world. This has occurred against increasingly urgent calls for international action to reduce fossil fuel dependence and CO_2 emissions (IPCC 2014). Multinational energy companies have often been accused of failing to operate in a socially responsible manner (Balmer 2010; Tuodolo 2015; McQueen 2015) and the reputations of some of

D. McQueen (✉)
Corporate and Marketing Communications, Bournemouth University,
Poole BH12 5BB, Dorset, UK
e-mail: dmcqueen@bournemouth.ac.uk

© The Author(s) 2017
A. Theofilou et al. (eds.), *Corporate Social Responsibility in the Post-Financial Crisis Era*, Palgrave Studies in Governance, Leadership and Responsibility, DOI 10.1007/978-3-319-40096-9_12

the largest global players have wilted under intense public scrutiny and a growing awareness of the impact of energy use and extraction on communities, ecosystems and the global climate. Such concerns have been widely publicised in relation to hydraulic fracturing or 'fracking' in the last decade in the USA and Australia (see Bosworth 2014) which has intensified the debate in the UK around proposed onshore shale gas exploration. In January 2013, David Cameron announced that local councils would be able to keep 100 percent of business rates they collected from shale gas sites, 'worth up to £1.7 million a year for a typical site' because the government was 'going all out for shale' (Gov.uk 2013). The Prime Minister argued that 'it will mean more jobs and opportunities for people, and economic security for our country' (Ibid.). At a time of continuing conflict and instability in the Middle East, the prospect of fostering domestic energy supplies, investment and economic independence would appear an obvious policy choice, but as a KPMG (2011) report makes clear the shale industry has to surmount tremendous reputational hurdles, particularly in the UK and Western Europe where 'the industry needs to control reputational risk and turn public opinion around' (p. 19).

Gas currently accounts for nearly half of the UK's total energy needs and around 30 percent of total electricity generated (DECC 2015). With North Sea gas production declining since 2000 and imports of gas now exceeding exports, the Conservative government, led by David Cameron, is pressing ahead with what has been described as a second 'dash for gas' (Elkins 2012). Inspired by the 'shale revolution' in the USA, which has helped dramatically reduce global oil and gas prices and given a boost to the US economy, the British government has put in place a series of policies designed to encourage shale gas extraction and thereby, it is hoped, greater energy independence. These policies include halving the tax rates on early profits from shale gas, offering at least £100,000 in community benefits per wellsite where hydraulic fracturing or 'fracking' takes place, and introducing industry-friendly regulatory changes, including the ability to drill beneath properties without the owner's permission (DECC 2016). This 'dash for gas' has been deeply controversial with environmentalists and civic groups, and since the first exploratory drilling site was established in Lancashire in 2011, hundreds of environmental organisations and community groups have offered vociferous opposition to the policy (see Jones et al. 2013).

The conservative government has, until now, appeared to pay scant attention to these groups and it continues to vigorously promote the economic and environmental benefits of onshore gas exploration. The government argues that shale gas, with lower CO_2 emissions than coal, can be a 'bridge' to renewables, as well as providing 65,000 jobs and energy security (DECC blog 2015). Those opposed to shale, or unconventional gas (UG), point to the dangers of widespread water and air pollution, increased earthquakes, drastically altered landscapes, various social and economic costs, and the wider impact on climate change of continuing our reliance on fossil fuels. This chapter provides an overview of a range of lobbying and public relations efforts by the oil and gas industry to portray shale gas exploration as safe and socially responsible in the face of determined and active opposition. It will outline some of the ways the industry has downplayed scientific doubts about the environmental and health impacts of fracking and related processes and successfully made its influence felt at the heart of government. It will also examine efforts to manage public perceptions of this highly contested development through a media strategy which has been effective, at least in part, in shaping broadcast coverage of the debate.

12.2 Definitions

Shale gas is natural gas, mainly composed of methane, found in shale rock beds often located between 1000 and 4000 metres below the ground. The gas is released by fracturing or 'fracking' the shale by drilling a borehole down into the earth and then pumping a mixture of water, sand and chemicals at high pressure into the shale, cracking the rocks and allowing the gas to flow back through the borehole and to the surface (Jones et al. 2015). This definition of high volume hydraulic fracturing (HVHF or 'fracking') is crucial because amongst many concerns expressed around shale gas exploration, the use of chemicals is amongst the most contentious. It is worth noting, for instance, that the government's public explanation of fracking often omits this aspect of the process, as in the following explanation found in the government's 'Guidance on Fracking' (Dec 2016): 'Hydraulic fracturing, known as fracking, is a technique used in the extraction of gas and oil from 'shale' rock formations by injecting water at high pressure' (p. 2). This omission of the word 'chemicals', a key detail in the information offered to the public, can be seen as symptomatic of a wider effort by the UK government and the fossil fuel industry to downplay potential hazards of fracking and present the case for shale gas exploration in the most positive light possible.

12.3 Scientific Disagreement

In fact, scientists appear divided, or at least uncertain, over the safety of hydraulic fracturing and related activity. While there is neither the time nor space here to review the scientific disagreements in detail, an outline of the areas of dispute is required to make sense of the efforts to present univocal versions of the science around fracking. The disagreements can be summarised around seven alleged impacts of 'fracking'—a term used henceforth to cover the entire process of UG exploration and production. These seven impacts are depletion and contamination of freshwater supplies; ground pollution and loss of biodiversity; the visual and physical effect on landscapes; increased seismic activity; air and noise pollution; the strain on local infrastructure and communities; and the wider contribution to man-made climate change.

A number of reports outline these and other threats in detail. For instance, The United Nations Environment Programme released a report in 2012 pointing out the dangers of methane leakage from fracking which has a Global Warming Potential (GWP) 'up to 72 times higher than CO_2 over a 20 year period' (UNEP 2012, p. 4). This and evidence of other environmental and health impacts led the report's authors to note that UG exploitation 'already includes instances of water contamination, leakages to soil, wide-scale land clearing and negative health impacts' and that 'increased extraction and use of UG is likely to be detrimental to efforts to curb climate change' (pp. 11–12). Whilst not ruling out fracking, it warns of 'unavoidable environmental impacts even if UG is extracted properly, and more so if done inadequately' (p. 11).

A report for the European Commission published in 2012 also noted 'high risk for people and environment' in terms of water contamination and depletion, air pollution, risk to biodiversity, noise impacts and traffic (AEA 2012, pp. v–vi). The report details how developing unconventional fossil fuel resources poses greater environmental risks than conventional gas development. Some recent studies have also argued that state support for unconventional oil and gas exploration is likely to be at the expense of the necessary huge investment in renewable sources of energy such as solar, wind and tidal required to reduce CO_2 emissions to acceptable levels (see Bosworth 2014). Hansen et al. (2013), for instance, argue that it would be 'foolhardy' for governments to encourage the development of any further fossil fuel extraction which may result in uncontrollable climate change. The danger underlined here and in other studies (see Tyndale Centre 2011) is that if states encourage unconventional oil and gas exploration our dependency on fossil fuels will simply be prolonged and the danger of runaway global warming will increase.

Induced seismic activity is another area of concern for those opposed to fracking. Scientific studies have clearly linked earthquakes with the underground disposal of wastewater from both conventional and unconventional oil and gas wells. Consequently, while hydraulic fracturing itself may not increase seismic activity, areas where fracking and associated wastewater disposal takes place have seen an enormous increase in tremors and quakes. The 2016 US Geological Survey observed, for example, that from 1950 to 2005, Oklahoma recorded an average of 1.5 earthquakes with a magnitude greater than 3.0 per year compared to 'several hundred M3.0+ earthquakes per year' in recent years (Petersen et al. 2016, p. 14). In fact, the very short-lived exploratory fracking by Cuadrilla Resources in Lancashire in 2011 was halted due to widely reported earth tremors in the seaside town of Blackpool. While these were relatively minor, at 1.5 and 2.3 on the Richter scale, Cuadrilla later admitted, following an investigation they commissioned, that hydraulic fracturing was the most likely cause.

While earthquakes, subsidence, noise, traffic and other threats to property values are of major concern, the dangers of water, air and land pollution from fracking have usually been most heavily prioritised in anti-fracking campaigns. These pollution issues have also been explored in numerous scientific reports and studies (see Jackson et al. 2015; TEDX 2016).

The Chartered Institute of Water and Environmental Management (2013), for instance, stated that the UK 'should not encourage fracking as a part of our energy mix until there is more evidence that operations can be delivered safely' (cited Ritchie et al. 2014, p. 3). A CHEM Trust report in 2015 entitled *Chemical Pollution from Fracking* warned of serious risks of local water, and land pollution and that fracking has the potential to massively impact the countryside and those who live in it—'be it people, livestock or wildlife' (p. 16).

Based on US figures, 2,400,000 gallons of fresh water, on average, per well is required to frack for shale gas, and the pressure on resources could be felt by communities that are vulnerable to water shortages and periodic droughts (see Harrison et al. 2014). As Jones et al. (2015) point out, these large volumes of water, mixed with a smaller volume of chemicals and lubricants, are pumped into boreholes where it is often difficult to predict their migration.

12.4 Public Opposition

In light of these and other environmental and health concerns, public opposition to fracking in the USA has increased significantly, rising from 40 percent to 51 percent in 2015 alone (Gallup 2016). Numerous states, towns and cities around the world have voted for a moratorium on fracking, including the states of Vermont and Maryland in the USA and Victoria and Tasmania in Australia. New York State voted to ban fracking after the release of a New York State Health Department (2014) report citing hundreds of peer-reviewed studies that pointed to chemical contamination, excess methane in water, surface spills, noise exposure and other health and environmental impacts. Many European countries have also shown little appetite for fracking with bans and moratoria in place in France, Germany, Netherlands, Czech Republic, Austria, Bulgaria, Scotland and Wales (Bloomberg 2014).

It may be that media coverage of fracking controversies and reports combined with the sustained efforts of anti-fracking activists are now having an impact on British public opinion. O'Hara et al.'s study of public attitudes in the UK to shale gas, for instance, shows a marked decline in support for fracking between 2013 and 2015 dropping from around 62 to 47 percent. Shale gas, the authors observe, 'remains the energy source the UK public are least likely to want in the UK's 2025 energy mix' (2015, p. 13). Their study shows that while shale was still considered a potentially cheap energy source that could bring significant economic benefits, growing numbers in the UK are opposed to its extraction, particularly amongst women who worry about the environmental impacts of fracking. The survey concludes that a growing proportion of the population does not want shale gas and that 'If the government pushes forwarded with its plans to fast track shale gas developments it must be prepared for significant levels of opposition from grass roots activists' (O'Hara et al. 2015, p. 14). Evidence of this opposition has already appeared in mainstream media coverage and prolific social media coverage of protests around exploratory drilling in Balcombe in West Sussex, Upton in Cheshire, Barton Moss in Salford and on the Fylde coast in Lancashire.

12.5   The Shale Gas Campaign

In 2013 the Institute of Directors identified the negative 'reputation' of fracking as one of the main barriers to enabling commercial production of onshore shale gas to go ahead in the UK. They recommended that 'the industry itself needs to develop a social licence to operate' and that 'more needs to be done to gain the confidence of local communities' (cited Jones et al. 2015, p. 383). Efforts to build public confidence in shale gas as a socially responsible and environmentally safe energy have taken a number of forms. Shale gas developers, such as Cuadrilla Resources, Dart Energy, Igas Energy and Ineos, have engaged several public relations firms, including Westbourne Communications, PPS Group, Bell Pottinger and Burson-Marsteller (Spinwatch 2015), to develop 'comprehensive, coherent and co-ordinated media relations campaigns in an attempt to win hearts and minds at both the local and national levels' (Jones et al. 2015, p. 387). The first element of this broad campaign had been underway for several years and involved gaining elite support amongst policy makers and academics. At the policy level the appointment of Lord John Browne Chairman, Board of Directors, Cuadrilla

Resources (until April 2015) in June 2010 as the government's 'Lead Non-Executive Director' at the Cabinet Office (Parliament.UK 2016) enabled a number of shale gas industry employees, supporters and advisors to be employed within relevant departments. Lord Browne's role in appointing business leaders as non-executive directors to the board of each government department included four appointees at the Treasury, three at the Department of Energy & Climate Change (DECC), four at the Department for Environment, Food and Rural Affairs (DEFRA) which oversees the Environment Agency and three in the Cabinet Office.

In addition to these appointments, Lord Browne has lobbied the government for exemptions from the Environment Agency regulations for the shale industry and worked with Lord Smith (former Chair of the Environment Agency) to reduce consultation time on waste permits and intervene with a council on planning permission for Cuadrilla (Friends of the Earth 2015). In fact, lobbying is a somewhat insufficient term for what appears to be a partnership arrangement, or alignment of goals between government and industry around shale gas (see Cave and Rowell 2014 for an elaboration of the embedding of corporate interests in government). The lobbying watchdog Spinwatch (2015) lists dozens of government advisors with close connections to the fossil fuel and shale gas industries. The Spinwatch report also shows 14 public relations firms 'hired by fracking companies', including Westbourne Communications, Weber Shandwick, Edelman, Burson-Marsteller and Bell Pottinger with personnel embedded through various roles in government or political parties. While such connections are often hidden to all but the most diligent researcher, in other cases they are in full public view. The Task Force on Shale Gas (TFSG) was charged with providing the government and public with 'an independent and impartial examination of both the potential benefits and risks linked to shale gas extraction', but received £650,000 from the fracking industry, including the leading shale gas companies Cuadrilla, Centrica, French oil company Total, and chemical giant Dow. These sponsorship details were made public on the task force's web page and hence no claim of subterfuge could be alleged.

Nevertheless, the 'independence' of a shale-industry-sponsored panel of four advised by five experts appears less certain on closer inspection. One of the panellists, Professor Ernest Rutter, wrote an article in

The Guardian in 2013 defending fracking in answer to Green Party councillor's article on the topic. A second panellist, Professor Nigel Brandon, has held a research position with BP. The third, Emma Duncan, was the deputy editor of *The Economist,* a freemarket-oriented magazine that has championed fracking. The fourth, Lord Chris Smith, is critical of the government's policy on renewables and carbon capture, but supportive of fracking. Amongst the five advisors was former Greenpeace director Stephen Tindale, known for his controversial support of genetically modified (GM) crops and fracking. According to the TFSG's constitution, also published on the website, 'the mission, goals, strategy and tactical plans for the Task Force' [is agreed] 'in consultation with a Secretariat provided by Edelman'. Public relations firm Edelman also provided the secretariat for The All Party Parliamentary Group on Unconventional Oil and Gas until 2014. Edelman, which operationalises and implements the TFSG mission and goals, represents Energy UK, a trade association representing 80 gas and electricity suppliers in the UK. Perhaps unsurprisingly, the task force panel concluded after a year of investigation that 'shale gas can be produced safely and usefully in the UK provided that the Government insists on industry-leading standards' and that exploratory drilling should begin (Task Force on Shale Gas 2015).

Lord Browne, a major stockholder and CEO of Cuadrilla, one of the funders of the shale gas taskforce, was, amongst other roles, chairman of the Royal Academy for Engineering until 2011. In 2012, the Royal Academy released a government-commissioned report on fracking. This was one of four key reports surveying the existing scholarship and assessing the risk of fracking in various domains which the government draws on to support the scientific case for shale gas. The Royal Academy report argued that the health, safety and environmental risks associated with fracking 'can be managed effectively in the UK as long as operational best practices are implemented and enforced through regulation' (The Royal Society and The Royal Academy of Engineering 2012, p. 4).

The Geological Society (2012) issued a report the same year broadly echoing the position of the Royal Society and Royal Academy of Engineering that shale gas can be extracted safely 'assuming wells are properly constructed' and provided that 'best practice is rigorously applied under an appropriate regulatory regime which addresses environmental and societal concerns' (p. 1). MacKay and Stone's (2013) report for DECC argued that shale gas' overall carbon footprint was comparable to gas extracted from conventional sources. It underplayed the potential threat of methane release, stating, 'if adequately regulated, local GHG [greenhouse gas] emissions from shale gas operations should represent only a small proportion of the total carbon footprint of shale gas, which is likely to be dominated by CO_2 emissions associated with its combustion' (p. 3). The fourth report, Public Health England's (2014) recommendations on the potential public health impacts of exposures to shale-gas-related chemical and radioactive pollutants, concluded using similar language to the three reports mentioned above: 'currently available evidence indicates that the potential risks to public health from exposure to the emissions associated with shale gas extraction will be low if the operations are properly run and regulated. In order to ensure this, regulation needs to be strongly and robustly applied' (p. 46).

One government report which is not cited by those promoting shale gas is the notoriously redacted Department for Environment, Food and Rural Affairs' *Shale Gas: Rural Economy Impacts* (2014) study which examined the 'potential economic, social and environmental impacts that are likely to be associated with an expansion in shale gas exploration'. The level of censorship (for want of a better word) can be measured by reading the recommendations (section 5) which are quoted in full here:

REDACTED
REDACTED
REDACTED
REDACTED
REDACTED
REDACTED
REDACTED
REDACTED
REDACTED
REDACTED
REDACTED. (DEFRA 2014, p. 13)

A year later, the government was forced to publish the report in full after the Information Commissioner ordered the government to do so.

The report provided some detail on likely water, noise, light and air pollution alongside possible short-term benefits and long-term costs to the local economy, rents, house prices and insurance premiums. The covering note to the full report appeared to discredit, or at least undermine, the contents:

> This paper is an early draft of an internal document; it is not analytically robust. [...] Containing no new evidence, the paper simply refers to data from overseas studies which cannot be used to predict impacts in the UK with any degree of reliability. (DEFRA 2015, p. 1)

12.6 Advocacy Coalitions and Sponsored Research

However, as Cairney et al. (2016) observe, 'evidence-based policy making' (EBPM) is a political process like any other, involving competition to decide what counts as evidence, how it should be evaluated and what policymakers should do with it. They explain that while science plays an important role, 'the link between scientific information and policy is not linear or unproblematic' (p. 3). As Cairney et al. (2016) remark, policymakers form 'advocacy coalitions' to join resources, coordinate their influence strategies, and translate their goals into policy. These contain 'people from a variety of positions (elected and agency officials, interest group leaders, researchers) who have similar policy beliefs and who coordinate activity over time (p. 9). A 'network' of academic experts is a core component of the 'advocacy coalitions' which emerge from the drive to formulate and enact energy policy. It is unsurprising, therefore, that some of the 'experts' on fracking most frequently cited in US and UK government reports emerge from fossil-fuel-funded institutes and research centres. The issue of 'sponsored research' is acute in the USA, where most scientific work is directed towards finding more efficient and cheaper ways of getting shale gas out of the ground, rather than on the environmental and public health effects. However, with cuts to publicly funded research, industry sponsorship is a rapidly growing practice in the UK (see Lander 2013). According to research by investigative reporter Maeve McClenaghan (2015),

80 percent of the Russell Group Universities received funding from the fossil fuel industry totalling £134,000,000 between 2010 and 2015. Just four, the University of Manchester, University of Cambridge, University of Oxford and Imperial University, received nearly 60 percent of this figure. The long-term reputational impacts on higher education institutions and academic research, more generally, of industry-sponsored research grants, are unclear. However, the danger of perceived 'sponsorship bias' is that it may discredit much of the research funded, or part-funded, by the oil and gas industries. Reputational damage to Higher Education institutions of this kind has already occurred in the USA several times. For example, New York State University's Buffalo Shale Resources and Society Institute (SRSI) was closed in November 2012 after allegations that a report on 'Environmental Impacts during Marcellus Shale Gas Drilling' was compromised by historical financial interests which may have influenced the authors' conclusions.

As Dr Stuart Parkinson, Executive Director of Scientists for Global Responsibility, points out, leading oil and gas corporations now have a major influence on the teaching and research in many of the UK's top universities. They can, in his view, 'steer' research agendas towards fossil-fuel-related R&D rather than urgently needed alternatives and thereby undermine progress in tackling climate change (cited McClenaghan 2015).

Research centres frequently cited by the government and in the media on the issue of fracking include Durham University's Energy Institute and the British Geological Survey based in Nottingham, which both receive sponsorship funds from a number of hydrocarbon and exploration companies. ReFINE—a 'fiercely independent' research consortium led jointly by Durham University and Newcastle University which focuses on the 'potential risks of shale gas and oil exploitation'—is primarily funded by Centrica (which bought a 25 percent stake in Cuadrilla in 2013) and shale gas developers Ineos.

12.7 The BBC's Coverage

How successful the strategy of funding research centres has been for the shale industry can be assessed by surveying the BBC's coverage of the controversial extraction process. If the government and shale industry's 'trusted experts' dominate coverage this might be a decisive factor in the battle for the 'hearts and minds' of the general public. An Ofcom poll conducted in 2015 showed that half of people surveyed regard the BBC's news outlets, across TV, radio and online, as their 'single most important source of news' with the highest rating for accuracy and trustworthiness (Ofcom 2015, p. 62). If industry-funded scientists are found to shape the scientific debate around shale gas on the BBC, this could play a critical role in persuading a sceptical or undecided population of the merits of shale gas development.

To assess this, a sample of BBC stories on hydraulic fracturing was downloaded from the BBC website to offer a snapshot of the coverage of the debate. The search terms 'fracking' and 'science' were entered into the BBC's website (in March 2015) for the period 1st January 2013 to 31st December 2015 and any irrelevant results (such as stories about 'tracking') were deleted. The search was confined to the top 20 stories published between 2013 and 2015 leading up the passing of the Infrastructure Bill in February 2015 and awarding of 93 Petroleum Exploration and Development Licences (PEDLs) after environmental assessment in December 2015. The onshore oil and gas licensing round was open to a period of six weeks public consultation from August 2015 on potential environmental impacts and was therefore a politically sensitive period in which hostile public opinion may have acted as a potential impediment to the government's plans to go 'all out for shale'.

So how is the science around fracking represented in this sample of BBC's coverage from 2013 to 2015? The 20 online articles and on-demand radio broadcasts were analysed and contributors' views coded as either broadly in favour, neutral or against. While most articles made some effort to offer a brief summary of positions in favour and against fracking, the majority of contributions were broadly in favour, or presented a view that evidence-based science supported the case for shale gas development. This can be seen, at one level, by a simple tally of contributors over the sample with ten scientific sources, six industry sources and nine political sources broadly in favour of fracking, while just two scientists, five politicians and six environmental groups were cited as broadly opposing the case for fracking. The coding revealed five scientific sources and four political sources offered broadly neutral positions and that the British Geological Survey offered both neutral and broadly pro-fracking positions. Significantly, some of the sources contributed to more than one pro-fracking story. Professor Richard Davies was cited twice, as was Professor Quentin Fisher of the University of Leeds and Professor Zoe Shipton of Strathclyde University (all frequent advocates for fracking in the media), while the British Geological Survey made contributions to a number of stories. All four sources have received research funding from oil and gas interests.

The range of contributors is of interest, with political sources outweighing scientific sources. Where party affiliation was identified, seven conservative sources dominated the pro-fracking argument with just one Labour, Member of the Scottish Parliament (MSP) Iain Gray, in favour. Political opposition to fracking came from four sources—two Scottish National Party (SNP) and one cross-party (Environmental Audit Committee) and one unknown (planning officers at Lancashire County Council). The two scientists cited as broadly against fracking were Professor Martin Mayfield of the University of Sheffield (briefly) and Professor Kevin Anderson of Manchester University who wrote to BBC *Inside Science* to complain, and was interviewed about, unbalanced coverage on fracking and climate change. The impression created across the 20 articles was that scientific studies supported the case for fracking, with very little <u>science</u> offered in the case against. Arguments against fracking were mostly cited by various environmental groups such as Greenpeace (three times), Friends of the Earth, Frack Off, WWF Scotland and National Trust.

The sense that the scientific evidence lies on one side of the debate is heightened by some of the BBC's own reporter's commentaries. The following is taken from one of the 20 reports published on 28 July 2014, in which the BBC's environmental analyst Roger Harrabin is quoted:

> If environmentalists succeed in stopping fracking in the UK by stirring up local objections they will actually make the greenhouse effect worse in the short term.

> This is because Britain will continue to use gas for heating and as a backup to capricious wind and solar electricity. If the industry can't get British gas it will import liquefied gas—and the energy needed to turn gas liquid makes it worse for the climate than home-produced gas.

The language employed here, 'stirring up local opposition', 'capricious wind and solar electricity' and 'worse for the climate', clearly favours the government and shale industry's narrative that shale can contribute to reducing the threat of climate change when, as we have seen, many evidence-based scientific studies suggest the opposite may be true (Tyndale Centre 2011; UNEP 2012; Harrison et al. 2014).

An examination of two radio broadcasts amongst the 20 stories reveals further lack of impartiality on the science around fracking. The first story which emerges as no.1 from the search for 'fracking' and 'science' on the BBC's homepage was a broadcast by *Inside Science* on 26 September 2013—a 'fracking special' meant to 'really understand the science surrounding the controversies'. The presenter, Adam Rutherford, 'sorts science fact from science fiction' by putting 'your frack FAQs to four experts'. We are first introduced to Kris Bone, a well engineering director at iGas, who is given five of the 15-minute feature to explain how the process worked from a coal-bed methane well in Warrington in Cheshire. Bone reassures listeners that 'fracking is not a new process' and has been around in the UK 'for at least 30 years' and used at around 200 onshore wells already: 'What is new is that it is in the deeper shales, which is a relatively new process in the UK'. Rutherford then introduces four experts who address some of the 'anxieties expressed by the public about fracking'. These are Professor Richard Davies from the Energy Institute; Dr David Rotherie, from the Open University; Professor Zoe Shipton, from the University of Strathclyde; and Professor Mike Stephenson from the British Geological Survey. These experts effectively dismiss concerns about water pollution and depletion, earthquakes and climate change. For instance, Richard Davies argues that 'the risk of contamination from fracking itself is incredibly low. There is not a single proven example of fracking causing contamination of groundwater'. David Rotherie supports this view, stating 'I don't think people's domestic water is at risk'. Zoe Shipton also argues that the 0.1–0.2 percent chemicals found in fracking slickwater were safe and could be compared to, for instance, the scale inhibitor found in your kettles and that these could be safely captured and treated on site.

Richard Davies addressed the issue of water scarcity and admitted the issue 'depends where you are' (the risk in Southern England and Karoo desert in South Africa was greater than in the North of England), but that the proposed water consumption for fracking was a tiny percentage of overall national consumption in the UK. On climate change, Dave Rotherie makes the case that domestic gas would create less CO_2 emissions than importing gas from abroad, and that shale gas is a 'very good stop gap' [...] 'otherwise we are going to be buying gas from the Russians for the next few decades'. Finally, on the issue of earthquakes, Mike Stephenson from the British Geological Survey admitted that the test drilling in Lancashire had probably caused very small tremors, but that, fracking, could actually 'save us from larger earthquakes, rather than causing earthquakes'.

In another *Inside Science* broadcast devoted partly to 'dispelling myths' around fracking on 11th June 2015, after a vote by European MEPs for a moratorium on fracking, the two scientists interviewed were Justin Rubinstein from the US Geological Survey and Zoe Shipton (again) from Strathclyde University. The introduction to the interview sets out the concern clearly: 'There is no doubt that in the US, earthquake activity has rocketed in the last decade', but Justin Rubenstein argues that:

> the increase in earthquakes certainly correlates with human activity and the increase does correlate with fracking, but correlation is not causation. We really don't think many of these earthquakes are directly related to fracking. Maybe in the order of 5–10 percent of these earthquakes are attributable to fracking. The process that we think is related to these earthquakes is a process called waste water disposal. And this is water that comes out when you're pulling out oil or gas.

The presenter, Adam Rutherford, puts aside the 5–10 percent of cases that may be caused by hydraulic fracturing directly and comments:

> Well that's very interesting [...] it is based on gas mining I suppose, but it is not actually fracking that is causing that increase.

This interpretation depends on the narrowest definition of fracking as only the actual cracking of rocks deep beneath the earth's surface, rather than the entire process around unconventional gas extraction which includes, in the USA at least, pumping water at high pressure, which stresses well integrity and underground waste water disposal.

Zoe Shipton, from Strathclyde University, argues that because waste water injection is 'unlikely' to be allowed, seismic events will be small and 'difficult to feel'. Returning to the Member of the European Parliament's (MEP's) largely 'symbolic' vote in support of a moratorium on fracking the presenter asks:

> Is this a mistake? Is this a vote in the sway of popular opinion rather than evidence-based policy?

Zoe Shipton replies:

> People are often not driven by the science. We can inform people about the science as much as we like, but the thing which makes people make their own minds up is their own values, fears and their concerns. There have been a number of reports including one by the Royal Society and Royal Academy of Engineering, that I was involved in, that have looked at the issues around environmental safety. The reports have largely found, or almost unanimously found, that this industry can be managed in a safe way if it is regulated properly and that the regulations in the UK are fit for purpose.

12.8   Conclusion

The BBC's charter requires that it offers balance and impartiality in the reporting of news and current affairs. In the case of reporting the scientific complexities and debates around fracking, it appears that the BBC is falling short of its obligations. The proposed introduction of fracking in the UK has so far passed the legislative hurdles and gained media and mainstream political support from the major parties. The government and sections of the media continue to frame shale gas as 'the cleanest fossil fuel' (DECC 2013, cited Jones et al. 2015). However, opposition to fracking continues to grow, and it may be that efforts to suppress dissenting scientific evidence by the government, the shale industry and the media will only amplify opposition and increase resistance to new technology. The various scientific doubts and uncertainties about fracking have not prevented the shale industry, the UK government and the BBC from presenting an optimistic and simplistic science-based case for UG. If shale gas exploration proceeds as planned in the UK, *any* evidence of negative impacts on communities, particularly accidents or contamination of water supplies in such a densely populated island, will only mobilise greater and more intense opposition to the shale industry and any government or group of experts attempting to defend it.

The danger is that a one-sided, industry-funded presentation of science research may affect not only the reputation of fossil fuel industries, but academic institutions and values as well. In this respect the shale industry has fallen short of its corporate social responsibility obligations to respect the views and livelihoods of communities and stakeholders in relation to the extraction of UG. Retreating behind narrow definitions of 'fracking', attempting to steer research and manage the debate in the media alongside intensive lobbying operations in the government may ultimately backfire and exacerbate public distrust of politicians, the mainstream media and the fossil fuel industry. A careful consideration of the impacts of continued hydrocarbon exploration (and particularly 'unconventional' oil and gas) on the environment, on communities and on long-term economic prosperity around the world at a time of growing climate insecurity is urgently required. This must remain a priority for any realistic discussion of corporate social responsibility—and is one that should be engaged with urgently by all organisations currently engaged in the promotion of shale gas development.

References

AEA. (2012). *Support to the identification of potential risks for the environment and human health arising from hydrocarbons operations involving hydraulic fracturing in Europe.* Retrieved March 28, 2016, from http://ec.europa.eu/environment/integration/energy/pdf/fracking%20study.pdf

Balmer, J. M. T. (2010). The BP deepwater horizon debacle and corporate brand exuberance. *Journal of Brand Management, 18*(2), 97–104.

Bloomberg. (2014, September 17). *Fracking in Europe: Fighting the revolution.* Retrieved March 29, 2016, from http://www.bloombergview.com/quicktake/fracking-europe

Bosworth, T. (2014). Unconventional and unburnable: Why going all out for shale gas is the wrong direction for the UK's energy policy. *Issues in Environmental Science and Technology: Fracking, 39,* 199–221.

Cairney, P., Fischer, M., & Ingold, K. (2016). Hydraulic fracturing policy in the UK: Coalition, cooperation and opposition in the face of uncertainty. In *Comparing Coalition Politics: Policy Debates on Hydraulic Fracturing in North America and Western Europe,* ed. C. Weible, T. Heikkila, K. Ingold and M. Fischer: Palgrave. Retrieved May 2015, from http://www.icpublicpolicy.org/conference/file/reponse/1435316621.pdf

Cave, T., & Rowell, A. (2014). *A quiet word: Lobbying, crony capitalism and broken politics in Britain.* London: The Bodley Head.

CHEM Trust. (2015*). Fracking pollution: How toxic chemicals from fracking could affect wildlife and people in the UK and EU.* Retrieved March 20, 2016, fromhttp://www.chemtrust.org.uk/wp-content/uploads/chemtrust-fracking-briefing-june2015.pdf

Department for Environment, Food & Rural Affairs (DEFRA). (2014). *Shale gas rural economy impacts.* Retrieved March 23, 2016, from https://www.gov.uk/government/uploads/system/uploads/attachment_data/file/408977/RFI6751_Draft_Shale_Gas_Rural_economy_impact_paper.pdf

Department for Environment, Food & Rural Affairs (DEFRA). (2015). *Draft shale gas rural economy impacts [Unredacted].* Retrieved March 23, 2016, from https://www.gov.uk/government/uploads/system/uploads/attachment_data/file/440791/draft-shale-gas-rural-economy-impact-report.pdf

Department of Energy and Climate Change (DECC). (2015). *UK energy statistics, Q2 2015.* Retrieved March 23, 2016, from https://www.gov.uk/government/uploads/system/uploads/attachment_data/file/463016/Press_Notice_September_2015.pdf

Department of Energy and Climate Change (DECC). (2016). *Guidance on fracking: Developing shale oil and gas in the UK.* Retrieved March 24, 2016, from https://www.gov.uk/government/publications/about-shale-gas-and-hydraulic-fracturing-fracking/developing-shale-oil-and-gas-in-the-uk

Department of Energy and Climate Change blog (DECC blog). (2015). *Shale gas—An inconvenient truth for the anti-fracking lobby.* Retrieved March 23, 2016, from https://decc.blog.gov.uk/2015/09/23/shale-gas-an-inconvenient-truth-for-the-anti-fracking-lobby/

Elkins, P. (2012, December 6). The UK's new dash for gas is a dangerous gamble. *New Scientist*. Retrieved March 23, 2016, from https://www.newscientist.com/article/dn22594-the-uks-new-dash-for-gas-is-a-dangerous-gamble/

Friends of the Earth. (2015, January 25). *Revealed: Secret government-industry plans to circumvent fracking opposition*. Retrieved March 24, 2016, from https://www.foe.co.uk/blog/revealed-secret-government-industry-plans-circumvent-fracking-opposition

Gallup. (2016, March 30). *Opposition to fracking mounts in the U.S.* Retrieved March 23, 2016, from http://www.gallup.com/poll/190355/opposition-fracking-mounts.aspx

Gov.uk. (2013, January 13). *Local councils to receive millions in business rates from shale gas developments*. Retrieved March 19, 2016, from https://www.gov.uk/government/news/local-councils-to-receive-millions-in-business-rates-from-shale-gas-developments

Hansen, J., Sato, M., Russell, G., & Kharecha, P. (2013). Climate sensitivity, sea level and atmospheric carbon dioxide. *Philosophical Transactions of the Royal Society A: Mathematical, Physical and Engineering Sciences, 371*(2001), 20120294. Retrieved March 20, 2016, from http://arxiv.org/abs/1211.4846

Harrison, G., Parkinson, S., & McFarlane, G. (2014). *Shale gas and fracking: Examining the evidence*. Scientists for Global Responsibility (SGR) and the Chartered Institute of Environmental Health (CIEH). Retrieved March 23, 2016, from http://www.sgr.org.uk/sites/sgr.org.uk/files/SGR-CIEH-Shale-gas-bfg.pdf

IPCC. (2014). Contribution of Working Groups I, II and III to the Fifth Assessment Report of the Intergovernmental Panel on Climate Change. In Core Writing Team, R. K. Pachauri, & L. A. Meyer (Eds.), *Climate change 2014: Synthesis report*. Geneva, Switzerland: IPCC. Retrieved March 19, 2016, from http://www.ipcc.ch/report/ar5/syr/

Jackson, R., Lowry, E., Pickle, A., Kang, M., DiGiulio, D., & Zhao, K. (2015). The depths of hydraulic fracturing and accompanying water use across the United States. *Environmental Science & Technology, 49*(15), 8969–8976.

Jones, P., Hillier, D., & Comfort, D. (2013). Fracking and public relations: Rehearsing the arguments and making the case. *Journal of Public Affairs, 13*(4), 1479–1854.

Jones, P., Hillier, D., & Comfort, D. (2015). The contested future of fracking for shale gas in the UK: Risk, reputation and regulation. *World Review of Entrepreneurship, Management and Sustainable Development, 11*(4), 337–390.

KPMG. (2011). *Shale gas a global perspective*. Retrieved March 13, 2016, from https://www.kpmg.com/Global/en/IssuesAndInsights/ArticlesPublications/Documents/shale-gas-global-perspective.pdf

Lander, R. (2013). *Knowledge and power: Fossil fuel universities*. Platform, People & Planet and 350.org. Retrieved March 26, 2016, from https://peopleand-planet.org/dl/fossil-free/knowledge-power-report.pdf

MacKay, D., & Stone, T. (2013). *Potential greenhouse gas emissions associated with shale gas extraction and use*. Department of Energy and Climate Change (DECC). Retrieved March 28, 2016, from https://www.gov.uk/government/uploads/system/uploads/attachment_data/file/237330/MacKay_Stone_shale_study_report_09092013.pdf

McClenaghan, M. (2015). Investigation: Top universities take £134m from fossil fuel giants despite divestment drive. *Greenpeace Energy Desk*. Retrieved March 14, 2016, from http://energydesk.greenpeace.org/2015/10/23/data-top-universities-take-134m-from-fossil-fuel-giants-despite-divestment--drive/

McQueen, D. (2015). CSR and new battle lines in online PR war: A case study of the energy sector. In A. Adi, D. Crowther, & G. Grigore (Eds.), *Online CSR corporate social responsibility in the digital age* (Developments in corporate governance and responsibility, Vol. 7, pp. 99–125). Bingley: Emerald Group Publishing Limited.

New York State Health Department. (2014). *A public health review of high volume hydraulic fracturing for shale gas development*. Retrieved March 24, 2016, from https://www.health.ny.gov/press/reports/docs/high_volume_hydraulic_fracturing.pdf

Ofcom. (2015, December 15). *News consumption in the UK: Research report*. Retrieved March 27, 2016, from http://stakeholders.ofcom.org.uk/binaries/research/tv-research/news/2015/News_consumption_in_the_UK_2015_report.pdf

O'Hara, S., Humphrey, M., Andersson-Hudson, J., & Knight, W. (2015). *Public perception of shale gas extraction in the UK: Two years on from the balcombe protests*. University of Nottingham. Retrieved March 17, 2016, from http://bettersociety.net/images/Public%20Perceptions%20of%20shale%20gas%20in%20the%20UK%20sept131015MH.WK.JA-H.pdf

Parliament.UK. (2016). *Lord Browne of madingley*. Retrieved March 17, 2016, from http://www.parliament.uk/biographies/lords/lord-browne-of-madingley/2172

Petersen, M., Mueller, C., Moschetti, M., Hoover, S., Llenos, A., Ellsworth, W., et al. (2016). *One-year seismic hazard forecast for the central and eastern United States from induced and natural earthquakes*. Reston, VA: U.S. Geological Survey. Retrieved March 30, 2016, from http://pubs.usgs.gov/of/2016/1035/ofr20161035.pdf

Public Health England. (2014). *Potential public health impacts of exposures to chemical and radioactive pollutants as a result of the shale gas extraction process.* Retrieved February 28, 2014, from https://www.gov.uk/government/uploads/system/uploads/attachment_data/file/332837/PHE-CRCE-009_3-7-14.pdf

Ritchie, H., Lloyd, G., & Griffiths, P. (2014). *A fracking good time? A planned approach to energy resilience in the UK and Ireland.* Paper presented to the Association of European Schools of Planning (AESOP) Annual Congress. "From control to co-evolution", July 9–12, University of Utrecht & University of Delft.

Spinwatch. (2015, April 29). *Access all areas: Westminster's (vast) fracking lobby exposed.* Retrieved January 10, 2016, from http://www.spinwatch.org/index.php/issues/climate/item/5765-access-all-areas-frackers-lobbyists-and-the-revolving-door

Task Force on Shale Gas. (2015). *Final conclusions and recommendations.* Retrieved February 10, 2016, from https://www.taskforceonshalegas.uk/news-and-events/final-conclusions-and-recommendations

TEDX. (2016). Chemicals in oil and gas operations—Peer-reviewed papers. *TEDX The endocrine disruption exchange.* Retrieved March 24, 2016, from http://www.endocrinedisruption.org/chemicals-in-natural-gas-operations/peer-reviewed-articles

The Geological Society. (2012). *Shale gas and fracking.* Retrieved March 23, 2016, from https://www.geolsoc.org.uk/Policy-and-Media/Resources/Shale-Gas-and-Fracking

The Royal Society and The Royal Academy of Engineering. (2012). *Shale gas extraction in the UK: A review of hydraulic fracturing.* Retrieved February 28, 2015, from http://www.raeng.org.uk/publications/reports/shale-gas-extraction-in-the-uk

Tuodolo, F. (2015). Corporate social responsibility: Between civil society and the oil industry in the developing world. *ACME: An International E-Journal for Critical Geographies, 8*(3), 530–541. Retrieved March 25, 2016, from http://ojs.unbc.ca/index.php/acme/article/view/850/706

Tyndale Centre. (2011). *Shale gas: An updated assessment of environmental and climate change impacts.* Retrieved March 20, 2016, from http://www.tyndall.ac.uk/sites/default/files/coop_shale_gas_report_update_v3.10.pdf

UNEP. (2012, November). Gas fracking: Can we safely squeeze the rocks? *Global Environmental Alert Service (GEAS).* Retrieved March 28, 2016, from http://www.unep.org/pdf/UNEP-GEAS_NOV_2012.pdf

13

For-Profits and Non-Profits: A Research on the Collaboration's Premises during the Financial Crisis

Andreea Angela Vonțea and Alin Stancu

13.1 Introduction

Given that companies confronted themselves with a more and more increased pressure due to globalization and intensified concerns regarding the equilibrium of power between corporation and society, over the years, corporate social responsibility (CSR) has become an issue discussed from a legal, economic, political, ethical and social viewpoint (Zaharia and Grundey 2011). The analytic interest in the field of CSR, as well as the practice of social responsibility, currently passes through a powerful rebound due to the important changes both in terms of the manner in which corporations define themselves and regarding the social expectations that revolve around for-profit organizations (Băleanu et al. 2011).

Companies make use of the concept of CSR from strategic considerations by selecting areas of interest that match the organizational values

A.A. Vonțea (✉) • A. Stancu
Bucharest University of Economic Studies, Bucharest, Romania
e-mail: andreea.vontea@mk.ase.ro

© The Author(s) 2017
A. Theofilou et al. (eds.), *Corporate Social Responsibility in the Post-Financial Crisis Era*, Palgrave Studies in Governance, Leadership and Responsibility, DOI 10.1007/978-3-319-40096-9_13

and confer opportunities in order to achieve marketing objectives. On the other hand, the organizations in question recognize that forming alliances with non-profit organizations and, implicitly, with a series of worthy causes can be mutually beneficial (Demetriou et al. 2010).

Contrary to expectations regarding the positive outcomes associated with CSR initiatives in terms of generating an optimal level of exposure and of determining some positive evaluations, such a result is difficult to be guaranteed (Bhattacharya et al. 2009). Along the time, there were produced some changes with regard to the manner in which corporate organizations support the activity of the ones from the non-profit sector. Increasingly more, in order to accomplish their objectives related to social responsibility, corporate organizations finance those non-profit organizations that are more visible concerning different communication activities (Ohreen and Petry 2012). The collaborative relationships between the for-profit organizations and the non-profit ones create a unique connection point between the objectives intended to be achieved by the two types of organizational entities, also offering a significant potential for generating innovative ways of "doing business by doing good" (Lee 2011).

Relationships between non-profit and for-profit entities involve some risks and benefits, especially for the involved non-profit organizations. Sometimes, the latter ones involve themselves in such agreements with a complete understanding of the implied consequences and potential costs. However, there appears an inherent risk somehow strengthened by these types of relationships, namely the imbalance of power that exists in the favour of corporations because they always involve themselves in partnerships with non-profit organizations as having a deliberate strategy of risk control. While the work with corporate partners can be associated with multiple advantages, non-profit organizations must be part of such relationships as having a significant preoccupation for maintaining their own level of autonomy (Baur and Schmitz 2012). The degree of achieving the objectives is also an important one. While the social objectives have the highest degree of importance for the overall activity of the non-profit organization, even the organizational objectives require a certain degree of attention. Consequently, the non-profit organizations' managers must adapt to the potential changes that characterize the market (Lefroy and Tsarenko 2014).

The most for-profit entities confront themselves with difficulties in identifying a certain non-profit organization or of a cause to match in a significant manner to the purpose and to the nature of their field of activity. For companies it is difficult to identify CSR activities with a high degree of matching that follows the exact sense of the definition because a great part of the important and desirable activities from a social view-point may prove as not to have a perfect match with the defining objectives of the for-profit organizations. Accordingly, companies should give more attention to the decision about the manner in which they implement CSR initiatives, rather than to focus on partners and on the derived activities (Kim et al. 2012).

Given that, by the current research endeavour, it is aimed to increase the degree of knowledge regarding the interactions between the corporate and the non-profit organizations, the managerial issue that we intend to address resides in the following question: 'In what manner can be improved the collaborative relationships between the corporate and the non-profit organizations in terms of the fundraising activity?'

13.2 Methodology

The purpose of the current research lies in analyzing the manner in which the corporate organizations interact with non-profit organizations in terms of the fundraising activity from the perspective of non-profit organizations' representatives during the forthcoming timeframe to the financial crisis.

The information collected for this qualitative research comes from multiple sources, being procured during the period of time comprised between April and July 2014. The research was projected during March 2014. In total, 12 personal interviews were held with representatives of corporate organizations from Romania, their answers being obtained by the use of the semi-structured interview technique. The average length of an interview was of approximately 60 minutes.

Concerning the working procedure, it is important to mention that, although the mention about the organizational affiliation (corporate in this case) of the interviewed persons is rendered as a reference for the endeavour of personal interviewing, for the identification of the source of the quotations from the interviews there were allocated randomly numbers from 1 to 12. Last but not least, all the mentions as proper names, related to the represented corporate organizations' field of activity et cetera, which could have led to the identification of the source were replaced with some generic ones.

The discussion's analysis derived from the interviews followed a series of successive phases. Each personal interview was recorded in an audio format, played back and transcribed. Within the initial phase, the transcripts were revised independently in an exploratory manner in order to identify key constructs and topics. Afterwards, depending on the topic of reference, their content was restructured and resumed, in the end being made a selection of the common elements, on the one hand and, on the other hand, of the areas of divergence that resulted from the subsequent statements. For analyzing complex phenomena and long-term dynamics, the comparative analysis is a procedure of a sizable usefulness (Eisenhardt 1989).

One of the elements of specificity of the current research is represented by the fact that the generic title of corporate organizations refers both to corporate organizations per se and to corporate foundations, the numerical ratio being of 8:4. Hence, this diversified composition of the sample was necessary in order to capture the respondents' differences in perceptions and interpretation.

The targeted corporate organizations represent a wide variety of industries—both from the Secondary Sector (production) and from the Tertiary one (services), the numerical ratio being of 4:8. With regard to the fields of activity, the manner of structuring the investigated sample was constituted as follows: commercializing industrial products—construction materials, PVC profiles and, respectively, automotive (three entities), commercializing tobacco products (one entity), banking (two entities), telecommunication services (two entities), consulting services and software programming engineering (one entity), life insurance (one entity), specialized medical assistance activities (one entity) and, respectively, commercializing products within the online environment (one entity).

It is also important to emphasize that all respondents were involved in activities related to the collaboration with non-profit organizations either directly (as decision makers/negotiators) or indirectly (as members of the execution/operational team). Given that the purpose of the current research resides in generating observations regarding a complex phenomenon—that is exploring the corporate organizations' conduct in terms of the interaction with the non-profit organizations and the investigation of its definitive influences—and there is aimed the development of a theoretical framework (rather than its testing), it can be considered that the adequate sampling method is represented by the theoretical sampling.

13.3 Results and Discussion

13.3.1 Prerequisites of Establishing Collaborative Relationships

A prime issue discussed is the one referring to the manner in which for-profit organizations act when there are taken into account alternatives of establishing collaborative relationships with non-profit entities—Their approach is a reactive one or there are other circumstances in which such processes are initiated by the commercial organization itself? Consequently, the interviews' content analysis reveals that the manifestation of a reactive position is the dominant one, the following example illustrating such an approach:

> For now, we stayed at the level at which, rather, we [as a corporate organization—A/N] wait for NGOs to 'come' with their proposals towards us instead of us to 'go' towards them. (Interview no. 12)

Nevertheless, two insertions reveal the existence of a proactive approach:

> […] in the end, [non-profit—A/N] organizations 'see', in major lines, which ones are the investments and the directions and try to approach and to adapt themselves—to come with particular offers and yes, for me this thing to happen seems to be a natural fact, but [as a corporate organization—A/N] we do not rely on it. Namely, it is important to have an initial screening that every company I think that puts it into practice in one way or another. We make it; it needs to be done. (Interview no. 11)

[…] there is also happening for us [as a corporate organization—A/N] to 'go' directly towards [non-profit—A/N] organizations … It is a selling exerted by us merely because, by ignorance, by an awareness, (Name of corporate organization) might not be considered a partner and then … you might want to be considered. You want to be part of that 'equation'. You see that you can create additional value. (Interview no. 9)

13.3.2 Eligibility Criteria

Once the stage represented by the primary selection of the potential non-profit collaborators was completed, there follows another important aspect, namely a process of assessing the non-profit organizations according to a series of criteria selected by the commercial organization, about which one of the interviewed persons affirms that:

Any type of partnership wanted by you [as a corporate organization—A/N] in the medium term has a phase of cognition and has a phase of 'understanding' and of 'listening'. So 'to understand' and 'to listen to' what does the [non-profit—N/A] organization—which ones are the elements either human and project related that animate and motivate the people form there and which are, how to say … the relationships and the manner in which it works 'inside' and, afterwards, by reference to the other ones. There exists a whole set of criteria that we follow because our auditors require these criteria to be transparent and explicit ones. (Interview no. 1)

In accordance with the arguments formulated by respondents, the most important one of them refers to the degree of alignment between the object of a potential collaborative relationship and the area within which the commercial organization decides to invest:

There exists 'openness', with the amendment that we do not accept any project and that, usually, we accept those projects that bind to our strategic interests too [as a corporate organization—A/N]. (Interview no. 12)

It is good that the cause [represented by a certain non-profit organization—A/N] match the three social categories supported by (Name of corporate organization). (Interview no. 2)

Any NGO can come as long as it is in line with the fields where we [as a corporate foundation—A/N] finance at this moment [...]. (Interview no. 7)

The motivation for which I do not accept certain projects or that is given by me [as a representative of a corporate organization—A/N] refers to the fact that they are not integrated within the CSR direction. I can't say that there is a direction, but in my mind and in our mind it is contoured. (Interview no. 6)

Complementing, another respondent argues in detail the idea about involvement:

[...] we [as a corporate foundation—A/N] seek to involve ourselves in the things for which we give money and are done by us too ... to contribute ... to have a sense ... To be something thought by us too! Not a 'ready-made' product! We do not do CSR! You do not come at me with a 'ready-made' product and you ask me for money [...]. I want to involve myself! I want to express my involvement when that product is conceived because I want it to be something that has to do with the things about which I am interested. If it is 'ready-made', the chances to be aligned to what we are interested in are extremely reduced ones. (Interview no. 10)

As mentioned by one of the interviewed persons, among the most important criteria concerning the assessment of the collaboration proposals, there can be included the one about the financial aspects required by a certain project's implementation. At the same time, it emphasizes the manner in which the represented organization addresses the potential costs associated with an involvement endeavour:

[...] the budget is not a thing to be neglected in all this effort. Our policy [as a corporate organization—A/N] is to not spend—so we don't have these costs 'on' the balance sheet, 'on' the operational budgets, but we use in full that facility allowed by the Fiscal Code [the mention integrated within Law no. 571/2003 regarding the Fiscal Code—A/N] according to which minimum of 3‰ of the turnover and 20% of the profit tax can be spent on sponsorship activities. (Interview no. 11)

The following two insertions still refer to financial aspects but, within this framework, there is highlighted the existence of a certain degree of flexibility regarding the manner in which the budgets are allocated, especially when certain requests are answered about which the for-profit entity is particularly interested in or when the projects are not too large scale ones:

> The conditions are flexible enough [...]. The things can be adapted long enough and, sometimes, throughout the project too; if we have money left, we reassign them. (Interview no. 4)
> It depends a lot on the amounts about which we talk. If there is subjected a small project, that does not have a major impact or it is not on the long run, then, for sure, there can be made an exception to the already approved budget. This is usually done—an adjustment. (Interview no. 2)

The normalization of the extent in which the non-profit organization depends on the financing obtained from the commercial organization is another issue referred to by two of the respondents:

> [...] [as a corporate foundation—A/N] we don't want our partners to rely exclusively on our financing because it isn't healthy. We try to help them relative to the part of organizational development. Namely, besides the project's financing per se, we also look at their organizational development needs. (Interview no. 7)
> They [as collaborator non-profit organizations—A/N] also have to come with a part of contribution because we don't want them to rely totally on the received money. (Interview no. 4)

Further, the financial aspects still make the object of the discussion, but two of the respondents connect this subject to the idea of experience:

> Financial results ... Certainly, any company investigates slightly the financial reports of the [non-profit—A/N] organizations with which it works. (Interview no. 11)
> [The collaborator non-profit organization—A/N] must have an extremely good experience so that to guarantee that the project in question, even though has considerable goals, will be able to succeed. Because it is about a major investment. (Interview no. 8)

To see that [the collaborator non-profit organization—A/N] has experience. Not to see that, all at once, it receives 50,000 euro and we find out
that it does not know to manage them. To see that it has done 'something'
... Experience regarding projects; these one counts quite a lot. (Interview
no. 4)

In their turn, non-profit organizations' type of projects implemented
or in progress represents another criterion the importance of which is
evoked by two of the respondents. The first one reiterates the idea regarding the obtained results, as well as the one about the alignment with the
represented organization's fields of interest:

At the most professional possible way, there needs to exist a portfolio criteria of the respective [non-profit—A/N] organizations; portfolio that should
reflect the type of projects that the Company wants to develop together
with this institution. A series of visible, sustainable results on the market
'on' the projects developed by the Company. (Interview no. 11)

Another two subjects, namely the type of projects previously held and
the impact associated with them, are again brought into discussion, at
the same time being made the connection with another criterion—the
sustainability—as points out another respondent:

[...] the organization's sustainability criteria—'What kind of projects did it
carried before?', 'What was their impact?'. (Interview no. 1)

Two other respondents refer to the same subject, emphasizing its definitive importance:

The first thing at which we look [as a corporate organization—A/N] is the
continuity in the project's logic. (Interview no. 12)

[As a corporate organization representative—A/N] I am looking at sustainability. My personal philosophy is that, instead of being 'the big thing
from a small point', it is better to be 'a significant part of something big',
something 'impactful'. And, usually, it is a healthy philosophy. (Interview
no. 9)

Another recurring subject derived from the one about the strategic alignment between the commercial organization's profile and the one of the potential non-profit collaborator is represented by approaching the projects from a long-term perspective, along with generating a standing impact (mention rendered, furthermore, within the previous insertion):

> We [as a corporate foundation—A/N] give them [to non-profit organizations—A/N] this grant, but we want to ensure ourselves that the project will be continued form a long term perspective. (Interview no. 4)
>
> [As a corporate organization—A/N] we want some relations on medium and long term with those [non-profit—A/N] organizations that manage themselves to see beyond the fiscal year that needs to be executed. [...] we want to work on a medium and long term. (Interview no. 1)
>
> [...] a very large number of beneficiaries, significant impact in the economic/social environment. (Interview no. 8)

The approaches regarding the dimensions of the non-profit organizations with which a commercial organization could have a collaboration relationship represent other selection criteria, as it is interesting to observe that the opinions expressed in such a framework vary a lot:

> Relative to the eligibility criteria there isn't a convention that refers to the size of the NGO or to the size in terms of budget/number of people. I [as a corporate foundation representative—A/N] am interested in the project per se. I am not interested if it's a large/small organization ... it doesn't seem relevant. (Interview no. 7)

As can be observed, the exemplified insertion expresses the fact that, in the discussed case, the emphasis is put on the project itself. The following insertion as well is built around the type of the project but, in this framework, the organization's dimension becomes a notable aspect:

> In general, the greater a [non-profit—A/N] organization, the less chances to collaborate, somewhat. [...] the chances to be exactly 'on' what we intend to do are quite reduced. (Interview no. 10)

With regard to the definitive characteristics of the collaborator non-profit organization's conduct, the interviews' content analysis reveals the fact that the most frequently mentioned is the one about reliability. Thus, two of the respondents affirm:

> It is about reliability, rigor and responsibility in budgets' spending. To exist a consciousness on every investment, on the amount of money spent. (Interview no. 11)
>
> [...] It would be desirable for that NGO to prove the reliability it has. So it's desirable for that NGO to be one that, indeed, has ... not necessarily awareness, but a proven reliability. It would be seen if it's an NGO that has a good reputation. (Interview no. 2)

Within the content of the second insertion previously rendered, there is mentioned the fact that awareness is also an aspect taken into account by the commercial organizations, but another interviewed person asserts something contrary:

> It doesn't matter the reputation of an organization ... We 'refused' ... Now it sounds so, 'condescending'... (Interview no. 10)

Moreover, one of the respondents mentions the careful approach of the organization in terms of an association decision:

> There is necessary, surely, to be careful relative to how we associate ourselves. (Name of brand from the corporate organization's portfolio) is a premium brand. So 'here' care must be considered. (Interview no. 3)

13.3.3 Conduct in Terms of Collaboration Relationships Involvement

The manner of putting into practice the interaction between the entities which represent the for-profit sector, respectively, the non-profit one is also an aspect of major importance. In order to support this idea, one of the respondents expresses an opinion about the conduct of a non-profit organization from a collaborative relationship:

[The non-profit organization—A/N] keeps its promises. I believe that this one is the most important think and the most important advice. Until it comes to promises, to ensure itself that it can deliver what it considered initially. (Interview no. 5)

According to another respondent's opinion, the information flow between the two types of organizations has, in its turn, a definitive role both for the non-profit collaborator from the perspective of the effectiveness associated with the project's implementation and for the for-profit one from the viewpoint of the practices of results' tracking:

[…] the transparency in the relationship with the NGO. As possible, [as a corporate organization—A/N] to receive as much information as possible about the respective project—how it is carried on, how it is quantified, which ones are its objectives, which ones are the indicators by which there is measured the achievement of those objectives, with what kind of results that project ends because we, in our turn, communicate further these results to our colleagues from the head office that make reporting to diverse entities and such information is very important for us. And another think that we look at is, of course, the impact. The impact meaning not necessarily how many hundreds of thousands of people heard the messages transmitted by the support given to the respective project but, concretely, how many people benefited or had won as that particular project was unfolded. We are not interested necessarily in reputation as we are interested in the effect—the concrete, practical result. (Interview no. 12)

Other angles of the discussion about the manner in which the information exchange is made but, on this occasion, strictly limited to the reporting activity are the following ones:

All our partners [as a corporate foundation—A/N] know that, when they apply and hence they obtain that funding, they will have to report on a monthly basis—both narrative and financial. All the projects are carefully monitored in order to be sure that money is used 'properly'. In this way, the things are transparent, the [non-profit—A/N] organizations must report—they are audited, they are verified. It is more difficult, there is more work for us, but it is even more rewarding. (Interview no. 7)

[As a corporate organization—A/N] we think in a complex manner—namely, we have to support the business. Everything you do must have either relevance as a direction—in order to refer ourselves to the business per se, and as a support factor for the business. Sure that everything is reflected in KPIs and in results; you depend on the latter ones. […] we are in an 'area' where we work with assessments and this one is a problem. (Interview no. 11)

The discussion concerning the guidelines that should be followed by the commercial entities within the context of collaboration with the non-profit ones refers, on the one hand, to the situation when the commercial entities approach this issue in an independent manner:

[As a corporate foundation—A/N] once at three years we develop a study with a—obviously—firm specialized in market research studies. (Interview no. 7)

On the other hand, there also appear circumstances under which the involvement areas (from the viewpoint of corporate social responsibility) are addressed in different degrees as a consequence of the recommendations formulated by the group of firms within which the organization is a part:

[…] ideas and projects that can come from the Group. (Interview no. 6)
[As a corporate organization—A/N] we relate to what it is recommended by the Group. (Interview no. 11)

Simultaneously, another interviewed person describes the notion of collaborative relationship as representing a comprehensive element relative to the financial value that corresponds to the supporting behaviour adopted by the commercial organization:

For me [as a corporate foundation representative—A/N], a strategic partnership doesn't mean 10,000 euro per year. Well, it can mean even 10,000. It can mean 40,000 euro per year. It means the linkage created together with (Name of corporate organization), which are 'there' for us and us for them, likewise … And we are 'friends' in the sense that we keep in touch, we keep ourselves informed about what each of us does, about what future plans we have and what we can do together. (Interview no. 5)

Further, another respondent evokes one of the most notable aspects that define the collaboration between the for-profit and non-profit organizations:

> [...] the Company's relationship with NGOs it is not made for this purpose per se—establishing a partnership. The Company's relationship is one with a wide variety of stakeholders—of interest factors or organizations/persons that, in a way or another, determine its activity or the smooth running of it. (Interview no. 1)

13.3.4 Communication Actions

The communication actions associated with a collaborative relationship between for-profit and non-profit organizations, from the respondents' perspective, divide themselves into two distinctive categories depending on the environment that corresponds to the transmitted message—the internal and the external communication. Even though, at first glance, the external communication seems to hold the main role in a context concerning CSR initiatives, two of the formulated arguments reflect contrary opinions regarding this assumption:

> [...] we [as a corporate organization—A/N] don't have a media budget allocated for the communication 'on' social responsibility initiatives. The unique manner of communication that is taken into account by us with priority consists of the internal communication towards all of our employees by the use of all the means that we have. (Interview no. 12)
>
> [As a corporate organization—A/N] we gave more attention to communicating inside the organization and, in general, the internal communication was much more developed because (Name of corporate organization), a good long time, was oriented towards the internal communication. (Interview no. 1)

The following two expressed viewpoints refer to the importance of allocating resources in order to support a non-profit organization or for implementing a collaborative relationship per se in comparison with the circumstance under which their destination would be assigned to promoting social involvement. Within the first example, there is made a reference to a potential good practice organizational conduct:

> [...] [As a corporate foundation—A/N] we don't spend three quarters of the budget on PR and a quarter on the project. Our money...—the majority—are directed towards projects. Important is to make the project and to have an object for discussion, and not vice versa. (Interview no. 7)

In the other example, there can be observed the fact that the approach of the subject is made through successive negations illustrated by a series of mentions about actions from the area of communicating by the use of advertising:

> In general, [as a corporate organization—A/N] we said that 'if we do something, it will be seen'. We haven't made an effort in order to communicate 'outside' visibly and aggressively because our achievements although, always, the communication part from the partnerships completed by us was an important part. We 'walk' the principle 'we tell what we do and we do what we tell', but we considered that 'putting' even financial resources into the communication part, does not make sense. The reason why we haven't made publicity, we haven't made advertising and we never paid for publicity and advertising spaces in order to 'erode' by this manner the resources that could be allocated to certain organizations or to a certain cause. (Interview no. 1)

Still about the role of communication, but this time from a diametrically opposed angle, states one of the interviewed persons:

> Usually, this is a clause of ours [as a corporate organization—A/N]—to be mentioned there appears something that 'talks' about the project financed by us. To be mentioned and, automatically, we have a certain type of advertising. Well, surely ... we speak about the major projects. Within the case of the small projects where you 'give' less, you don't have ... you can't have this 'pretence'. But, by reference to the major projects, it is normal to mention you. Where there is made advertising for the project, 'there' are we present. (Interview no. 8)

In seven of the 12 interviews conducted with representatives of commercial organizations, there were multiple mentions about aspects such as visibility, reputation or brand awareness, the statements being made predominantly in an indirect manner. Two of the most relevant mentions are the following ones:

> Of course that for a company is important to have also visibility for what it intends to do in terms of social involvement. […] the brand's visibility and its attached values related to defining that company as a socially involved one. This is what we aim at. […] because there are involved some funds, obviously that there should be identified a justification from a non-commercial viewpoint too, but it—this non-commercial—has an equivalence in the visibility as a brand. (Interview no. 11)
>
> Obviously that the main reason, from my point of view, is awareness. This is also a trend … We all [as corporate organizations—A/N] want to associate ourselves with some good causes, to increase awareness. (Interview no. 6)

13.4 Discussion and Further Research

The focal aspect that derives from the prerequisites of establishing collaborative relationships between entities from the for-profit and, respectively, the non-profit sectors refers to the manner in which corporate organizations address the identification of the potential collaborators. The interview's content analysis indicates the fact that the dominant approach is the reactive one in the sense that the endeavour's initiation for establishing collaboration relationships is made by the non-profit organizations. Nevertheless, there are situations within which the role of initiator belongs to the corporate ones. In particular, it is interesting to observe that, in one of the interviews, the notion of selling process is associated with CSR initiatives and, implicitly, with the involvement intent in collaborative relationships with non-profit entities.

Regarding the eligibility criteria that substantiate the selection of collaborator non-profit organizations, the actions of formulating and communicating them in an objective manner can be considered essential ones. In consonance with this thing, one of the respondents brings into discussion the justification of such a conduct in the sense that there is mentioned the auditing process and, implicitly, its binding nature.

From the viewpoint of the issues that represent the object of the criteria depending on which corporate organizations decide to collaborate with non-profit organizations, it may be concluded that the existence of a strategic alignment is the most important one of these. Thereby, for corporate organizations it is extremely important, between what represents the object of a potential collaborative relationship and the directions followed by it in terms of its CSR conduct, to have an alignment. Moreover, as the analysis of the interview's content indicates, it is necessary that this matching to be a strategic one by its nature so that it contributes to the achievement of the objectives associated with the manner in which organizations carry out their commercial activity.

The financial aspects associated with corporate organizations' involvement into collaborative relationships with non-profit organizations represent another particularity depending on which such an interaction takes place or not. Firstly, corporate organizations' option for collaboration depends on the financial results obtained in the sense that their support is filtered by the fiscal facilities conferred by law. Secondly, the flexibility degree of the budget allocated to sponsorship activities influences, in its turn, in a direct manner the decision regarding the association of the two types of entities. Again, the financial component is brought into discussion so that other two respondents recall the necessity of normalizing the extent to which non-profit organizations depend on the corporate financing because depending entirely on them may constitute a significant drawback of their own sustainability.

The interviews' content analysis reveals the fact that another criterion considered by corporate organizations as to be a definitive one relative to establishing a collaborative relationship is represented by approaching projects from a medium- or long-term perspective and, consequently, generating a significant impact. Within the same context and, at the same time, in connection with the financial area, the respondents' statements also evoke that the non-profit organizations' history regarding their experience in terms of managing projects and, implicitly, their budgets is one of the monitored criteria.

The discussion about the dimensions of the non-profit organizations that have the status of a potential collaborator can be looked at as depending on two distinct plans. The first plan is the one at which, from the perspective of corporate organizations, the aspect regarding the proposed project's characteristics is the one that prevails in comparison with the one about dimensions. By reference to the second plan, besides the elements that individualize the proposed project, the emphasis is put on the type of organizations of whose portfolio it is part of. Thus, one of the respondents expresses its preference regarding the work with international organizations due to the fact that their degree of formalization is an aspect that facilitates the manner in which the information exchange is addressed.

Reliability is an attribute that is an integral part of the main elements that characterize the conduct of non-profit organizations with which corporate entities may establish a collaboration relationship, according to the viewpoints expressed by the respondents. This attribute, on the one hand, refers to the manner in which non-profit organizations approach or relate themselves to the financial contribution offered by the financing corporate organizations. On the other hand, as stated by another respondent, the reliability derives from acquiring a good reputation by the non-profit organization.

As one of the interviewed persons says, fulfilling the assumed commitments is one of the principles of good practice that determine the proper collaboration between the corporate organizations and the non-profit ones. One of the recurring subjects in terms of the manner of implementing the information exchange between entities refers to the reporting process. The consistency of the feedback received by the corporate organizations is an aspect that influences the interaction from both a current and a future perspective relative to the probability of continuing the collaborative relationship.

Another characteristic of the corporate organization's conduct regarding the involvement into collaborative relationships with non-profit organizations refers to the manner of approaching the fields associated with the manifestation of a socially responsible behaviour. Thereby, these can be taken into account either on the basis of the own organizational considerations or as a further step related to the international recommendations. Beyond these aspects, the corporate organization's conduct is a variable and diverse one by the manner of implementing the social involvement endeavours.

Amongst the elements of characterizing the communication associated with the interaction between corporate organizations and the non-profit ones, there can be found the one that refers to the environment to which there are addressed the concerned actions—the internal environment or the external one. The respondents' assertions indicate that orienting the communication actions towards the internal environment represents a consistent part of the totality of such endeavours, as one of the interviewed persons highlights the priority character of such an initiative. In the case of the communication directed towards the external environment, there can be observed the existence of a consensus of the respondents in terms of the necessity of allocating resources for supporting the non-profit organizations' activity in comparison with the case in which resources are watched as the object of certain actions that promote elements regarding corporate organizations' identity. Notwithstanding, there are some opinions by which, practically, is confirmed the fact that the communication actions that derive from the implementation of a collaborative relationship between corporate organizations and the non-profit ones have a high degree of importance. Consequently, in more than half of the interviews, within the discussion about the communication actions derived from a collaborative relationship, the respondents' mentions referred—even though in an indirect manner—to a series of terms of which meaning was related to promoting the identity of the represented organizations.

References

Băleanu, T. E., Chelcea, L., & Stancu, A. (2011). The social responsibility of the top 100 Romanian companies. An analysis of corporate websites. *Amfiteatru Economic, 13*(29), 235–248.

Baur, D., & Schmitz, H. P. (2012). Corporations and NGOs: When accountability leads to co-optation. *Journal of Business Ethics, 106*(1), 9–21.

Bhattacharya, C. B., Korschun, D., & Sen, S. (2009). Strengthening stakeholder–company relationships through mutually beneficial corporate social responsibility initiatives. *Journal of Business Ethics, 85*(2), 257–272.

Demetriou, M., Papasolomou, I., & Vrontis, D. (2010). Cause-related marketing: Building the corporate image while supporting worthwhile causes. *The Journal of Brand Management, 17*(4), 266–278.

Eisenhardt, K. M. (1989). Building theories from case study research. *Academy of Management Review, 14*(4), 532–550.

Kim, N., Sung, Y., & Lee, M. (2012). Consumer evaluations of social alliances: The effects of perceived fit between companies and non-profit organizations. *Journal of Business Ethics, 109*(2), 163–174.

Lee, L. (2011). Business-community partnerships: Understanding the nature of partnership. *Corporate Governance: The International Journal of Business in Society, 11*(1), 29–40.

Lefroy, K., & Tsarenko, Y. (2014). Dependence and effectiveness in the nonprofit-corporate alliance: The mediating effect of objectives achievement. *Journal of Business Research, 67*(9), 1959–1966.

Ohreen, D. E., & Petry, R. A. (2012). Imperfect duties and corporate philanthropy: A Kantian approach. *Journal of Business Ethics, 106*(3), 367–381.

Zaharia, R. M., & Grundey, D. (2011). Corporate social responsibility in the context of financial crisis: A comparison between Romania and Lithuania. *Amfiteatru Economic, 13*(29), 195–206.

Index[1]

---

[1] Note: Page numbers with "n" denote notes.

© The Author(s) 2017

A. Theofilou et al. (eds.), *Corporate Social Responsibility in the Post-Financial Crisis Era*, Palgrave Studies in Governance, Leadership and Responsibility, DOI 10.1007/978-3-319-40096-9

.

Printed by Printforce, the Netherlands

.